Personal Identity

21·95

PERSONAL IDENTITY

Second Edition

Edited by
JOHN PERRY

UNIVERSITY OF CALIFORNIA PRESS
Berkeley   Los Angeles   London

University of California Press, one of the most distinguished university presses in the United States, enriches lives around the world by advancing scholarship in the humanities, social sciences, and natural sciences. Its activities are supported by the UC Press Foundation and by philanthropic contributions from individuals and institutions. For more information, visit www.ucpress.edu.

University of California Press
Berkeley and Los Angeles, California

University of California Press, Ltd.
London, England

Chapter 16 is reprinted from the American Philosophical Quarterly, Vol. 7, No. 4 (October 1970), pp. 269–85, by courtesy of the editor and of Professor Shoemaker.

ISBN 978–0-520–25642–2 (pbk. : alk. paper)

The Library of Congress has cataloged an earlier edition of this book as follows:

Library of Congress Cataloging-in-Publication Data

Perry, John, 1943–.
   Personal Identity / edited by John Perry.
      p.   cm.
   Topics in philosophy ; 2
   Includes bibliographical references.
   ISBN 978–0-520–02960–6 (pbk. : alk. paper)
   1. Personality—Addresses, essays, lectures.   I. Title.   II. Series
BD331.P46   1975
126—dc18   74079770

Manufactured in the United States of America

17   16   15   14   13   12   11   10
10   9   8   7   6   5   4   3   2

The paper used in this publication meets the minimum requirements of ANSI/NISO Z39.48–1992 (R 1997) (*Permanence of Paper*).

Contents

PART IV: ABANDONMENT OF PERSONAL IDENTITY

PART V: PERSONAL IDENTITY AND SURVIVAL

PART VI: THE UNITY OF CONSCIOUSNESS

Part VII: SELECTIONS FOR THE SECOND EDITION

Preface to the Second Edition

The view that personal identity consists in links of memory has twice been the focus of considerable attention from philosophers. The first time was after Locke put forward the view in the second edition of his *Essay Concerning Human Understanding* (1790). Major philosophers of the eighteenth century, including Joseph Butler, David Hume, Thomas Reid, and Samuel Clarke and Anthony Collins, in their *Controversy,* provided vigorous discussions of personal identity, more or less explicitly devoted to Locke's view.

The second period began in the middle of the twentieth century and continues. H. P. Grice, Anthony Flew, Anthony Quinton, Bernard Williams, Sydney Shoemaker, and Derek Parfit among many others provided important discussions and new versions of the memory theory. Shoemaker's work, in his book *Self-Knowledge and Self-Identity* and many subsequent writings, has been particularly influential. These discussions are the foundation of work on the topic since the 1970s.

The first edition of this anthology attempted to bring together key sources from these two periods, along with some expository and critical materials, for the convenience of students and scholars. In that, it seems to have been largely successful; the book has been widely adopted in courses and seminars, and, judging from citations of it in many footnotes, has provided a helpful resource for many subsequent writers in the field.

Still, with time I have come to regret that certain things weren't included. I'm happy that the University of California Press has decided to publish a second edition, and I thank Lindsie Bear for her help with this project.

The biggest regret was not including Sydney Shoemaker's

seminal paper "Persons and Their Pasts." Shoemaker's rather Wittgensteinian take on the problem in *Self-Knowledge and Self-Identity,* and in the article "Personal Identity and Memory," included in the anthology, was crucial in reestablishing the problem of personal identity. But his later work, more supportive of the memory theory, has eclipsed this early work in importance; an enormous portion of works on personal identity since "Persons and Their Pasts" start with its problems and employ its concepts. So I have added this important article.

In the eighteenth century, Samuel Clarke and Anthony Collins were involved in a two-year controversy (1706–8), exchanging four letters of increasing length. The controversy began with Clarke's review of a book by Henry Dodwell; some of Clarke's criticisms of Dodwell appeared to apply also to certain of John Locke's views, and Clarke's review provoked a reply from Locke's protégé, Anthony Collins. The exchange covered Collins' Locke-inspired views on materialism ("thinking matter"), personal identity, and the afterlife. The *Controversy* went through five editions in the eighteenth century. A number of important twentieth- and twenty-first-century themes, about both materialism and personal identity, are covered, with considerable imagination and sophistication. In particular, Clarke was the first to put forward the "fissioning" or "reduplication" argument against the memory theory—an argument brought back into the debate by Bernard Williams (1956–57).

In 1975 I had heard of Clarke and Collins' correspondence but hadn't seen a copy; there is no modern edition of it. For this edition, William Uzgalis has selected the key passages about personal identity from their letters, and I'm very happy to be able to add this important material to the anthology. I have also added a fine article by Uzgalis that helps us understand the controversy and its connection with Butler's criticisms of Locke.

Finally, I have included a discussion of mine that deals with Williams' "The Self and the Future." I've found it useful in teaching, and hope that others will too.

John Perry
October 2007
Palo Alto, California

PART I

INTRODUCTION

John Perry

1

The Problem of Personal Identity

PERSONS AND PUZZLES

Imagine the following. Elected to the Senate from your home
state, you have become a key member of the Committee on
Health, Education, and Welfare. This committee meets tomorrow
to vote on a bill to fund a feasibility study of a new method
for manufacturing shoes, which is alleged to produce a high
quality, inexpensive shoe that never wears out. Your support of
the bill is essential; it has faced the bitter and unflagging oppo-
sition of the American Cobblers Association (ACA), led by their
high pressure lobbyist Peter Pressher, and a number of committee members intend to vote against it.

The morning of the committee vote you wake up, open
your eyes, and glance at the clock on the shelf beyond the bed.
Something seems strange. The bump in the covers you take to
be your feet seems strangely distant. As you get out of bed you
hit your head on a shelf that used to be a good three or four
inches above it. You notice you are wearing a leather apron,
which you are certain you didn't wear to bed. Puzzled, you go
to the mirror. Staring out you see not your familiar clean-shaven
face and squatty body, but the strapping frame and bearded
countenance of Peter Pressher.

You don't know what to think. Are you dreaming? Is this
some kind of a trick? But you perform various tests to eliminate
these possibilities. No doubt can remain: the body you have
looks just like the body Peter Pressher normally has; it seems to
be that very body.

Hearing laughter, you turn toward your living room. There on the sofa sits a person who looks exactly like you. That is exactly like you used to look, down to the inevitable magenta hollyhock (your state's flower) in the lapel. Before you can speak, he says,

"Surprised, Senator? I've made sacrifices for the Cobblers before. Getting this squatty body must take the prize. But I'll vote to kill that bill this afternoon, and it will be worth it . . ."

He speaks with your own deep and resonant voice, but the syntax and the fanatic overtones are unmistakably those of . . .

"Peter Pressher! . . ."

"Right, Senator, it's me. But as far as the rest of the world will ever know, it's really you. We snuck into your apartment last night and my brother Bimo, the brain surgeon, carefully removed your brain and put it in my body—or should I say your body. And vice-versa. It's a new operation he's pioneering; he calls it a "body-transplant.""

"You'll never get away with it . . ."

"Forget it. You have two choices. You can go around telling people that you're you, in which case I will sue you and my family, thinking they are your family, will sign papers to have you put away. Or you can start acting like me—become Peter Pressher—we think you'd make a good lobbyist. Almost as good a lobbyist as I'll make a senator!"

An incredible story? Let's hope so. Impossible? In one sense, yes. Physicians cannot now perform body-transplants with human beings. But in another sense the case is perfectly possible. The day when such operations can be performed may not be so far away.[1] Such an operation is possible in the sense of being conceivable. The story was not self-contradictory or incoherent. As a piece of science fiction, it's pretty mild stuff.

This case is of a genre of fiction characteristic of philosophical discussion about personal identity. In the pages that follow, the reader will meet a prince who appropriates the body of a cobbler (Locke and Shoemaker), a thin puritanical Scot and a fat apolaustic Pole who exchange bodies (Quinton), and two fellows named "A" and "B" who are told that their bodies and brains are to be shuffled, and asked to choose ahead of time which of the survivors is to be tortured and which rewarded

(Williams). Butler owes his interest in personal identity to concern about the afterlife, which is a puzzle case of sorts. If there is an afterlife, what will make the persons who exist then identical with the persons they used to be on earth? Surely not identity of the body involved. And this is just the feature all such puzzle cases have in common: we are presented, at different times, with the same person (or what is alleged to be the same person), but not the same live human body.

Why are such cases puzzling, and why is the puzzlement of philosophical interest? Because they seem to disprove the view that a person is just a live human body. If we can have the same person on two different occasions when we don't have the same live human body, then it seems that a person cannot be identified with his body, and personal identity cannot be identified with bodily identity. This is puzzling simply because the assumption that the two go together plays a large role in our daily lives. We make it when we identify others on the basis of appearance, or observed movements, or fingerprints. What is the justification for this assumption? The abandonment of the simple theory that personal identity is just bodily identity carries with it the need to formulate an alternative account of personal identity. On such attempts this anthology focuses.

But perhaps we are moving too fast. Are we so sure that the puzzle cases prove what they are alleged to? Perhaps the events imagined have been wrongly described, and the right description would go something like this:

You are a senator from your home state. One morning you wake up on the sofa, seeming to remember being Peter Pressher, a lobbyist for the ACA. A man emerges from a bedroom, who seems to remember being you. But subsequent tests—fingerprints, testimony of close friends, comparison of medical records, etc.— establishes, to your delight and his dismay, that you are a duly elected senator with delusions (which you keep quiet about) of having been a lobbyist, while he is a lobbyist with delusions of having been a senator. His situation is rather ironic. He willingly participated in a scheme where his brain (and so various of his psychological characteristics) were exchanged for your brain (and so various of your psychological characteristics). He seems to have thought that would somehow constitute a "body transfer," and he would wind up in the Senate. (He was taught this by a philosophy professor in college, whom he is suing.) What actually happened, of course, is that two people underwent radical changes in character and personality, and acquired delusive memories, as a result of brain surgery.

How shall we decide between these two descriptions? In a sense, they do not disagree about what happened—which sounds emanated from which bodies, and so forth. So neither can be proven incorrect by reference to the occurrence of these events. But in another sense they are blatantly contradictory, and one must be wrong.

The philosophers who discuss this type of case come to opposite conclusions. Quinton and Locke and Shoemaker would say of our case that the senator acquired the lobbyist's body and not his psychological characteristics. Williams gives very strong arguments in favor of this conclusion, but in the end rejects it, and sticks hesitantly with the view that bodily identity is a necessary condition of personal identity.

This shows, perhaps, that it is only *after* doing some thinking about our concept of a person, will we be able to settle on one description or the other as being the right one (if even then). But the puzzle cases do at least provide us with a motivation for doing this thinking.

In this anthology, the reader will find attempts by eleven philosophers to solve, dissolve, or shed light on some aspect of the problem of personal identity. Puzzle cases play a central role in some of these discussions, but they are not the only issue. I make no attempt in the remainder of this introduction to discuss, or even catalog, all of the controversies found herein. I do try, in the next section, to provide a framework within which theories may be stated and issues joined. In the remainder, I compare the structures of the three versions of the memory-theory, and I discuss the selections by Locke, Butler, and Hume. Locke's essay is of special interest, for it is both historically the first and logically the simplest of the theories of personal identity proposed, and it is wise to initiate one's study of the problem by determining just what the weaknesses of his view are. Butler's essay includes the important criticism that Locke's analysis, and others which employ the concept of memory, are circular. But it also includes criticisms of considerably less value. I have defended Locke against these at some length, because I think the confusions thus uncovered are usefully exposed, as they crop up again and again in discussions of personal identity. And my reason for discussing Hume is much the same, although here the confusions emerge not in criticisms of the views of others, but in a misinterpretation of the nature of his own theory.

PERSONS AND PERSON-STAGES; IDENTITY AND UNITY

In studying the problem of personal identity, we are learning about our own concept of a person, trying to articulate and analyze knowledge we in a sense already have. For we all make judgments about personal identity in daily life with no problem, and even in the puzzle cases we may have strong "intuitions" about what to say. When we philosophize, we are trying to discover what principles are implicit in these judgments, how they are related to one another, and why they are important. When the principles we confidently employ in everyday life are thus clarified and analyzed, we will not only be in a better position to see what to say about puzzling cases, but also to assess the importance and utility of the concept we have, and perhaps even to make some changes.

But what kind of principles are these? What kind of question is "what is personal identity?" To try to get clear about this, I want to spend a little time on an example of a person who is ignorant in a somewhat different way, of the "identity conditions" of a much different kind of thing.

Suppose you are introducing the game of baseball to a friend. You want him to acquire the concept of a *baseball game*. You take him to a large field in which there are four games going on at the same time, walk around the field watching the different games, and familiarize him with different types of baseball events or plays: double plays, home runs, triples, and so forth. He gets the hang of this quite well, and can soon use such sentences as "A single was just hit" quite as well as you can. Does he have the concept of a baseball game?

He may not. Suppose further conversation reveals that he is

under the impression that all the events on the field were events in a single game. Clearly, he did not have mastery of the concept of a baseball game. Again, suppose he thought that each *inning* constituted a game by itself, so that thirty-six rather than four games had been played on the field during the afternoon. Or suppose he thought that each game was just part of a longer whole, which would continue the following day. Clearly, he would not have mastered the concept of a baseball game.

What is it he doesn't know? We can represent the mistakes he makes as wrong judgments about identity. He gives wrong answers to questions of the form "Is this the same game as that?" where "this" and "that" identify games by indicating events that occur on different parts of the field, or at different times. It is because we can represent his problem this way that we might say, "He doesn't know the identity conditions of a baseball game."

Thus in order to completely master the concept of a baseball game, your friend will have to, in a sense, learn the answer to this question:

(I) Under what conditions are baseball events, events in one game?

The friend, of course, will not learn to answer such a question as such. Probably most umpires and league officials could not rattle off an explicit answer. But he will learn to make correct judgments, given adequate information, about whether baseball events are so related, and in this sense he will know the conditions under which baseball events belong to one game.

It seems to make perfectly good sense to ask for an explicit answer to the question, however. To answer it, we would follow something akin to the hypothetico-deductive method used in science, first trying a simple hypothesis (perhaps that baseball events belong to the same game if they occur on the same diamond and within three hours of one another), and deducing its consequences for various actual and imagined baseball events. If it doesn't give us the right answers for certain cases (as the suggested hypothesis does not), we amend it or abandon it entirely and start over. With luck, we eventually arrive at a hypothesis that handles correctly all the cases we have clear intuitions about. We might then feel free to appeal to the hypothesized conditions to decide cases about which we have unclear or conflicting intuitions, or we might find that the most satisfactory hypothesis deems them to be truly indeterminate.

The conditions called for in (I) are relational; our theory has to specify a relation that can obtain between baseball events. It is important to note that this will not be the relation of *identity.* Our ultimate goal is to analyze the relation *is the same baseball game as,* which is just the relation of identity restricted to baseball games. But we do this by finding a relation that does not hold between baseball games at all, but between baseball events. We can clarify the connection between the relation we are trying to analyze and the one we need to find, in the following way. Let R be the relation between baseball events belonging to one game, and E and E' be baseball events. Then,

E has R to E'   if and only if   the game in which E
                                         is an event is the
                                         same baseball game as
                                         the game in which E' is
                                         an event.[2]

I shall call R the *unity relation* for baseball games. Then we can repeat our point in this way. Baseball events that belong to the same game will not in general be identical, but the unity relation will obtain between them. The game in which they are both events will be identical with itself, but the unity relation will not obtain between it and itself.

It is sometimes useful to analyze questions like (I) into two further subquestions, which I state in a general form:

(i) What relation obtains between simultaneous K-events
    that are events belonging to the same K;
(ii) What relation obtains between K-stages that are stages
    of the same K.

A K-stage is a set containing all and only those K-events which belong to a given K at a given time. Thus in asking the second question we presuppose an answer to the first.

I believe this general framework should be applied to the concept of a person, and the question of personal identity. This may not be obvious. After all, baseball games are not "things" in the ordinary sense, but "processes." And they break up easily into discrete events, most of which begin with a pitch and end with a noise from the umpire. But persons are not processes, and there is no one natural way to break up a person's life into discrete events. But although a person is not commonly thought of as a process, we can think of his *life* or *personal history* as a process, a sequence of events, and the concept of a personal history is intimately associated with the concept of a person; someone could not be said to have mastered the concept of a person if he could not say, given the requisite information, whether two events belonged to *the history* of one person. It will not then be necessary in this introduction to argue for the identification of a person with his personal history in this sense. We will leave that question to one side, and introduce the notion of an "event belonging to a person" as shorthand for the familiar notion of an "event belonging to the personal history of a person."

While it's true that events in a person's life do not naturally break up into discrete episodes, or break up equally naturally in a variety of ways, this again seems insufficient to reject the framework. Any way we break up the phenomena we describe with our concept of a person, the framework can be applied.

Can we imagine someone in a position, relative to the concept *person,* analogous to the position of the student of baseball, relative to the concept, *game of baseball?* Such a person would be able to make judgments expressed in such sentences as "Someone is smoking," "Someone is thinking," "Someone is walking." But he would not have the ability, or perhaps only a limited ability, to make such combined judgments as "Someone is walking and the same person is smoking," "Someone is thinking and the same person was just now walking," even given information which would be more than adequate for the rest of us to make such judgments. We may imagine him to have various *alternative* concepts for individuating persons—perhaps he has the concept of a *deca-person,* which corresponds to what we would call a "ten-year slice of a person stretching one year divisible by ten to the next." Or per-

haps he simply has no thoughts on the matter. There is no readily apparent reason why a person could not be in this situation,
although there may not be as many obvious and plausible ways
to go wrong individuating persons as there are in the case of
baseball games.

At any rate, we can certainly *ask* the questions (i) and (ii)
for our concept of a person, just as we can *ask* them for any
concept of a kind of object which persists through time. If a
philosopher could show us that they could not be non-trivially
answered, that would be an important and interesting result, and
not a proof that it was wrong to ask them in the first place.

I suggest, then, that the main technical problems for a
theory of personal identity is answering questions (i) and (ii) (or
more precisely the questions we get when we take, as the value
of the variable "K" in those questions, the word "person"). I
say "technical problem," for there are other questions, perhaps
in the end more important, which naturally arise: why should
the concept that answers to the conditions specified by some
theory or other play the important role that our concept of a
person does play? How do we ever know that the specified relation obtains between person-events? And so forth.

Now philosophers have concentrated on the second sort of
question in thinking about personal identity, and the reader will
find little discussion, in most of the following essays, of the
problem of personal identity "at a time." But recent scientific
and medical work has produced *actual* puzzle cases relevant to
this problem: cases in which we are not sure whether one or
two persons are associated with a particular human body *at one
time.* In the last selection, Thomas Nagel discusses these fascinating experiments.

Some of the authors here anthologized speak of giving the
"criteria" of personal identity. I believe this word is used in two
importantly different ways. In one sense, "criteria of identity"
are just what I have called the unity relations, between simultaneous events, or nonsimultaneous person-stages. This, I believe,
is the way Quinton uses the phrase. But the root meaning of
"criterion" is "way of knowing," and other authors use it with
something more like its original meaning. We might discover that
person-stages are stages of the same person not by observing

directly that the unity relation holds between them, but by in-
ferring this from the holding of another relation between them.
That other relation would be our *evidence* for the unity relation's holding. Now some philosophers believe that there can
be such evidence which has a privileged status, which is somehow
"conceptually guaranteed" to be, if not infallible, at least reliable, and use the word "criterion" for such evidence. This is
the way Shoemaker uses the phrase "criterion of identity."[3]

This difference can be crucial. For example, Shoemaker
says he wants to consider "the view that memory provides a
criterion of personal identity, or, as H. P. Grice expressed it
some years ago, that 'the self is a logical construction and is to
be defined in terms of memory'" (p. 119). But it's pretty clear
that Grice's view is that the *unity relation* for persons can be defined in terms of memory. This is not just an alternative way of
saying that memory is a "criterion," in Shoemaker's sense, of
identity. And the view that the unity relation can be defined in
terms of memory would not obviously imply the view that memory is the sole criterion of personal identity, as Shoemaker's later
arguments seem to suggest.

On the other hand, the two uses of "criteria" are surely
related, for in general there is an important connection between
our ways of knowing something and what we thereby come to
know.

LOCKE'S THEORY

Locke's statement of the problem of personal identity, and
his pioneering attempt to define personal identity in terms of
memory, have exercised remarkable influence on later discussions
of the subject. In this anthology, Reid and Butler criticize Locke,
while Quinton and Grice attempt to vindicate the spirit of his
theory, if not the letter. Other papers, though not so explicitly
concerned with Locke, grapple with themes that he originated:
the possibility of body exchanges, the role of memory in personal identity, and so forth.

Locke defines a person as "a thinking intelligent being, that
has reason and reflection, and can consider itself as itself, the
same thinking thing, in different times and places" (p. 39). This

makes it an essential property of persons that they have the power of *reflection,* and I believe Locke is best interpreted as thinking that their having this power makes it possible for them to "consider themselves as themselves, the same thinking thing, in different times and places." We must then see what reflection is, and how this power is connected to judgments of personal identity.

Let us take the word "experience" broadly. If we think of person-event as being identifiable by a live human body, a time, and a property, then we may think of experiences as that subset of person-events in which the relevant property is a *mental* or *psychological.* There seems to be two "ways" in which one can come to know the truth of a sentence reporting an experience, e.g., "Someone is thinking." One might *observe,* with one's sense of vision, or touch, or, perhaps, hearing or smell or taste, that someone was having an experience. I might see that you are thinking. (We won't worry about whether this is "direct observation" or an "inference"; Locke thought the latter.) But if the someone who is doing the thinking is myself, I won't find out that "someone is thinking" by use of any of my five senses. I can tell whether I am thinking when I am blindfolded, my nose and ears plugged, my fingers numb, and my tongue shot full of Novocaine. It seems then I must find out in some other way. Locke thought this other way was a sort of sixth or "inner sense" which he called "reflection" (the sense of this word is captured by the more modern "introspection"). Locke's controversial belief that reflection is best thought of as a sense—like vision or hearing—is not crucial. What is important seems less controversial: that we do have such a way of finding out about the occurrence of experiences, and that all the experiences we find out about in this way are our *own.* I can be "reflectively aware" of the occurrence of my own experiences, but not of yours.

This latter fact is not, according to Locke, an accident, but a consequence of the meaning of "my experience." We mean by "my experiences" simply "those experiences the occurrence of which I can be aware of reflectively." I take this to be a plausible reconstruction of what Locke is getting at when he says, "When we see, hear, smell, taste, feel, meditate, or will anything, we know that we do so. Thus it is always as to our present sensations and perceptions: and by this every one is to himself that which he calls *self"* (p. 39). Thus Locke seems to have hinted at an answer to the first of the questions which, following the format sketched in the last section, we can pose for a theory of personal identity:

> Under what conditions do simultaneous experiences belong to the same person?

Locke's answer: if one is a reflective awareness of the other. The problem with the suggestion is that it gives us only a sufficient condition, and a condition, furthermore, which is only relevant to "linking" experiences that are on "different levels." It doesn't tell us anything at all about the conditions under which a given act of seeing and a given act of hearing belong to the same person. Locke doesn't develop the hint, and I know of no obvious way to plausibly elaborate it.

Locke goes on to formulate an answer to the second question; it is on this that he spends the remainder of his chapter, and it is his ideas here that have influenced later theorists. When Locke speaks of the "consciousness that always accompanies thinking," it seems that he has this reflective awareness in mind; and he says "as far as this consciousness can be extended backwards to any past action or thought, so far reaches the identity of that person." But what does Locke have in mind by reflective awareness of *past* experiences? We are aware of the past not through any sense faculty, but through our faculty of memory. What we now remember, we may have seen; but we now remember it, or remember seeing it; we don't now *see* something that happened in the past. Similarly, one would suppose we now remember an experience, or perhaps remember being reflectively aware of an experience, but are not now reflectively aware of the occurrence of a past experience.

Locke must mean something like this: "Any experience I can remember being reflectively aware of, is mine, i.e., one that happened to me." Thus the distinction between knowing of present experiences by our five external senses and knowing of them by our sixth inner sense is carried over into memory; all and only experiences I can remember having been aware of in this latter way were mine.

The second of the questions we can pose for a theory of personal identity is

> Under what conditions are person-stages stages of the same person?

A person-stage is a set of simultaneous experiences all of which belong to one person. Locke really doesn't have a right to make use of such a notion until he gives us a plausible answer to the first question, which he doesn't do. But let's waive this, allow him the notion of a person-stage, and see what we can make of his suggestion. I believe the following is a fair reconstruction:

> Person-stages belong to the same person, if and only if the later could contain an experience which is a memory of a reflective awareness of an experience contained in the earlier.

This has shortcomings, some obvious, some not so obvious. First, it requires us to be able to remember everything that ever happened to us. This is absurd—although Locke defended it, perhaps in the spirit of conceptual innovation, in the face of good counterexamples he himself provides (p. 48). On the face of it, Locke has given us too stringent a necessary condition for an earlier experience to belong to a person. Reid gives several irresistible counterexamples, the most famous being the case of the brave officer (p. 114). Quinton and Grice attempt, among other things, to reach a plausible account by weakening Locke's condition in response to examples like Reid's. By the time we reach Grice's third version, things have become pretty complex, and I want to briefly compare the various versions of the memory theory with which we are presented, in a way that may make the motivations behind and structure of the more complex versions easier to grasp.

LOCKE, QUINTON, AND GRICE

I want to bring out the similarities and differences in the ways that Locke, Quinton, and Grice use memory in their analyses of personal identity. In doing so, I shall ignore interesting and important differences. For example, I shall ignore Quinton's incorporation of similarity of character into his account, and I shall ignore the differences between Quinton's "soul-phases" and Grice's "total temporary states (t.t.s's)," pretending that all three philosophers couch their accounts in terms of "person-stages," even though not one of the three uses that term. And I shall use Grice's term "contains a memory of" in place of Locke's "extending consciousness backwards," and Quinton's "recollection."

We can compare Locke, Quinton, and Grice most easily by beginning with an account of personal identity in terms of memory that no one has ever put forward, and developing their views as responses to objections to this orphan theory. I shall call this account "Proto-Locke," as it resembles Locke's view most closely.

According to Proto-Locke, person-stages A and B belong to the same person if and only if A actually contains a memory of an experience contained in B. There are plenty of perfectly clear cut counterexamples to Proto-Locke; successive attempts to patch things up will lead us from this simplest of memory theories to the most subtle and complex.

The most obvious counterexample is sleep. Wilson is asleep; his current person-stage contains only a rather vaguely blissful experience. Wilson does not remember seeing Wynn hit a home run earlier in the day. But surely, it was he, the same person, who was at Dodger Stadium not six hours ago.

Locke apparently saw this sort of objection. He speaks, not simply of the past thoughts and actions to which we extend our consciousness but those to which it *could* be so extended. Wilson could remember the game. So we come to an analysis one level of complexity beyond Proto-Locke, which maintains that the unity relation is:

R_L: A does contain *or could contain* a memory of an experience contained in B.

Now let us return again to Proto-Locke, and examine a-nother sort of counterexample, Reid's famous Brave Officer Paradox. Suppose as a boy Jones was flogged for stealing apples; this he remembers later while performing a brave deed as an officer; this brave deed he remembers even later, as a general. But by then he has forgotten the flogging. According to Proto-Locke, the brave officer is the boy, and the general is the brave officer, but the general is not the boy. This is absurd, and Proto-Locke fails again.

The first sort of amendment won't solve this problem. For the general might not only not remember the flogging but might not be *able* to remember it, no matter how hard he tried, or how often reminded. Indeed, Reid's general was in just this state.

An amendment to Proto-Locke, which resolves the Brave Officer Paradox, is made by Quinton. Quinton's suggested unity relation is the *ancestral* of Proto-Locke's. An explanation of the notion of the ancestral of a relation follows. Take two objects, a and z, and a relation R. If there is a sequence of objects, a, b, c, . . . w, x, y, z, such that a has R to b, b has R to c, and so on, until finally x has R to y, and y has R to z, then a and z are related by the *ancestral of R*. The string can be as long or short as need be. Some examples of ancestral relations: while 6 does not have the relation, *next number after* to 2, it does have the ancestral of this relation to 2, in virtue of the sequence, 6, 5, 4, 3, 2; while my great-grandparent does not have the relation, *parent of*, to me, he does have the ancestral of the parent relation, in virtue of the sequence, my great-grandfather, my grandmother, my mother, me. The ancestral of the parent relation is the same as the relation we call "being an ancestor of," and that's where the notion of the ancestral got its name.

This then is Quinton's suggestion:

R_Q: There is a sequence of person-stages, of which A is the first member and B the last, such that A contains a memory of an experience contained in the second, the second contains a memory of an experience contained in the third, and so on, until finally the second to the last contains a memory of an experience contained in B.

(Actually, remember, Quinton talks about soul-phases and rec-ollection, and builds in also a condition of character similarity from soul-phase to soul-phase in the sequence.)

Quinton's relation, it is important to notice, is the ancestral of Proto-Locke's, and not the ancestral of R_L. This fact is hard to explain, since both Locke and Grice had seen the necessity for using links of *possible* memory. Perhaps Quinton's notion of recollection has built in such merely possible memory, and our interpretation of him is unfair. At any rate, it seems that Quinton's account is responsive only to counterexamples of the Brave Officer kind. It resolves the Brave Officer Paradox, in fact, only on the assumption that the brave officer is an insomniac con-sumed with memories of his most recent past.

If we combine the improvements over Proto-Locke suggest-ed by Locke and Quinton, we obtain the following suggestion:

> R_X: There is a sequence of person-stages, of which A is the first member and B the last, such that A could contain a memory of an experience contained in the second, the second could contain a memory of an experience contained in the third, and so on, until finally the second to the last could contain a memory of an experience contained in B.

R_X is the ancestral of R_L, rather than merely of Proto-Locke.

R_X corresponds precisely to one put forward, and rejected, by Grice, on page 87 below. This may not be obvious, since Grice uses a somewhat different approach: he is trying to analyze the sentence "Someone heard a noise," rather than to analyze the unity relation directly. His suggestion is:

a (past) hearing of a noise is an element in a t.t.s., which is a member of a series of t.t.s's, such that every member of the series would, given certain conditions, contain as an element a memory of some experience which is an element in the preceding member.

If A and B are both members of a series of the sort Grice de-scribes, then a sequence of the sort required by R_X could be formed, by dropping from the series those t.t.s's occurring later than A or earlier than B. And if A and B are members of a sequence of the sort required by R_X, that string will itself form a series of the sort required by Grice. Given that "t.t.s." is Grice's version of a person-stage, and "would, given certain conditions, contain," is supposed to just mean "could contain," we can see that Grice's suggestion amounts to R_X.

But Grice rejects this suggestion. We can illustrate the sorts of reasons he had by the Senile General Case. The senile general's biography is just like the brave officer's, except the senile general *can* remember being flogged as a child, and *cannot* remember performing a brave deed as an officer, nor can he remember anything subsequent to his performance of the brave deed. And while he performed the brave deed, he remembered the flogging. R_X obtains between the senile general stage of this person and the flogged child stage, and between the brave officer stage and the flogged child stage, but not between the senile general stage and the brave officer stage. So the senile general and the brave officer are both the person who was flogged as a child, but are not each other, which is absurd.

Grice adds another layer of complexity to take care of this sort of case. Before taking the ancestral of Locke's relation, he disjoins it with its converse, so the basic relation is

R_Y: *A* contains, or could contain, a memory of an experience contained in *B*, or *B* contains, or could contain, a memory of an experience contained in *A*.

The ancestral of R_Y we can express this way:

R_G: There is a sequence of person-stages (not necessarily in the order they occur in time, and not excluding repetitions), the first of which is *A* and the last of which is *B*, such that each person-stage in the sequence either (i) contains, or could contain, a memory of an experience contained in the next, or (ii) contains an experience of which the next person-stage contains a memory, or could contain a memory.

Again, this is not quite the way Grice put it. As his final analysis of "Someone heard a noise," he suggests:

a (past) hearing of a noise is an element in a t.t.s. which is a member of a series of t.t.s's such that every member of the series either would, given certain conditions, contain as an element a memory of some experience which is an element in some previous member, or contains as an element some experience a memory of which would, given certain conditions, occur as an element in some subsequent member; there being no subset of members which is independent of the rest. [P. 88]

Grice is describing the series with time order kept intact, so that it is not necessarily a successor or predecessor in the series to which a given t.t.s. is linked by a possible memory. The two conditions, the one in Grice's paragraph and R_G, are equivalent: the sequence required by R_G can be obtained from the series required by Grice by shifting the order of the t.t.s's so that each is linked to its successor in the string, ignoring their order in time, and listing again a member already used if necessary to keep the sequence going; the series required by Grice can be obtained from the sequence required by R_G by simply listing its members in the order they occur in time.

R_G allows us, in effect, to change directions and thus ignore time order when linking the person-stages. The sequence, the senile general stage, the flogged child stage, the brave officer stage, satisfies the requirements, so that the senile general turns out to be the brave officer after all.

Even if Grice's theory is immune from all counterexamples, there are other sorts of objections to be considered, which would apply to his account as much as to simpler ones. For example, Butler claims that memory theories of personal identity must be circular, since the notion of memory presupposes that of personal identity (p. 100). And Butler also claims that, if Locke's theory were correct, our belief in personal identity would be an illusion, for Locke does not require identity of substance, and without this there is no identity, in the true sense, at all. This objection would apply to Quinton and Grice also, and because it is not well treated in the other essays, I shall discuss it here.

LOCKE AND BUTLER ON SUBSTANCE

Locke is very explicit in saying that identity of "immaterial substance" is neither a necessary nor a sufficient condition for personal identity. He did not, however, jettison the notion of substance entirely; he thought that at every moment of a person's life, or at least at every conscious moment, he must be in "vital union" with some immaterial substance or other. Locke thought we must be in vital union with immaterial substances to think, just as we must be in vital union with material substances —i.e., the atoms that make up our body at any given time—to reach or walk or stand up.

But what did Locke mean by "substance?" Although various conceptions of substance occur in Locke's *Essay*, and it's not always clear what he has in mind, it is pretty clear what he means in the chapter on personal identity. When Locke denies, early in the chapter, that in the case of a material object or a plant, identity of substance is a necessary condition of identity of material object, or identity of plant, he is denying that the material object or plant need always, throughout its history, be composed of the same material atoms. The concept of substance is of the ultimate things in a causal sense: those things whose properties and relationships explain (or would explain, if known) the properties and relationships of the larger composite entities we deal with as human beings. And when he denies, a little later on, that identity of immaterial substance is a necessary condition of personal identity, he is thinking of immaterial substances analogously, as sort of "immaterial atoms." Locke thought of a person as a complex of material and immaterial atoms in "vital union" with one another.

Unlike Descartes, Locke did not identify a person with the immaterial substance which is, at any given time, a "part" of him, and in virtue of which he has the property of thought, etc. If he had, his claim that identity of immaterial substance was not required for personal identity would be paradoxical.[4] It is true that *thinking* is according to Locke a defining property of persons, and he also says that immaterial substances *think;* they "think in us." But I don't believe this need get him into trouble. The sense in which immaterial substances are said to think is analogous to the sense in which our hands can be said to grasp things; if I say that I grasped the pencil, and also that my hand grasped the pencil, I am not committed to identifying myself with my hand.

Butler thought that Locke's denial of the requirement of identity of substance doomed his analysis of personal identity. He reasoned that if personal identity does not require identity of substance, then personal identity is not a case of identity or "sameness" in the "strict and philosophic sense of that word." And nothing, he thought, could be clearer than that it is. For if personal identity is only the "loose and common" variety of identity, and not the "strict and philosophical kind," it follows that "our present self is not, in reality, the same with the self of yesterday, but another self of person coming in its room, and mistaken for it; to which another self will succeed tomorrow" (p. 102). And from this many absurdities follow, for example, "the person of today is really no more interested in what will befall the person of tomorrow, than in what will befall any other person" (p. 102). And of particular interest to Butler, it would follow that "the inquiry concerning a future life [is] of no consequence at all to us the persons who are making it" (p. 99).

Locke draws an analogy between the identity of persons and the identity of vegetables, pointing out that in neither case is the identity of the substances which make up the individual necessary to its identity. But according to Butler, this linking of the inquiry into the identity of persons with questions about vegetables is a signal that something has gone seriously wrong with Locke's account. Butler says that when someone speaks of (say) a tree that was planted in this spot fifteen years ago, being the *same tree* that is now in this spot, even if what he says is quite true by our ordinary lights, still, "he means only the same as to all the purposes of property and uses of common life, and not that the tree has been all that time the same *in the strict philosophic sense of that word*" (p. 100, italics added). This is clear, for as Locke himself points out, identity of the trees is consistent with diversity of substance. But Butler goes on, "in a strict and philosophical manner of speech, no man, no being, no anything can be the same with that, with which it has indeed nothing the same" (p. 101).

What are we to say of Butler's criticism? One wonders, in the first place, what the so-called "strict and philosophical" sense of 'sameness' has to do with sameness or identity. A connection is made in the text: "it being a contradiction in terms, to say that they are [the same] when no part of their substance, and no one of their properties, is the same" (p. 101). Now there is an important principle, which we will call the *indiscernibility of the identical*: if A and B are identical, one and the same, then every property of A's is a property of B's and vice versa. But why does Butler doubt that this condition is met in the case of the tree?

One might think that it is obviously not met. After all, consider the tree planted fifteen years ago. It was small. But the tree in front of us is not small. So, even though we say in the "loose and common sense" that they are the same, that this tree is the very one we planted, they are not the same in the "strict and philosophical sense" for their properties differ.

This had better not be what Butler has in mind. Even if the tree had retained a number or even all of the original material particles it had, and thus exemplified sameness in the strict and philophical sense, it might still have grown. So the strict and philosophical sense would no more escape violation of the indiscernibility of the identical than the loose and common sense, were the above argument correct.

And, more importantly, the argument is not correct. Both the tree we planted, and this tree, *are* large; both this tree, and the one we planted, *were* small (or, as we might alternatively put it, both have "tenselessly" the property of being large *in 1972*, and of being small *in 1920*). There is no property the one *has*, and the other *lacks*, and no property the one *had* the other *lacked*. There is a property "the one" *had* that "the other" *does not have*. But that's no violation of the indiscernibility of the identical, and does not mean that there is more than one tree involved. For in exactly the same sense, there is also a property which "the one" had and "the one" does not now have. The tree we planted here fifteen years ago *had* the property of being small, but the tree we planted here fifteen years ago no longer *has* it, having grown up.

Butler says that the tree planted and the tree now seen do

not have properties in common, given that they have no material particles in common, "because it is allowed that the same property cannot be transferred from one substance to another." If by "transfer of properties" we mean something like one object's smallness becoming the very smallness of another object, then we might agree, without inquiring too closely into the sense of what we are admitting, that this cannot happen. But so what? Transfer of properties in this mysterious sense is not required by the doctrine that the tree planted is the tree seen, and the properties of the former the properties of the latter. The configuration of material particles that used to make up the tree does not need to "transfer its smallness" to later configurations of particles; it's quite satisfactory if they possess their own "smallness" or "middle-sizedness" or whatever. The tree now before us, which is not small at all, has the property of having been small, but not because any properties have been transferred. It *has* the property of having been small simply because it *had* the property of being small, because the configuration of material particles that now constitutes this tree is related in certain ways (the unity relation for tree-stages) to smaller past configurations.

So Butler's "strict and philosophical" sense of "sameness" seems to have little to do with the ordinary notion of sameness or identity. It not only seems to be not a necessary condition of identity, but also not a sufficient condition. We would not say that the tree we planted here fifteen years ago and the elm on the far side of the driveway are one and the same tree, even if we were assured by responsible horticulturists that the ultimate material particles which made up the tree we planted when we planted it had made their way across the lawn over the years, and now made up the elm.

Since it is the immaterial substances which Locke took to explain the properties of persons that are definitive, Butler presumably thought Locke should have required identity of immaterial substance for personal identity. Perhaps, even granting the unsure connection between Butler's special kind of identity and ordinary identity, there are reasons for thinking personal identity must be a case of the former. But on this question Locke speaks well enough for himself. Using the term "body" technically, to mean a particular configuration of material particles,

Locke observes:

The question being what makes the same person; and whether it be the same identical substance, which always thinks in the same person, which, in this case, matters not at all: different substances, by the same consciousness (where they do partake in it) being united into one person, as well as different bodies by the same life are united into one animal, whose identity is preserved in that change of substances by the unity of continued life." [p. 40]

We don't know or care whether we are, throughout our lives, in "vital union" with one or many immaterial substances; we are willing to affirm or deny personal identity in complete ignorance of this question. Hence identity of immaterial substance is neither a necessary nor sufficient condition for personal identity. This is Locke's point; Butler seems not to face up to it at all.

Butler's own view seems to be that each individual person has an essence, a mental property which all his states of consciousness exemplify, and no one else's do (p. 100). And I think he would say that, in virtue of this fact, there was identity of substance wherever there was personal identity. Locke is entitled to object this in two places. First, this notion of substance seems at best tenuously related to that notion of substance used by Locke when he denied that identity of substance is a necessary condition of personal identity. Second, Butler is certainly wrong in thinking that all my or anyone else's conscious states have such a special property that sets them off from conscious states belonging to others, a point well made by Hume (p. 161).

We are left with Butler's claim that if personal identity were not identity in the so called strict and philosophical sense, our concern with our own futures and pasts would be inexplicable. Butler thought that when the logical implications of Locke's "hasty observations" on the topic were laid bare, this would be obvious:

that our substance is indeed continually changing; but whether this be so or not, is nothing to the purpose, since it is not substance, but consciousness alone, which constitutes personality; which consciousness, being successive, cannot be the same in any two moments, nor consequently the personality constituted by it. And hence it must follow, that it is a fallacy on ourselves, to charge our present selves with anything we did, or to imagine our present selves interested in anything which befell us yesterday, or that our present self will be interested in what will befall us tomorrow. ... [P. 102]

Butler's argument rests on the denial of identity in the ordinary sense between the person who worries today and the person who acts tomorrow. Although some of the philosophers who "developed" Locke's views agreed with Butler about this, there is no reason to, as we have seen. Locke could simply grant Butler his notion of strict and philosophical identity, but point out that since we are concerned with our future, and our present person-stages do not have the relations appropriate to strict and philosophical identity with our later ones, Butler must be wrong in thinking that strict and philosophical identity has anything to do with our special concern for our pasts and futures.

While this may be sufficient to blunt Butler's criticism, the issues here run somewhat deeper, as a study of Williams and Parfit will show.

HUME'S THEORY

I shall conclude with a few remarks about Hume, whose famous essay is unique in its mixture of insight and enigma. I believe Hume offers an interesting if sketchy theory of personal identity, a *causal* theory, disguised as the revolutionary discovery that there is no such thing as personal identity. I want to remove the disguise and reveal the theory, as fair game for amendment and elaboration, or criticism and rejection.

According to Hume, what is really true in cases we describe as cases of "personal identity" is this: distinct perceptions ("perception" is Hume's most general word for a mental event) bear a certain relation of resemblance or causation to one another. The perceptions themselves are not identical, says Hume, nor can any one entity be discovered or proven to exist, which is in any way involved in both perceptions. Thus, he says, a case of personal identity is not a case of identity at all. He does not regard this as the common sense view, nor the received view among philosophers, but as a philosophical discovery.

Why did Hume think that, strictly speaking, it is a mistake to talk about personal identity?

It's a mistake if there really is no identity when we say there is, and Hume thought that if we thought a bit about what might be meant by "identity," we should see that this is so. We must then look at what Hume has to say about identity. He discusses this topic in an earlier chapter of his *Treatise*, "On Skepticism With Regard to the Senses."

Hume's empiricism included pretty rigid adherence to the doctrine that for every idea there is a corresponding impression. Ideas and impressions are both "perceptions"; they differ in "vivacity and strength." Impressions include sensations and hallucinations; ideas include ordinary imaginings, visual imagery, and so forth, and also *concepts*, which Hume perhaps thought of as a species of image. And this raises a problem. What impression corresponds to our idea of identity? Hume says,

One single object conveys the idea of unity, not that of identity . . . [P. 159].

On the other hand, a multiplicity of objects can never convey this idea, however resembling they may be supposed. The mind always pronounces the one not to be the other, and considers them as forming two, three, or any determinate number of objects, whose existences are entirely distinct and independent. [P. 159]

So Hume thinks that we can find impressions corresponding to unity, and impressions corresponding to number or diversity, but no impression corresponding to identity, which is somehow a "mean" between these two ideas.

But then he does manage to find an impression which, in a way, corresponds to our idea of identity. Suppose I have a single impression for a period of time, say, from 10:01 to 10:03. To say it is a single impression, is to imply that it is uninterrupted and unchanging. Now there are two ways I can "survey" such an impression. I can think of it as it actually occurred, first thinking of what went on in my mind at 10:01, and then thinking of what went on in my mind a second later, and so on. "Surveyed" in such a way, this single impression corresponds to the idea of *unity*. But I could also think, at one time, of the impression I had at 10:01, and of the impression I had at 10:03. To do this I would have to "multiply" the impression in my mind, and so, "surveyed" in this way, such an impression corresponds to the idea of *number*. Such an invariable and uninterrupted impression, which is capable of being "surveyed" in either of these ways, corresponds to a "medium betwixt unity and number," and that is *identity*. Thus our idea of identity is of the "invariableness and uninterruptedness of any object, thro a suppos'd variation of time, without any break of the view, and without being oblig'd to form the idea of multiplicity or number" (p. 160).

Given this analysis of identity, Hume launches an ingenious exploration of the causes or our attributing identity to impressions that are not parts of an invariable and uninterrupted series. The core of the explanation is simply that we mistakenly attribute identity in cases in which, though there is no invariableness, there is close resemblance, and to cases in which, although there is interruption, the series as a whole resembles a series of perceptions we have had which are uninterrupted. It's clear that Hume intends this as a purely empirical, psychological explanation of a mistake we make, which has its origin in the constitution of the human mind.

If Hume's analysis of identity were correct, he would be right in denying that cases of personal identity are cases of identity at all. The perceptions which we count as the perceptions of a single person—e.g., the perceptions, past and present, which I consider mine—do not form an invariable or uninterrupted series. And there seems to be no particular reason to believe in an "unknown substance" which in some way would provide the invariability and uninterruptedness required.

But Hume's analysis of identity is wrong. The search for an impression of identity is unnecessary, the problem produced when one is not found, illusory, and the impression Hume finally comes up with, irrelevant. We can see that something is fishy right off. Why does Hume think that an impression corresponding to our idea of unity is easier to come by than one corresponding to identity? Does my impression of a deck of cards correspond to my idea of unity? or multiplicity? There is a single deck, but a number of cards. In general, it doesn't make sense to ask, "Is X seeing one thing or many things?" It only makes sense to ask "Is X seeing one F or many Fs" where F is a word or phrase like "card" or "deck of cards," or "man" or "arm" or "tree" or "branch." And these pairs of examples illustrate, with different substitutions for "F" we may get different answers, even given the same person and the same act of seeing. And so it is with identity, and for the same reasons. If I see two baseball events, I may be getting impressions of the same game, but of different innings. So Hume goes wrong in asking for an impression of identity *simpliciter.*

Suppose then we ask, "What impression or impressions correspond to our idea of *the same person*?" The question is still somewhat fishy. Consider two impressions of Richard Nixon, had by someone who saw him at ages 15 and 60. Does this pair of impressions somehow correspond to our idea of "the same person?" I cannot see any important sense in which it does. For all the person who has the impressions knows, he may have been seeing different people; nothing *in the impressions* show this not to be the case. Impressions *of* the same person are not necessarily impressions that correspond to our idea of the same person. If we demanded, that any two impressions of the same person, be such that one could tell, just by examination of those impressions, whether or not they are impressions of the same person, we will be driven to analyzing personal identity in terms of exact similarity, and then be disappointed to find that it never occurs. But the demand is wrong.

Can any sense be made of Hume's search for an impression? I think so. Having the concepts expressed by a word is in *some* way connected with understanding what the world must be like for sentences in which the word occurs to be true. It is this that was appealed to in the second section of this introduction, when we said that the student of baseball wouldn't have mastery of the concept of a baseball game, unless, given adequate information, he could make correct judgments about whether baseball events belong to the same game. And one might plausibly think that this means knowing what impressions one would or could have if such sentences were true.

If this is true, and is the kernel of truth behind Hume's demand for an impression corresponding to our idea of identity, then what he should do, to analyze the concept of personal identity, is ask what we require of the world for two person-events to belong to the same person. But now this is just what Hume tells us, although he describes himself not as offering an analysis of what we ordinarily mean by personal identity, but rather a discovery about what we mistakenly call personal identity. He offers an answer to the question he should have asked, but did not: person events belong to the same person if they are linked by the relations of causation and resemblance. We can take Hume's theory of what we have instead of personal identity as a theory of what personal identity is. As such, it seems to me to have considerable merit in its emphasis on causation, although of course Hume gives us nothing like a thoroughly worked out version of the theory.

CONCLUDING REMARKS

I have tried to outline a framework for consideration of theories of personal identity, and to uncover some of the more pervasive confusions which have led philosophers like Hume and Butler astray. But the topic of personal identity consists in many more controversies than those discussed or alluded to in this introduction. The essays here anthologized constitute a good introduction to the more important and central controversies. But even they do not exhaust the topic of personal identity, and the interested student should be drawn into the vast and rewarding literature (some of which is listed at the end of this volume) from which they are selected.

NOTES

1. See the remarks of Christiaan Barnard, quoted in *Newsweek,* December 23, 1968, p. 46.

2. This formula would need revision if we were to take into account certain odd cases. See my paper, "Can the Self Divide?" *Journal of Philosophy* (September 7, 1972).

3. See Sydney Shoemaker, *Self-Knowledge and Self-Identity* (Ithaca, Cornell University Press, 1958), chap. 1.

4. Shoemaker makes such a criticism in *Self-Knowledge and Self-Identity,* pp. 45 ff.

PART II

VERSIONS OF
THE MEMORY THEORY

John Locke

2

Of Identity and Diversity

1. *Wherein Identity Consists.* — Another occasion the mind often takes of comparing, is the very being of things; when, considering anything as existing at any determined time and place, we compare it with itself existing at another time, and thereon form the ideas of identity and diversity. When we see anything to be in any place in any instant of time, we are sure (be it what it will) that it is that very thing, and not another, which at that same time exists in another place, how like and undistinguishable soever it may be in all other respects: and in this consists identity, when the ideas it is attributed to vary not at all from what they were that moment wherein we consider their former existence, and to which we compare the present. For we never finding, nor conceiving it possible, that two things of the same kind should exist in the same place at the same time, we rightly conclude, that, whatever exists anywhere at any time, excludes all of the same kind, and is there itself alone. When therefore we demand whether anything be the same or no, it refers always to something that existed such a time in such a place, which it was certain at that instant was the same with itself, and no other. From whence it follows, that one thing cannot have two beginnings of existence, nor two things one beginning; it being

The selection is chapter 27 of Locke's *Essay Concerning Human Understanding.* The *Essay* was first published in 1690; this chapter first appeared in the second edition, 1694. The numbering of the first ten sections varies from edition to edition; the popular edition by A. C. Fraser assigns the number 10 to both section 8 and section 10.

impossible for two things of the same kind to be or exist in the same instant, in the very same place, or one and the same thing in different places. That, therefore, that had one beginning, is the same thing; and that which had a different beginning in time and place from that, is not the same, but diverse. That which has made the difficulty about this relation has been the little care and attention used in having precise notions of the things to which it is attributed.

2. *Identity of Substances*—We have the ideas but of three sorts of substances: 1. God. 2. Finite intelligences. 3. Bodies. First, God is without beginning, eternal, unalterable, and everywhere; and therefore concerning his identity there can be no doubt. Secondly, Finite spirits having had each its determinate time and place of beginning to exist, the relation to that time and place will always determine to each of them its identity, as long as it exists. Thirdly, The same will hold of every particle of matter, to which no addition or subtraction of matter being made, it is the same. For, though these three sorts of substances, as we term them, do not exclude one another out of the same place, yet we cannot conceive but that they must necessarily each of them exclude any of the same kind out of the same place; or else the notions and names of identity and diversity would be in vain, and there could be no such distinctions of substances, or anything else one from another. For example: could two bodies be in the same place at the same time, then those two parcels of matter must be one and the same, take them great or little; nay, all bodies must be one and the same. For, by the same reason that two particles of matter may be in one place, all bodies may be in one place; which, when it can be supposed, takes away the distinction of identity and diversity of one and more, and renders it ridiculous. But it being a contradiction that two or more should be one, identity and diversity are relations and ways of comparing well founded, and of use to the understanding.

Identity of Modes.—All other things being but modes or relations ultimately terminated in substances, the identity and diversity of each particular existence of them too will be by the same way determined: only as to things whose existence is in succession, such as are the actions of finite beings, v.g., motion and thought, both which consist in a continued train of succession: concerning their diversity there can be no question; because each perishing the moment it begins, they cannot exist in different times, or in different places, as permanent beings can at different times exist in distant places; and therefore no motion or thought, considered as at different times, can be the same, each part thereof having a different beginning of existence.

3. *Principium Individuationis.*—From what has been said, it is easy to discover what is so much inquired after, the principium individuationis; and that, it is plain, is existence itself, which determines a being of any sort to a particular time and place, incommunicable to two beings of the same kind. This, though it seems easier to conceive in simple substances or modes, yet, when reflected on, is not more difficult in compound ones, if care be taken to what it is applied: v.g., let us suppose an atom, i.e., a continued body under one immutable superfices, existing in a determined time and place; it is evident, that considered in any instant of its existence, it is in that instant the same with itself. For, being at that instant what it is, and nothing else, it is the same, and so must continue as long as its existence is continued; for so long it will be the same, and no other. In like manner, if two or more atoms be joined together into the same mass, every one of those atoms will be the same, by the foregoing rule: and whilst they exist united together, the mass, consisting of the same atoms, must be the same mass, or the same body, let the parts be ever so differently jumbled. But if one of these atoms be taken away, or one new one added, it is no longer the same mass or the same body. In the state of living creatures, their identity depends not on a mass of the same particles, but on something else. For in them the variation of great parcels of matter alters not the identity: an oak growing from a plant to a great tree, and then lopped, is still the same oak; and a colt grown up to a horse, sometimes fat, sometimes lean, is all the while the same horse: though, in both these cases, there may be a manifest change of the parts; so that truly they are not either of them the same masses of matter, though they be truly one of them the same oak, and the other the same horse. The reason whereof is, that, in these two cases, a mass of matter, and a living body, identity is not applied to the same thing.

4. *Identity of Vegetables.*—We must therefore consider wherein an oak differs from a mass of matter, and that seems to me to be in this, that the one is only the cohesion of par-

ticles of matter any how united, the other such a disposition of them as constitutes the parts of an oak; and such an organization of those parts as is fit to receive and distribute nourishment, so as to continue and frame the wood, bark, and leaves, etc., of an oak, in which consists the vegetable life. That being then one plant which has such an organization of parts in one coherent body, partaking of one common life, it continues to be the same plant as long as it partakes of the same life, though that life be communicated to new particles of matter vitally united to the living plant, in a like continued organization conformable to that sort of plants. For this organization being at any one instant in any one collection of matter, is in that particular concrete distinguished from all other, and is that individual life, which existing constantly from that moment both forwards and backwards, in the same continuity of insensibly succeeding parts united to the living body of the plant, it has that identity which makes the same plant, and all the parts of it, parts of the same plant, during all the time that they exist united in that continued organization, which is fit to convey that common life to all the parts so united.

5. *Identity of Animals.*—The case is not so much different in brutes, but that any one may hence see what makes an animal and continues it the same. Something we have like this in machines, and may serve to illustrate it. For example, what is a watch? It is plain it is nothing but a fit organization or construction of parts to a certain end, which, when a sufficient force is added to it, it is capable to attain. If we would suppose this machine one continued body, all whose organized parts were repaired, increased, or diminished by a constant addition or separation of insensible parts, with one common life, we should have something very much like the body of an animal; with this difference, that, in an animal the fitness of the organization, and the motion wherein life consists, begin together, the motion coming from within; but in machines, the force coming sensibly from without, is often away when the organ is in order, and well fitted to receive it.

6. *The Identity of Man.*—This also shows wherein the identity of the same man consists; viz., in nothing but a participation of the same continued life, by constantly fleeting particles of matter, in succession vitally united to the same organized

body. He that shall place the identity of man in anything else, but like that of other animals, in one fitly organized body, taken in any one instant, and from thence continued, under one organization of life, in several successively fleeting particles of matter united to it, will find it hard to make an embryo, one of years, mad and sober, the same man, by any supposition, that will not make it possible for Seth, Ismael, Socrates, Pilate, St. Austin, and Caesar Borgia, to be the same man. For, if the identity of soul alone makes the same man, and there be nothing in the nature of matter why the same individual spirit may not be united to different bodies, it will be possible that those men living in distant ages, and of different tempers, may have been the same man: which way of speaking must be, from a very strange use of the word man, applied to an idea, out of which body and shape are excluded. And that way of speaking would agree yet worse with the notions of those philosophers who allow of transmigration, and are of opinion that the souls of men may, for their miscarriages, be detruded into the bodies of beasts, as fit habitations, with organs suited to the satisfaction of their brutal inclinations. But yet I think nobody, could he be sure that the soul of Heliogabalus were in one of his hogs, would yet say that hog were a man or Heliogabalus.

7. *Identity Suited to the Idea.*—It is not therefore unity of substance that comprehends all sorts of identity, or will determine it in every case; but to conceive and judge of it aright, we must consider what idea the word it is applied to stands for: it being one thing to be the same substance, another the same man, and a third the same person, if person, man, and substance, are three names standing for three different ideas; for such as is the idea belonging to that name, such must be the identity; which, if it had been a little more carefully attended to, would possibly have prevented a great deal of that confusion which often occurs about this matter, with no small seeming difficulties, especially concerning personal identity, which therefore we shall in the next place a little consider.

8. *Same Man.*—An animal is living organized body; and consequently the same animal, as we have observed, is the same continued life communicated to different particles of matter, as they happen successively to be united to that organized living body. And whatever is talked of other definitions, ingenious

observation puts it past doubt, that the idea in our minds, of which the sound man in our mouths is the sign, is nothing else but of an animal of such a certain form: since I think I may be confident, that, whoever should see a creature of his own shape or make, though it had no more reason all its life than a cat or a parrot, would call him still a man; or whoever should hear a cat or a parrot discourse, reason, and philosophize, would call or think it nothing but a cat or a parrot; and say, the one was a dull irrational man, and the other a very intelligent rational parrot. A relation we have in an author of great note, is sufficient to countenance the supposition of a rational parrot. His words are:

I had a mind to know, from Prince Maurice's own mouth, the account of a common, but much credited story, that I had heard so often from many others, of an old parrot he had in Brazil, during his government there, that spoke, and asked, and answered common questions, like a reasonable creature: so that those of his train there generally concluded it to be witchery or possession; and one of his chaplains, who lived long afterwards in Holland, would never from that time endure a parrot, but said they all had a devil in them. I had heard many particulars of this story, and assevered by people hard to be discredited, which made me ask Prince Maurice what there was of it. He said, with his usual plainness and dryness in talk, there was something true, but a great deal false of what had been reported. I desired to know of him what there was of the first. He told me short and coldly, that he had heard of such an old parrot when he had been at Brazil; and though he believed nothing of it, and it was a good way off, yet he had so much curiosity as to send for it: that it was a very great and a very old one; and when it came first into the room where the prince was, with a great many Dutchmen about him, it said presently, What a company of white men are here! They asked it, what it thought that man was, pointing to the prince. It answered, Some General or other. When they brought it close to him, he asked it, D'ou venez-vous? It answered, De Marinnan. The Prince, A qui estes-vous? The parrot, A un Portugais. The Prince, Que fais-tu là? Je garde les poulles. The Prince laughed, and said, Vous gardez les poulles? The parrot answered, Oui, moi, et je sçai bien faire; and made the chuck four or five times that people use to make to chickens when they call them. I set down the words of this worthy dialogue in French, just as Prince Maurice said them to me. I asked him in what language the parrot spoke, and he said in Brazilian. I asked whether he understood Brazilian; he said no: but he had taken care to have two interpreters by him, the one a Dutchman that spoke Brazilian, and the other a Brazilian that spoke Dutch; that he asked them separately and privately, and both of them agreed in telling him just the same thing that the parrot had said. I could not but tell this odd story, because it is so much out of the way, and from the first hand, and what may pass for a good one; for I dare say this prince at least believed himself in all he told me, having ever passed for a very honest and pious man: I leave it to naturalists to reason, and to other men to believe, as they please upon it; however, it is not, perhaps, amiss to relieve or enliven a busy scene sometimes with such digressions, whether to the purpose or no.

Same Man.—I have taken care that the reader should have the story at large in the author's own words, because he seems to me not to have thought it incredible; for it cannot be imagined that so able a man as he, who had sufficiency enough to warrant all the testimonies he gives of himself, should take so much pains, in a place where it had nothing to do, to pin so close not only on a man whom he mentions as his friend, but on a prince in whom he acknowledges very great honesty and piety, a story which, if he himself thought incredible, he could not but also think ridiculous. The prince, it is plain, who vouches this story, and our author, who relates it from him, both of them call this talker a parrot: and I ask any one else who thinks such a story fit to be told, whether—if this parrot, and all of its kind, had always talked, as we have a prince's word for it this one did—whether, I say, they would not have passed for a race of rational animals; but yet, whether, for all that, they would have been allowed to be men, and not parrots? For I presume it is not the idea of a thinking or rational being alone that makes the idea of a man in most people's sense, but of a body, so and so shaped, joined to it; and if that be the idea of a man, the same successive body not shifted all at once, must, as well as the same immaterial spirit, go to the making of the same man.

9. *Personal Identity.*—This being premised, to find wherein personal identity consists, we must consider what person stands for; which, I think, is a thinking intelligent being, that has reason and reflection, and can consider itself as itself, the same thinking thing, in different times and places; which it does only by that consciousness which is inseparable from thinking, and, as it seems to me, essential to it: it being impossible for any one to perceive without perceiving that he does perceive. When we see, hear, smell, taste, feel, meditate, or will anything, we know that we do so. Thus it is always as to our present sensations and perceptions: and by this every one is to himself that which he calls self; it not being considered, in this case, whether the same self be continued in the same or divers substances. For, since consciousness always accompanies thinking, and it is that which makes every one to be what he calls self, and thereby distinguishes himself from all other thinking things: in this alone consists personal identity, i.e., the sameness of a rational being; and as far as this consciousness can be extended backwards to any past action or thought, so far reaches the identity of that person;

it is the same self now it was then; and it is by the same self with this present one that now reflects on it, that that action was done.

10. *Consciousness Makes Personal Identity.*—But it is further inquired, whether it be the same identical substance? This, few would think they had reason to doubt of, if these perceptions, with their consciousness, always remained present in the mind, whereby the same thinking thing would be always consciously present, and, as would be thought, evidently the same to itself. But that which seems to make the difficulty is this, that this consciousness being interrupted always by forgetfulness, there being no moment of our lives wherein we have the whole train of all our past actions before our eyes in one view, but even the best memories losing the sight of one part whilst they are viewing another; and we sometimes, and that the greatest part of our lives, not reflecting on our past selves, being intent on our present thoughts, and in sound sleep having no thoughts at all, or at least none with that consciousness which remarks our waking thoughts; I say, in all these cases, our consciousness being interrupted, and we losing the sight of our past selves, doubts are raised whether we are the same thinking thing, i.e., the same substance or no. Which, however reasonable or unreasonable, concerns not personal identity at all: the question being, what makes the same person, and not whether it be the same identical substance, which always thinks in the same person; which, in this case, matters not at all: different substances, by the same consciousness (where they do partake in it) being united into one person, as well as different bodies by the same life are united into one animal, whose identity is preserved in that change of substances by the unity of one continued life. For it being the same consciousness that makes a man be himself to himself, personal identity depends on that only, whether it be annexed solely to one individual substance, or can be continued in a succession of several substances. For as far as any intelligent being can repeat the idea of any past action with the same consciousness it had of it at first, and with the same consciousness it has of any present action; so far it is the same personal self. For it is by the consciousness it has of its present thoughts and actions, that it is self to itself now, and so will be the same self, as far as the same consciousness can extend to actions past

or to come; and would be by distance of time, or change of substance, no more two persons, than a man be two men by wearing other clothes to-day than he did yesterday, with a long or a short sleep between: the same consciousness uniting those distant actions into the same person, whatever substances contributed to their production.

11. *Personal Identity in Change of Substances.*—That this is so, we have some kind of evidence in our very bodies, all whose particles, whilst vitally united to this same thinking conscious self, so that we feel when they are touched, and are affected by, and conscious of good or harm that happens to them, are a part of ourselves; i.e., of our thinking conscious self. Thus, the limbs of his body are to every one a part of himself; he sympathizes and is concerned for them. Cut off a hand, and thereby separate it from that consciousness he had of its heat, cold, and other affections, and it is then no longer a part of that which is himself, any more than the remotest part of matter. Thus, we see the substance whereof personal self consisted at one time may be varied at another, without the change of personal identity; there being no question about the same person, though the limbs which but now were a part of it, be cut off.

12. But the question is, "Whether, if the same substance, which thinks, be changed, it can be the same person; or, remaining the same, it can be different persons?"

Whether in the Change of Thinking Substances.—And to this I answer: First, This can be no question at all to those who place thought in a purely material animal constitution, void of an immaterial substance. For, whether their supposition be true or no, it is plain they conceive personal identity preserved in something else than identity of substance; as animal identity is preserved in identity of life, and not of substance. And therefore those who place thinking in an immaterial substance only, before they can come to deal with these men, must show why personal identity cannot be preserved in the change of immaterial substances, or variety of particular immaterial substances, as well as animal identity is preserved in the change of material substances, or variety of particular bodies: unless they will say, it is one immaterial spirit that makes the same life in brutes, as it is one immaterial spirit that makes the same person in men; which the Cartesians at least will not admit, for fear of making brutes thinking things too.

13. But next, as to the first part of the question, "Whether, if the same thinking substance (supposing immaterial substances only to think) be changed, it can be the same person?" I answer, that cannot be resolved, but by those who know what kind of substances they are that do think, and whether the consciousness of past actions can be transferred from one thinking substance to another. I grant, were the same consciousness the same individual action, it could not: but it being a present representation of a past action, why it may not be possible that that may be represented to the mind to have been, which really never was, will remain to be shown. And therefore how far the consciousness of past actions is annexed to any individual agent, so that another cannot possibly have it, will be hard for us to determine, till we know what kind of action it is that cannot be done without a reflex act of perception accompanying it, and how performed by thinking substances, who cannot think without being conscious of it. But that which we call the same consciousness, not being the same individual act, why one intellectual substance may not have represented to it, as done by itself, what it never did, and was perhaps done by some other agent; why, I say, such a representation may not possibly be without reality of matter of fact, as well as several representations in dreams are, which yet whilst dreaming we take for true, will be difficult to conclude from the nature of things. And that it never is so, will by us, till we have clearer views of the nature of thinking substances, be best resolved into the goodness of God, who, as far as the happiness or misery of any of his sensible creatures is concerned in it, will not, by a fatal error of theirs, transfer from one to another that consciousness which draws reward or punishment with it. How far this may be an argument against those who would place thinking in a system of fleeting animal spirits, I leave to be considered. But yet, to return to the question before us, it must be allowed, that, if the same consciousness (which, as has been shown, is quite a different thing from the same numerical figure or motion in body) can be transferred from one thinking substance to another, it will be possible that two thinking substances may make but one person. For the same consciousness being preserved, whether in the same or different substances, the personal identity is preserved.

14. As to the second part of the question, "Whether the

same immaterial substance remaining, there may be two distinct
person?" which question seems to me to be built on this, whether the same immaterial being, being conscious of the action of
its past duration, may be wholly stripped of all the consciousness of its past existence, and lose it beyond the power of ever
retrieving it again; and so as it were beginning a new account
from a new period, have a consciousness that cannot reach beyond this new state. All those who hold pre-existence are evidently of this mind, since they allow the soul to have no remaining consciousness of what it did in that pre-existent state, either
wholly separate from body, or informing any other body; and
if they should not, it is plain experience would be against them.
So that personal identity reaching no further than consciousness
reaches, a pre-existent spirit not having continued so many ages
in a state of silence, must needs make different persons. Suppose
a Christian Platonist or a Pythagorean should, upon God's having
ended all his works of creation the seventh day, think his soul
hath existed ever since; and would imagine it has revolved in
several human bodies, as I once met with one, who was persuaded his had been the soul of Socrates; (how reasonably I will not
dispute; this I know, that in the post he filled, which was no
inconsiderable one, he passed for a very rational man, and the
press has shown that he wanted not parts or learning;) would
any one say, that he, being not conscious of any of Socrates'
actions or thoughts, could be the same person with Socrates?
Let any one reflect upon himself, and conclude that he has in
himself an immaterial spirit, which is that which thinks in him,
and, in the constant change of his body keeps him the same:
and is that which he calls himself: let him also suppose it to be
the same soul that was in Nestor or Thersites, at the siege of
Troy (for souls being, as far as we know anything of them, in
their nature indifferent to any parcel of matter, the supposition
has no apparent absurdity in it), which it may have been, as
well as it is now the soul of any other man: but he now having
no consciousness of any of the actions either of Nestor or
Thersites, does or can he conceive himself the same person with
either of them? Can he be concerned in either of their actions?
attribute them to himself, or think them his own, more than the
actions of any other men that ever existed? So that this consciousness not reaching to any of the actions of either of those

men, he is no more one self with either of them, than if the
soul or immaterial spirit that now informs him had been created,
and began to exist, when it began to inform his present body,
though it were ever so true, that the same spirit that informed
Nestor's or Thersites' body were numerically the same that now
informs his. For this would no more make him the same person
with Nestor, than if some of the particles of matter that were
once a part of Nestor, were now a part of this man; the same
immaterial substance, without the same consciousness, no more
making the same person by being united to any body, than the
same particle of matter, without consciousness united to any
body, makes the same person. But let him once find himself
conscious of any of the actions of Nestor, he then finds himself
the same person with Nestor.

15. And thus may we be able, without any difficulty, to
conceive the same person at the resurrection, though in a body
not exactly in make or parts the same which he had here, the
same consciousness going along with the soul that inhabits it.
But yet the soul alone, in the change of bodies, would scarce to
any one but to him that makes the soul the man, be enough to
make the same man. For should the soul of a prince, carrying
with it the consciousness of the prince's past life, enter and inform the body of a cobbler, as soon as deserted by his own soul,
every one sees he would be the same person with the prince,
accountable only for the prince's actions: but who would say it
was the same man? The body too goes to the making the man,
and would, I guess, to everybody determine the man in this
case; wherein the soul, with all its princely thoughts about it,
would not make another man: but he would be the same cobbler to every one besides himself. I know that, in the ordinary
way of speaking, the same person, and the same man, stand
for one and the same thing. And indeed every one will always
have a liberty to speak as he pleases, and to apply what
articulate sounds to what ideas he thinks fit, and change them
as often as he pleases. But yet, when we will inquire what
makes the same spirit, man, or person, we must fix the ideas
of spirit, man, or person in our minds, and having resolved
with ourselves what we mean by them, it will not be hard
to determine in either of them, or the like, when it is the
same, and when not.

16. *Consciousness makes the same Person.*—But though the same immaterial substance or soul does not alone, wherever it be, and in whatsoever state, make the same man; yet it is plain, consciousness, as far as ever it can be extended, should it be to ages past, unites existences and actions, very remote in time into the same person, as well as it does the existences and actions of the immediately preceding moment: so that whatever has the consciousness of present and past actions, is the same person to whom they both belong. Had I the same consciousness that I saw the ark and Noah's flood, as that I saw an overflowing of the Thames last winter, or as that I write now; I could no more doubt that I who write this now, that saw the Thames overflowed last winter, and that viewed the flood at the general deluge, was the same self, place that self in what substance you please, than that I who write this am the same myself now whilst I write (whether I consist of all the same substance, material or immaterial, or no) that I was yesterday; for as to this point of being the same self, it matters not whether this present self be made up of the same or other substances; I being as much concerned, and as justly accountable for any action that was done a thousand years since, appropriated to me now by this self-consciousness, as I am for what I did the last moment.

17. *Self Depends on Consciousness.*—Self is that conscious thinking thing, whatever substance made up of (whether spiritual or material, simple or compounded, it matters not), which is sensible or conscious of pleasure and pain, capable of happiness or misery, and so is concerned for itself, as far as that consciousness extends. Thus every one finds, that, whilst comprehended under that consciousness, the little finger is as much a part of himself as what is most so. Upon separation of this little finger, should this consciousness go along with the little finger, and leave the rest of the body, it is evident the little finger would be the person, the same person, and self then would have nothing to do with the rest of the body. As in this case it is the consciousness that goes along with the substance, when one part is separate from another, which makes the same person, and constitutes this inseparable self; so it is in reference to substances remote in time. That with which the consciousness of this present thinking thing can join itself, makes the same person, and is one self with it, and with nothing else; and so attributes to itself,

and owns all the actions of that thing as its own, as far as that consciousness reaches, and no further; as every one who reflects will perceive.

18. *Objects of Reward and Punishment.*—In this personal identity is founded all the right and justice of reward and punishment; happiness and misery being that for which every one is concerned for himself, and not mattering what becomes of any substance not joined to, or affected with that consciousness. For as it is evident in the instance I gave but now, if the consciousness went along with the little finger when it was cut off, that would be the same self which was concerned for the whole body yesterday, as making part of itself, whose actions then it cannot but admit as its own now. Though, if the same body should still live, and immediately from the separation of the little finger have its own peculiar consciousness, whereof the little finger knew nothing; it would not at all be concerned for it, as a part of itself, or could own any of its actions, or have any of them imputed to him.

19. This may show us wherein personal identity consists: not in the identity of substance, but, as I have said, in the identity of consciousness; wherein if Socrates and the present mayor of Queenborough agree, they are the same person: if the same Socrates waking and sleeping do not partake of the same consciousness, Socrates waking and sleeping is not the same person. And to punish Socrates waking for what sleeping Socrates thought, and waking Socrates was never conscious of, would be no more of right, than to punish one twin for what his brother-twin did, whereof he knew nothing, because their outsides were so like, that they could not be distinguished; for such twins have been seen.

20. But yet possibly it will still be objected, suppose I wholly lose the memory of some parts of my life, beyond a possibility of retrieving them, so that perhaps I shall never be conscious of them again; yet am I not the same person that did those actions, had those thoughts that I once was conscious of, though I have now forgot them? To which I answer, that we must here take notice what the word I is applied to; which, in this case, is the man only. And the same man being presumed to be the same person, I is easily here supposed to stand also for

the same person. But if it be possible for the same man to have distinct incommunicable consciousness at different times, it is past doubt the same man would at different times make different persons; which, we see, is the sense of mankind in the solemnest declaration of their opinions; human laws not punishing the mad man for the sober man's actions, nor the sober man for what the mad man did, thereby making them two persons: which is somewhat explained by our way of speaking in English, when we say such an one is not himself, or is beside himself; in which phrases it is insinuated, as if those who now, or at least first used them, thought that self was changed, the selfsame person was no longer in that man.

21. *Difference between Identity of Man and Person.* —But yet it is hard to conceive that Socrates, the same individual man, should be two persons. To help us a little in this, we must consider what is meant by Socrates, or the same individual man.

First, it must be either the same individual, immaterial, thinking substance; in short, the same numerical soul, and nothing else.

Secondly, or the same animal, without any regard to an immaterial soul.

Thirdly, or the same immaterial spirit united to the same animal.

Now, take which of these suppositions you please, it is impossible to make personal identity to consist in anything but consciousness, or reach any further than that does.

For, by the first of them, it must be allowed possible that a man born of different women, and in distant times, may be the same man. A way of speaking, which whoever admits, must allow it possible for the same man to be two distinct persons, as any two that have lived in different ages, without the knowledge of one another's thoughts.

By the second and third, Socrates, in this life and after it, cannot be the same man any way, but by the same consciousness; and so making human identity to consist in the same thing wherein we place personal identity, there will be no difficulty to allow the same man to be the same person. But then they who place human identity in consciousness only, and not in something else, must consider how they will make the infant

Socrates the same man with Socrates after the resurrection. But whatsoever to some men makes a man, and consequently the same individual man, wherein perhaps few are agreed, personal identity can by us be placed in nothing but consciousness (which is that alone which makes what we call self), without involving us in great absurdities.

22. But is not a man drunk and sober the same person? why else is he punished for the fact he commits when drunk, though he be never afterwards conscious of it? Just as much the same person as a man that walks, and does other things in his sleep, is the same person, and is answerable for any mischief he shall do in it. Human laws punish both, with a justice suitable to their way of knowledge; because, in these cases, they cannot distinguish certainly what is real, what counterfeit: and so the ignorance in drunkenness or sleep is not admitted as a plea. For, though punishment be annexed to personality, and personality to consciousness, and the drunkard perhaps be not conscious of what he did, yet human judicatures justly punish him, because the fact is proved against him, but want of consciousness cannot be proved for him. But in the great day, wherein the secrets of all hearts shall be laid open, it may be reasonable to think, no one shall be made to answer for what he knows nothing of; but shall receive his doom, his conscience accusing or excusing him.

23. *Consciousness Alone Makes Self.*—Nothing but consciousness can unite remote existences into the same person: the identity of substance will not do it; for whatever substance there is, however framed, without consciousness there is no person: and a carcass may be a person, as well as any sort of substance be so without consciousness.

Could we suppose two distinct incommunicable consciousnesses acting the same body, the one constantly by day, the other by night; and, on the other side, the same consciousness, acting by intervals, two distinct bodies; I ask, in the first case, whether the day and the night man would not be two as distinct persons as Socrates and Plato? And whether, in the second case, there would not be one person in two distinct bodies, as much as one man is the same in two distinct clothings? Nor is it at all material to say, that this same, and this distinct consciousness, in the cases above mentioned, is owing to the same and distinct immaterial substances, bringing it with them to those bodies; which, whether true or no, alters not the case; since it is evident the personal identity would equally be determined by the consciousness, whether that consciousness were annexed to some individual immaterial substance or no. For, granting that the thinking substance in man must be necessarily supposed immaterial, it is evident that immaterial thinking thing may sometimes part with its past consciousness, and be restored to it again, as appears in the forgetfulness men often have of their past actions: and the mind many times recovers the memory of a past consciousness, which it had lost for twenty years together. Make these intervals of memory and forgetfulness to take their turns regularly by day and night, and you have two persons with the same immaterial spirit, as much as in the former instance two persons with the same body. So that self is not determined by identity or diversity of substance, which it cannot be sure of, but only by identity of consciousness.

24. Indeed it may conceive the substance whereof it is now made up to have existed formerly, united in the same conscious being; but, consciousness removed, that substance is no more itself, or makes no more a part of it, than any other substance; as is evident in the instance we have already given of a limb cut off, of whose heat, or cold, or other affections, having no longer any consciousness, it is no more of a man's self, than any other matter of the universe. In like manner it will be in reference to any immaterial substance, which is void of that consciousness whereby I am myself to myself: if there be any part of its existence which I cannot upon recollection join with that present consciousness, whereby I am now myself, it is in that part of its existence no more myself, than any other immaterial being. For whatsoever any substance has thought or done, which I cannot recollect, and by my consciousness make my own thought and action, it will no more belong to me, whether a part of me thought or did it, than if it had been thought or done by any other immaterial being anywhere existing.

25. I agree, the more probable opinion is, that this consciousness is annexed to, and the affection of, one individual immaterial substance.

But let men, according to their diverse hypotheses, resolve

of that as they please; this very intelligent being, sensible of
happiness or misery, must grant that there is something that is
himself that he is concerned for, and would have happy; that
this self has existed in a continued duration more than one instant, and therefore it is possible may exist, as it has done,
months and years to come, without any certain bounds to be set
to its duration; and may be the same self by the same consciousness continued on for the future. And thus, by this consciousness, he finds himself to be the same self which did such or such
an action some years since, by which he comes to be happy or
miserable now. In all which account of self, the same numerical
substance is not considered as making the same self; but the
same continued consciousness, in which several substances may
have been united, and again separated from it; which, whilst
they continued in a vital union with that wherein this consciousness then resided, made a part of that same self. Thus any part
of our bodies vitally united to that which is conscious in us,
makes a part of ourselves: but upon separation from the vital
union by which that consciousness is communicated, that which
a moment since was part of ourselves, is now no more so than
a part of another man's self is a part of me: and it is not impossible but in a little time may become a real part of another
person. And so we have the same numerical substance become
a part of two different persons; and the same person preserved
under the change of various substances. Could we suppose any
spirit wholly stripped of all its memory or consciousness of past
actions, as we find our minds always are of a great part of ours,
and sometimes of them all; the union or separation of such a
spiritual substance would make no variation of personal identity,
any more than that of any particle of matter does. Any substance vitally united to the present thinking being, is a part of
that very same self which now is; anything united to it by a
consciousness of former actions, makes also a part of the same
self, which is the same both then and now.

    26. *Person a Forensic Term.*—Person, as I take it, is the
name for this self. Wherever a man finds what he calls himself
there, I think, another may say is the same person. It is a forensic term, appropriating actions and their merit; and so belongs
only to intelligent agents capable of a law, and happiness, and

misery. This personality extends itself beyond present existence to what is past, only by consciousness, whereby it becomes concerned and accountable, owns and imputes to itself past actions, just upon the same ground and for the same reason that it does the present. All which is founded in a concern for happiness, the unavoidable concomitant of consciousness; that which is conscious of pleasure and pain, desiring that that self that is conscious should be happy. And therefore whatever past actions it cannot reconcile or appropriate to that present self by consciousness, it can be no more concerned in, than if they had never been done; and to receive pleasure or pain, i.e., reward or punishment, on the account of any such action, is all one as to be made happy or miserable in its first being, without any demerit at all: for supposing a man punished now for what he had done in another life, whereof he could be made to have no consciousness at all, what difference is there between that punishment, and being created miserable? And therefore, conformable to this, the apostle tells us, that, at the great day, when every one shall "receive according to his doings, the secrets of all hearts shall be laid open." The sentence shall be justified by the consciousness all persons shall have, that they themselves, in what bodies soever they appear, or what substances soever that consciousness adheres to, are the same that committed those actions, and deserve that punishment for them.

27. I am apt enough to think I have, in treating of this subject, made some suppositions that will look strange to some readers, and possibly they are so in themselves. But yet, I think they are such as are pardonable, in this ignorance we are in of the nature of that thinking thing that is in us, and which we look on as ourselves. Did we know what it was, or how it was tied to a certain system of fleeting animal spirits; or whether it could or could not perform its operations of thinking and memory out of a body organized as ours is: and whether it has pleased God, that no one such spirit shall ever be united to any one but such body, upon the right constitution of whose organs its memory should depend; we might see the absurdity of some of these suppositions I have made. But, taking as we ordinarily now do, (in the dark concerning these matters,) the soul of a man for an immaterial substance, independent from matter, and

indifferent alike to it all, there can, from the nature of things, be no absurdity at all to suppose that the same soul may at different times be united to different bodies, and with them make up for that time one man, as well as we suppose a part of a sheep's body yesterday should be a part of a man's body tomorrow, and in that union make a vital part of Meliboeus himself, as well as it did of his ram.

28. *The Difficulty from ill Use of Names.*—To conclude: Whatever substance begins to exist, it must, during its existence, necessarily be the same: whatever compositions of substances begin to exist, during the union of those substances the concrete must be the same; whatsoever mode begins to exist, during its existence it is the same; and so if the composition be of distinct substances and different modes, the same rule holds: whereby it will appear, that the difficulty or obscurity that has been about this matter rather rises from the names ill used, than from any obscurity in things themselves. For whatever makes the specific idea to which the name is applied, if that idea be steadily kept to, the distinction of anything into the same, and divers, will easily be conceived, and there can arise no doubt about it.

29. *Continued Existence makes Identity.*—For, supposing a rational spirit be the idea of a man, it is easy to know what is the same man, viz., the same spirit, whether separate or in a body, will be the same man. Supposing a rational spirit vitally united to a body of a certain conformation of parts to make a man, whilst that rational spirit, with that vital conformation of parts, though continued in a fleeting successive body, remain, it will be the same man. But if to any one the idea of a man be but the vital union of parts in a certain shape, as long as that vital union and shape remain in a concrete no otherwise the same, but by a continued succession of fleeting particles, it will be the same man. For, whatever be the composition whereof the complex idea is made, whenever existence makes it one particular thing under any denomination, the same existence continued, preserves it the same individual under the same denomination.

Anthony Quinton

3

The Soul

1. THE SOUL AND SPIRITUAL SUBSTANCE

Philosophers in recent times have had very little to say about the soul. The word, perhaps, has uncomfortably ecclesiastical associations, and the idea seems to be bound up with a number of discredited or at any rate generally disregarded theories. In the history of philosophy the soul has been used for two distinct purposes: first, as an explanation of the vitality that distinguishes human beings, and also animals and plants, from the broad mass of material objects, and, secondly, as the seat of consciousness. The first of these, which sees the soul as an ethereal but nonetheless physical entity, a volatile collection of fire-atoms or a stream of animal spirits, on some views dissipated with the dissolution of the body, on others absorbed at death into the cosmic soul, and on others again as capable of independent existence, need not detain us. The second, however, the soul of Plato and Descartes, deserves a closer examination than it now usually receives. For it tends to be identified with the view that in each person there is to be found a spiritual substance which is the subject of his mental states and the bearer of his personal identity. But on its widest interpretation, as the nonphysical aspect of a person, its acceptance need not involve either the existence of a spiritual substance over and above the

This article is reprinted from *The Journal of Philosophy,* vol. 59, no. 15 (July 1962), by courtesy of the editor and of A. Quinton.

mental states that make up a person's inner, conscious life or the proposition that this spiritual substance is what ultimately determines a person's identity through time. When philosophers dismiss the soul it is usually because they reject one or both of these supposed consequences of belief in it.

It is worth insisting, furthermore, that the existence of a spiritual substance is logically distinct from its being the criterion of personal identity. So the strong, and indeed fatal, arguments against the substance theory of personal identity do not at the same time refute the proposition, self-evident to Berkeley and many others, that there can be no conscious state that is not the state of some subject.

As a criterion of identity spiritual substance has three main weaknesses. First, it is regressive in just the same way as is an account of the identity of a material object through time in terms of its physical components. No general account of the identity of a kind of individual thing can be given which finds that identity in the presence of another individual thing within it. For the question immediately arises, how is the identity through time of the supposed identifier to be established? It, like the thing it is supposed to identify, can present itself at any one time only as it is at that time. However alike its temporally separate phases may be, they still require to be identified as parts of the same, continuing thing. In practice we do identify some wholes through their parts, normally where the parts are more stable and persistent unities than the wholes they compose and where, in consequence, the parts are more readily identifiable, as, for example, when we pick out one person's bundle of laundry from the bundles of others after the labels have been lost. But this can be only a practical expedient, not a theoretical solution.

A second difficulty is to find any observable mental entity that can effectively serve as a criterion in this case. The only plausible candidate is that dim, inchoate background, largely composed of organic sensations, which envelops the mental states occupying the focus of attention. This organic background is a relatively unchanging environment for the more dramatic episodes of conscious life to stand out against. But both the fixity and the peripheral status of this background are only relative. It does change, and it, or its parts, can come or be brought into the focus of attention. Even if its comparatively undisturbed persistence of character suggests it as a criterion, its vagueness makes it even less accessible to public application than the general run of mental criteria and leaves it with little power to distinguish between one person and another. The organic background is, of course, as regressive a criterion as any other part of a person's mental life. Its only virtues are that it is observable and that it does seem to be a universal constituent of the momentary cross sections of a person's experience. In this last respect it is preferable to most distinguishable features of a person's mental life. For, generally speaking, the parts of a complex and enduring thing are not necessary to the identity of that thing. Just as a cathedral is still the same cathedral if a piece has been knocked off it, whatever the piece may be, so a person is the same person if he ceases to have a particular belief or emotion, whatever that belief or emotion may be.

Finally, if it is held that the spiritual substance is nevertheless a permanent and unaltering constituent of a person's conscious life, it follows that it must be unobservable and so useless for purposes of identification. Suppose that from its very first stirrings my consciousness has contained a continuous whistling sound of wholly unvarying character. I should clearly never notice it, for I can only notice what varies independently of my consciousness—the whistles that start and stop at times other than those at which I wake up and fall asleep. It is this fact that ensured from the outset that Hume's search for a self over and above his particular perceptions was bound to fail. The unobservability of spiritual substance, and its consequent inapplicability as a criterion, can also be held to follow directly from taking its status as substance seriously, as an uncharacterized substratum for qualities and relations to inhere in with no recognizable features of its own.

But to admit that spiritual substance cannot possibly be the criterion of a person's identity and that it cannot be identified with any straightforwardly observable part of a person's mental life does not mean that it does not exist. It has seemed self-evident to many philosophers that every mental state must have an owner. To believe this is not to commit oneself to the existence of something utterly unobservable. If it is true, although both subjects and mental states are unobservable in isolation, each can be observed in conjunction with the other. There is a comparison here with the relations and observability of the positions and qualities of material things. One cannot be aware of a color except as present at some place and at some time or of a position except as the place and time where some discernible characteristics are manifested. So it might be argued that one can be aware of a conscious subject only as in some mental state or other and of a mental state only as belonging to some subject or other. Critics of the Berkeleyan principle sometimes suggest that it is no more than a faulty inference from the subject-object structure of the sentences in which mental facts are reported. It would certainly be a mistake to infer that a conscious subject is something entirely distinct from all its states from the linguistic fact that we commonly assign mental states to owners. We say of a chair that it has a back, a seat, arms, and legs, but this should not and does not lead us to conclude that the chair is something over and above the parts that it has, appropriately arranged. A more usual argument for the principle starts from the premise that mental states are acts that cannot be conceived without an agent in the same way as there cannot be a blow without a striker or a journey without a traveler. The premise of this argument has been much criticized by recent philosophers. A feeling of depression or a belief in the trustworthiness of a friend is not a precisely datable occurrence but a more or less persisting dispositional state. Nor is it an instance of agency in the sense of being the intentional execution of a decision. But these mistaken implications do not affect the validity of the argument under consideration. A disposition requires a possessor as much as an act requires an agent, and the blow I get from a swinging door still presupposes the existence of the door even though it did not mean to hit me.

The strength of the argument lies in the fact that we can assert the existence of some mental state, a feeling of anger let us say, only when we are in a position to assert either that we ourselves are angry or that somebody else is. We have given no sense to the words "discovering the existence of a mental state that is not my own or anyone else's." The nearest we come to speaking in this way is when we say, for example, "there is a sadness about the place," when walking about some ruins in a contemplative frame of mind. What we mean in this case is that the place inclines us to feel sad and might well give rise to the same inclination in others. And this capacity for producing sad feelings in myself and others, as a disposition, has its own substance, so to speak: the broken columns and collapsed walls with which it is bound up.

The subject in this rather thin and formal sense is not borne down in the ruin of that concept of spiritual substance in which it is proposed as the determinant of personal identity. It could be argued that it is a loose way of referring to the related series of other mental states or to the body or both with which any given mental state is universally associated by our manner of reporting such states. If it is something distinct from both of these, as it has traditionally been believed to be, it is not properly to be called the soul. It could not exist without any states at all, and even if it could it would be an emotionally useless form of survival of bodily death. Its existence, in fact, is irrelevant to the problem of the soul, which is that of whether a person is essentially mental in character and so distinct from his body, a connected sequence of mental states and not a physical object. It is irrelevant whether the sequence of mental states composing a person on this theory presupposes a distinguishable subject or not.

Spiritual substance cannot be the criterion of personal identity, and it may or may not be presupposed by the existence of conscious mental states. Whether as part or presupposition of our mental life, it should not be identified with the soul when this is conceived as the nonbodily aspect of a person. The well-founded conviction that there is no spiritual substance in the first sense and widespread doubts as to its existence in the second should not be allowed to obscure the issue of whether there is a unitary nonbodily aspect to a person and, if there is, whether it is the fundamental and more important aspect. Locke saw that spiritual substance could not account for personal identity and, although he believed in its existence, speculated whether it might not have been possible for God to endow a material substance with the power of thinking. Yet he clearly believed in the soul as the connected sequence of a person's conscious states, regarded this sequence as what a person essentially was, and held it to be capable of existing independently of the body. I want to consider whether an empirical concept of the soul, which, like Locke's, interprets it as a sequence of mental states logically distinct from the body and is neutral with regard to the problem of the subject, can be constructed.

2. THE EMPIRICAL CONCEPT OF THE SOUL

It will be admitted that among all the facts that involve a person there is a class that can be described as mental in some sense or other. Is it enough to define the soul as the temporally extended totality of mental states and events that belong to a person? It will not be enough to provide a concept of the soul as something logically distinct from the body if the idea of the series of a person's mental states involves some reference to the particular human body that he possesses. In the first place, therefore, a nonbodily criterion of personal identity must be produced. For if the soul were the series of mental states associated with a given body, in the sense of being publicly reported by it and being manifested by its behavior, two temporally separate mental states could belong to the history of the same soul only if they were in fact associated with one and the same human body. This notion of the soul could have no application to mental states that were not associated with bodies. The soul must, then, be a series of mental states that is identified through time in virtue of the properties and relations of these mental states themselves. Both the elements of the complex and the relations that make an identifiable persisting thing out of them must be mental. To establish the possibility of such a mental criterion of identity will be the hardest part of the undertaking.

Locke's criterion of memory has been much criticized, and it is certainly untenable in some of the interpretations it has been given. It will not do to say that two mental states belong to the same soul if and only if whoever has the later one can recollect the earlier one if the possibility of recollection involved is factual and not formal. For people forget things, and the paradox of the gallant officer is generated in which he is revealed as identical with both his childish and his senile selves while these are not identical with each other. However, a more plausible criterion can be offered in terms of continuity of character and memory. Two soul-phases belong to the same soul, on this view, if they are connected by a continuous character and memory path. A soul-phase is a set of contemporaneous mental states belonging to the same momentary consciousness. Two soul-phases are directly continuous if they are temporally juxtaposed, if the character revealed by the constituents of each is closely similar, and if the later contains recollections of some elements of the earlier. Two soul-phases are indirectly continuous and connected by a continuous character and memory path if there is a series of soul-phases all of whose members are directly continuous with their immediate predecessors and successors in the series and if the original soul-phases are the two end points of the series. There is a clear analogy between this criterion and the one by means of which material objects, including human bodies, are identified. Two object-phases belong to the same object if they are connected by a continuous quality and position path. Direct continuity in this case obtains between two temporally juxtaposed object-phases which are closely similar in qualities and are in the same position or in closely neighboring positions. Indirect continuity is once again the ancestral of direct continuity. There is no limit to the amount of difference in position allowed by the criterion to two indirectly continuous object-phases, but in normal discourse a limit is set to the amount of qualitative difference allowed by the requirement that the two phases be of objects of the same kind. Character in the mental case corresponds to quality in the physical and memory to spatial position. The soul, then, can be defined empirically as a series of mental states connected by continuity of character and memory.

Now there is an objection to the idea that memory can be any sort of fundamental criterion of identity which rests on the view that a memory criterion presupposes a bodily criterion. I shall defer the consideration of this issue, however, until two less serious difficulties have been met. These are that the construction suggested requires an exploded Cartesian dualism about the nature of mental states and, arising out of this, that a person's character is not clearly distinguishable from his body. The former, Rylean, objection can be met without difficulty. Even if the most extreme and reductive version of logical behaviorism were correct, even if a person's mental states were simply and solely behavioral dispositions, actual or potential, his character a complex property of these dispositions, and his memory a particular disposition to make first-person statements in the past tense without inference or reliance on testimony, the empirical concept of the soul would still apply to something distinct from any particular human body, though some body or other, not necessarily human perhaps, would be required to manifest the appropriate dispositions in its behavior and speech. In other words, an extreme, reductive, logical behaviorism is perfectly compatible with reincarnation, with the manifestation by one body of the character and memories that were previously manifested by another body that no longer exists. The second objection is that the soul as here defined and the body cannot be clearly distinguished, since the possession of some sorts of character trait requires the possession of an appropriate sort of body. I do not see that there is much empirical foundation for this to start with. It would be odd for a six-year-old girl to display the character of Winston Churchill, odd indeed to the point of outrageousness, but it is not utterly inconceivable. At first, no doubt, the girl's display of dogged endurance, a world-historical comprehensiveness of outlook, and so forth, would strike one as distasteful and pretentious in so young a child. But if she kept it up the impression would wear off. We do not, after all, find the story of Christ disputing with the doctors in the temple literally unintelligible. And a very large number of character traits seem to presume nothing about the age, sex, build, and general physical condition of their host. However, even if this were an empirically well-founded point, it would not be a relevant one. It would merely show that the possession of a given trait of character required the possession of an appropriate *kind* of body, a large one or a male one or an old one, and not the possession of a *particular* body. As things are, characters can survive large and even emotionally disastrous alterations to the physical type of a person's body, and these changes may have the effect of making it hard for others to recognize the continuity of character that there is. But courage, for example, can perfectly well persist even though the bodily conditions for its more obvious manifestations do not.

3. MENTAL AND BODILY CRITERIA OF IDENTITY

In recent philosophy there have been two apparently independent aspects to the view that the mind is logically dependent on the body. On the one hand, there are the doctrines that hold mental states either to be or necessarily to involve bodily states, whether bodily movement and dispositions thereto or neural events and configurations. With these doctrines, I have argued, the empirical concept of the soul can be reconciled. On the other hand, many philosophers have insisted that the basic and indispensable criterion of personal identity is bodily. Even mind-body dualists like Ayer, who have accepted the existence of a categorially clear-cut class of mental events, have sometimes taken this position. In his first treatment of the problem he appears at first to give a mental account of the concept of a person as being a series of experiences. But the relation that connects them in his theory involves an indispensable reference to a particular persisting human body. A person is made up of those total mental states which contain organic sensations belonging to one particular human body, presumably to be identified itself in terms of continuity of qualities and spatial position. Ayer draws the conclusion that properly follows from this and from any other account of personal identity that involves reference to a particular human body, namely that the notion of a person's disembodied existence is a self-contradictory one and, further, that even the association of a personality with different bodies at different times is inconceivable. These conclusions may well seem to constitute a reductio ad absurdum of the bodily criterion of personal identity rather than a disproof of the possibility of a person's survival of death. To explore them a little further will help to present the claims of mental as against bodily criteria in a clearer light.

At the outset it must be admitted that the theory of a bodily criterion has a number of virtues. It has, first, the theoretical attraction of simplicity, in that it requires only one mode of treatment for the identification through time of all enduring things, treating human beings as just one variety of concrete objects. Second, it has a practical appeal, in that its application yields uncontentiously correct answers in the very great majority of the actual cases of personal identification with which we are called upon to deal. Finally, it has the merit of realism, for it is, in fact, the procedure of identification that we do most commonly apply. Even where, for lack of relevant evidence, it is inapplicable, as in the case of the Tichborne claimant, it would not be supposed that the result of applying other criteria such as memory would conflict with what the bodily evidence would have shown if it had been forthcoming. Is there anything better to set against these powerful recommendations in favor of a bodily criterion than that it entails that things many people have wanted very deeply to say about the survival of death are inconsistent? A supporter of the bodily criterion might argue that it was so much the worse for them, that their inconsistent assertions arose from attempting to assert and deny at the same time that a person no longer existed.

It does seem strange, all the same, to say that all statements about disembodied or reincarnated persons are self-contradictory. Is it really at all plausible to say this about such familiar things as the simpler type of classical ghost story? It may be argued that there are plenty of stories which are really self-contradictory and yet which can be, in a way, understood and enjoyed, stories about time machines, for example. To try to settle the case we had better consider some concrete instances. Suppose I am walking on the beach with my friend A. He walks off a fair distance, treads on a large mine that someone has forgotten to remove, and is physically demolished in front of my eyes. Others, attracted by the noise, draw near and help to collect the scattered remains of A for burial. That night, alone in my room, I hear A's voice and see a luminous but intangible object, of very much the shape and size of A, standing in the corner. The remarks that come from it are in A's characteristic style and refer to matters that only A could have known about. Suspecting a hallucination, I photograph it and call in witnesses who hear and see what I do. The apparition returns afterwards and tells of where it has been and what it has seen. It would be very peculiar to insist, in these circumstances, that A no longer existed, even though his body no longer exists except as stains

on the rocks and in a small box in the mortuary. It is not essential for the argument that the luminous object look like *A* or
that it speak in *A*'s voice. If it were a featureless cylinder and
spoke like a talking weighing machine we should simply take
longer becoming convinced that it really was *A*. But if continuity
of character and memory were manifested with normal ampli-
tude, we surely should be convinced.

Consider a slightly different case. I know two men *B* and *C*.
B is a dark, tall, thin, puritanical Scotsman of sardonic tempera-
ment with whom I have gone on bird-watching expeditions. *C*
is a fair, short, plump, apolaustic Pole of indestructible enterprise and optimism with whom I have made a number of more
urban outings. One day I come into a room where both appear
to be, and the dark, tall, thin man suggests that he and I pursue
tonight some acquaintances I made with *C*, though he says it
was with him, a couple of nights ago. The short, fair, plump,
cheerful-looking man reminds me in a strong Polish accent of a
promise I had made to *B*, though he says it was to him, and
which I had forgotten about, to go in search of owls on this
very night. At first I suspect a conspiracy, but the thing continues far beyond any sort of joke, for good perhaps, and is accompanied by suitable amazement on their part at each other's
appearance, their own reflections in the mirror, and so forth.

Now what would it be reasonable to say in these circumstances: that *B* and *C* have changed bodies (the consequence of
a mental criterion), that they have switched character and memories (the consequence of a bodily criterion), or neither? It
seems to me quite clear that we should not say that *B* and *C*
had switched characters and memories. And if this is correct, it
follows that bodily identity is not a logically complete criterion
of personal identity; at best it could be a necessary condition of
personal identity. Of the other alternatives, that of refusing to
identify either of the psychophysical hybrids before us with *B*
or *C* may seem the most scrupulous and proper. But the refusal
might take a number of different forms. It might be a categor-
ical denial that either of the hybrids is *B* or *C*. It might, more
sophisticatedly be an assertion that the concept of personal
identity had broken down and that there was no correct answer,
affirmative or negative, to the question: which of these two is

B and which *C?* It might, uninterestingly, be a state of amazed and inarticulate confusion.

What support is there for the conclusion required by the empirical concept of the soul, that *B* and *C* have substituted bodies? First of all, the rather weak evidence of imaginative literature. In F. Anstey's story *Vice Versa* the corpulent and repressive Mr. Bultitude and his athletic and impulsive schoolboy son are the victims of a similar rearrangement. The author shows not the smallest trace of hesitation in calling the thing with the father's character and memories the father and the thing with the father's body the son. (Cf. also Conan Doyle's *Keinplatz Experiment.*) A solider support is to be found by reflecting on the probable attitude after the switch of those who are most concerned with our original pair, *B* and *C,* as persons, those who have the greatest interest in answering the question of their personal identity: their parents, their wives, their children, their closest friends. Would they say that *B* and *C* had ceased to exist, that they had exchanged characters and memories or that they had exchanged bodies? It is surely plain that if the character and memories of *B* and *C* really survived intact in their new bodily surroundings those closely concerned with them would say that the two had exchanged bodies, that the original persons were where the characters and memories were. For why, after all, do we bother to identify people so carefully? What is unique about individual people that is important enough for us to call them by individual proper names? In our general relations with other human beings their bodies are for the most part intrinsically unimportant. We use them as convenient recognition devices enabling us to locate without difficulty the persisting character and memory complexes in which we are interested, which we love or like. It would be upsetting if a complex with which we were emotionally involved came to have a monstrous or repulsive physical appearance, it would be socially embarrassing if it kept shifting from body to body while most such complexes stayed put, and it would be confusing and tiresome if such shifting around were generally widespread, for it would be a laborious business finding out where one's friends and family were. But that our concern and affection would follow the character and memory complex and not its original bodily associate is surely clear. In the case of general shifting about we should be in the position of people trying to find their intimates in the dark. If the shifts were both frequent and spatially radical we should no doubt give up the attempt to identify individual people, the whole character of relations between people would change, and human life would be like an unending sequence of shortish ocean trips. But, as long as the transfers did not involve large movements in space, the character and memory complexes we are concerned with could be kept track of through their audible identification of themselves. And there is no reason to doubt that the victim of such a bodily transfer would regard himself as the person whom he seems to remember himself as being. I conclude, then, that although, as things stand, our concept of a person is not called upon to withstand these strains and, therefore, that in the face of a psychophysical transfer we might at first not know what to say, we should not identify the people in question as those who now have the bodies they used to have and that it would be the natural thing to extend our concept of a person, given the purposes for which it has been constructed, so as to identify anyone present to us now with whoever it was who used to have the same character and memories as he has. In other words the soul, defined as a series of mental states connected by continuity of character and memory, is the essential constituent of personality. The soul, therefore, is not only logically distinct from any particular human body with which it is associated; it is also what a person fundamentally is.

It may be objected to the extension of the concept of personal identity that I have argued for that it rests on an incorrect and even sentimental view of the nature of personal relations. There are, it may be said, personal relationships which are of an exclusively bodily character and which would not survive a change of body but which would perfectly well survive a change of soul. Relations of a rather unmitigatedly sexual type might be instanced and also those where the first party to the relationship has violent racial feelings. It can easily be shown that these objections are without substance. In the first place, even the most tired of entrepreneurs is going to take some note of the character and memories of the companion of his later nights at work. He will want her to be docile and quiet, perhaps, and to remember that he takes two parts of water to one of scotch, and no ice. If she ceases to be plump and red-headed and vigorous he may lose interest in and abandon her, but he would have done so anyway in response to the analogous effects of the aging process. If he has any idea of her as a person at all, it will be as a unique cluster of character traits and recollections. As a body, she is simply an instrument of a particular type, no more and no less interesting to him than a physically identical twin. In the case of a purely sexual relationship no particular human body is required, only one of a more or less precisely demarcated kind. Where concern with the soul is wholly absent there is no interest in individual identity at all, only in identity of type. It may be said that this argument cuts both ways: that parents and children are concerned only that they should have round them children and parents with the same sort of character and memories as the children and parents they were with yesterday. But this is doubly incorrect. First, the memories of individual persons cannot be exactly similar, since even the closest of identical twins must see things from slightly different angles; they cannot be in the same place at the same time. More seriously, if more contingently, individual memories, even of identical twins, are seldom, if ever, closely similar. To put the point crudely, the people I want to be with are the people who remember me and the experiences we have shared, not those who remember someone more or less like me with whom they have shared more or less similar experiences. The relevant complexity of the memories of an individual person is of an altogether different order of magnitude from that of the bodily properties of an entrepreneur's lady friend. The lady friend's bodily type is simply enough defined for it to have a large number of instances. It is barely conceivable that two individual memories should be similar enough to be emotionally adequate substitutes for each other. There is the case of the absolutely identical twins who go everywhere together, side by side, and always have done so. Our tendency here would be to treat the pair as a physically dual single person. There would be no point in distinguishing one from the other. As soon as their ways parted sufficiently for the question of which was which to arise, the condition of different memories required for individuation would be satisfied.

It may be felt that the absolutely identical twins present a certain difficulty for the empirical concept of the soul. For suppose their characters and memories to be totally indistinguishable and their thoughts and feelings to have been precisely the same since the first dawning of consciousness in them. Won't the later phase of one of the twins be as continuous in respect of character and memory with the earlier phases of the other as they are with his own earlier phases? Should we even say that there are two persons there at all? The positional difference of the two bodies provides an answer to the second question. Although they are always excited and gloomy together, the thrills and pangs are manifested in distinct bodies and are conceivable as existing separately. We might ignore the duality of their mental states, but we should be able in principle to assert it. As to the matter of continuity, the environment of the two will be inevitably asymmetrical, each will at various times be nearer something than the other, each will block some things from the other's field of vision or touch; so there will always be some, perhaps trivial, difference in the memories of the two. But even if trivial, the difference will be enough to allow the application in this special case of a criterion that normally relies on radical and serious differences. However alike the character and memories of twin no. 1 on Tuesday and twin no. 2 on Wednesday, they will inevitably be less continuous than those of twin no. 2 on the two days.

4. MEMORY AND BODILY IDENTITY

I must now return to the serious objection to the use of memory as a criterion of personal identity whose consideration was postponed earlier. This has been advanced in an original and interesting article on personal identity published by Sydney S. Shoemaker in *The Journal of Philosophy*.* He argues that memory could not be the sole or fundamental criterion for the iden-

*"Personal Identity and Memory." 56, 22 (Oct. 22, 1959): 868.

tity of other people, because in order to establish what the memories of other people are I have to be able to identify them in a bodily way. I cannot accept sentences offered by other people beginning with the words "I remember" quite uncritically. I must be assured, first, that these utterances really are memory claims, that the speaker understands the meaning of the sentences he is using, and, secondly, that his memory claims are reliable. Mr. Shoemaker contends that it is essential, if either of these requirements is to be satisfied, for me to be able to identify the maker of the apparent memory claims in an independent, bodily way. In order to be sure that his remarks really are intended as memory claims, I have to see that he generally uses the form of words in question in connection with antecedent states of affairs of which he has been a witness. And to do this I must be assured that he is at one time uttering a memory sentence and at another, earlier, time is a witness of the event he purports to describe; in other words I must be able to identify him at different times without taking his apparent memories into account. The point is enforced by the second requirement about the conditions under which I can take his memory claims as trustworthy. To do this I must be able to establish at least that he was physically present at and, thus, in a position to observe the state of affairs he now claims to recollect.

There is a good deal of force in these arguments, but I do not think they are sufficient to prove that the soul is not logically distinct from the particular body with which it happens to be associated at any given time. In the first place, the doubt about the significance of someone's current memory claims is not one that I must positively have laid to rest before taking these claims as evidence of his identity. The doubt could seriously arise only in very special and singular circumstances. If someone now says to me, "I remember the battle of Hastings," I will presume him to be slightly misusing the words, since I have good reasons for thinking that no one now alive was present at that remote event. I shall probably take him to be saying that he remembers that there was such a thing as the battle of Hastings, having learnt of it at school, or that it took place in 1066, that Harold was killed at it, that it was the crucial military factor in the Norman conquest, and so forth. But if, on being questioned, he says that these reinterpretations distort the meaning he intended, that he remembers the battle of Hastings in the same way as he remembers having breakfast this morning, if perhaps a little more dimly, then I cannot reasonably suppose that he doesn't understand the meaning of his remark though I may well think that it is false, whether deliberately or not. Mr. Shoemaker admits that in a case of apparent bodily transfer the significance of a person's memory claims could be established by considering the way in which he used memory sentences after the transfer had taken place. So at best this part of his argument could prove that in order to identify people we need to be able to make at least local applications of the criterion of bodily identity. They must be continuous in a bodily way for a period of time sufficient to enable us to establish that they are using memory sentences correctly. But in view of the somewhat strained and artificial character of the doubt in question, I am inclined to reject even this modest conclusion. At best it is a practical requirement: people must be sufficiently stable in a bodily way for me to be able to accumulate a large enough mass of apparent memory claims that are prima facie there to infer from the coherence of these apparent claims that they really are memory claims and not senseless noises.

The reliability of the memory claims of others is a more substantial issue. For, unlike significance, it is a feature of apparent memory claims that we commonly do have serious reason to doubt. It must be admitted, further, that if I have independent reasons for believing that Jones's body was physically present at an event that Jones now claims to remember, I have a piece of strong evidence in support of the correctness of his claim. It is not, of course, conclusive. Even if he were looking in the direction at the time, he might have been in a condition of day-dreaming inattentiveness. The question is, however: is it in any sense a necessary condition for the correctness of my acceptance of a man's present memory claim that I should be able, in principle, to discover that the very same body from which the claim under examination now emerges was actually present at the event now purposedly remembered? I cannot see that it is. To revert to the example of a radical psychophysical exchange between B and C. Suppose that from B's body memory claims emerge about a lot of what I have hitherto confidently taken to be C's experiences. I may have good reason to believe that C's body was present at the events apparently recalled. If the claims are very numerous and detailed, if they involve the recollection of things I didn't know B had seen although I can now establish that they were really present for C to observe, and if the emission of apparent C memories from B's body and vice versa keeps up for a fair period, it would be unreasonable not to conclude that the memory claims emerging from B's body were in fact correct, that they were the memory claims of C not of B, and that therefore the person with B's body was in fact not now B but C. Here again a measure of local bodily continuity seems required. I shall not say that C inhabits B's body at all unless he seems to do so in a fairly substantial way and over a fair period of time. But as long as the possibility of psychophysical exchange is established by some salient cases in which the requirement of local bodily continuity is satisfied I can reasonably conjecture that such exchange has taken place in other cases where the translocation of memory claims is pretty short-lived. At any rate it is only the necessity of local bodily continuity that is established, not the necessary association of a person with one particular body for the whole duration of either. Bodily continuity with a witness is a test of the reliability of someone's memory claims, and it is an important one, but it is not a logically indispensable one.

5. THE PROBLEM OF DISEMBODIMENT

Nothing that I have said so far has any direct bearing on the question whether the soul can exist in an entirely disembodied state. All I have tried to show is that there is no necessary connection between the soul as a series of mental states linked by character and memory and any particular continuing human body. The question now arises: must the soul be associated with some human body? The apparent intelligibility of my crude ghost story might seem to suggest that not even a body is required, let alone a human one. And the same point appears to be made by the intelligibility of stories in which trees, toadstools, pieces of furniture, and so on are endowed with personal characteristics. But a good deal of caution is needed here. In the first place, even where these personal characteristics are not associated with any sort of body in the physiological sense, they are associated with a body in the epistemological sense; in other words, it is an essential part of the story that the soul in question have physical manifestations. Only in our own case does it seem that strictly disembodied existence is conceivable, in the sense that we can conceive circumstances in which there would be some good reason to claim that a soul existed in a disembodied state. Now how tenuous and nonhuman could these physical manifestations be? To take a fairly mild example, discussed by Professor Malcolm, could we regard a tree as another person? He maintains with great firmness that we could not, on the rather flimsy ground that trees haven't got mouths and, therefore, could not be said to speak or communicate with us or make memory claims. But if a knothole in a tree trunk physically emitted sounds in the form of speech, why should we not call it a mouth? We may presume that ventriloquism, hidden record-players and microphones, dwarfs concealed in the foliage, and so forth have all been ruled out. If the remarks of the tree were coherent and appropriate to its situation and exhibited the type of continuity that the remarks of persons normally do exhibit, why shouldn't we regard the tree as a person? The point is that we might, by a serious conceptual effort, allow this in the case of one tree or even several trees or even a great many nonhuman physical things. But the sense of our attribution of personality to them would be logically parasitic on our attributions of personality to ordinary human bodies. It is from their utterances and behavior that we derive our concept of personality, and this concept would be applicable to nonhuman things only by more or less far-fetched analogy. That trees should be personal pre-supposes, then, the personality of human beings. The same considerations hold in the extreme case of absolutely minimal embodiment, as when a recurrent and localized voice of a recognizable tone is heard to make publicly audible remarks. The voice might give evidence of qualitative and positional continuity sufficient to treat it as an identifiable body, even if of an excessively diaphanous kind. The possibility of this procedure, however, is contingent on there being persons in the standard, humanly embodied sense to provide a clear basis for the acquisition of the concept that is being more or less speculatively applied to the voice.

Whatever the logic of the matter, it might be argued, the causal facts of the situation make the whole inquiry into the possibility of a soul's humanly or totally disembodied existence an entirely fantastic one. That people have the memories and characters that they do, that they have memories and characters at all, has as its causally necessary condition the relatively undisturbed persistence of a particular bit of physiological apparatus. One can admit this without concluding that the inquiry is altogether without practical point. For the bit of physiological apparatus in question is not the human body as a whole, but the brain. Certainly lavish changes in the noncerebral parts of the human body often affect the character and perhaps even to some extent the memories of the person whose body it is. But there is no strict relationship here. Now it is sometimes said that the last bit of the body to wear out is the brain, that the brain takes the first and lion's share of the body's nourishment, and that the brains of people who have starved to death are often found in perfectly good structural order. It is already possible to graft bits of one human body on to another, corneas, fingers, and, even, I believe, legs. Might it not be possible to remove the brain from an otherwise worn-out human body and replace it either in a manufactured human body or in a cerebrally untenanted one? In this case we should have a causally conceivable analogue of reincarnation. If this were to become possible and if the resultant creatures appeared in a coherent way to exhibit the character and memories previously associated with the brain that had been fitted into them, we could say that the original person was still in existence even though only a relatively minute part of its original mass and volume was present in the new physical whole. Yet if strict bodily identity is a necessary condition of personal identity, such a description of the outcome would be ruled out as self-contradictory. I conclude, therefore, not only that a logically adequate concept of the soul is constructible but that the construction has some possible utility even in the light of our knowledge of the causal concitions of human life.

H. P. Grice

4

Personal Identity

I propose to discuss first the nature of the main question which philosophers have been asking, when they have concerned themselves with the problem of Personal Identity. Then I shall ask whether it is possible to maintain a Pure Ego theory of the Self; and finally I shall state and attempt to defend a form of Logical Construction theory. In fulfilling the first part of my programme I shall try to state rather dogmatically what I think to be the question really at issue between philosophers, irrespective of whether such philosophers would admit that this is the question or would agree with my formulation of it. I shall hope that the later sections of my article may provide some justification for my views about the nature of the question.

A. — The Question.*

If we reflect on sentences in which the word "I" (or "me," etc.) occurs, we can, I think, distinguish at least three different classes of sentences, in each of which the use of the word "I" is different.

(1) Sentences such as "I am hearing a noise," "I am thinking about the immortality of the soul."

---

*In what I say in this section, and elsewhere, I am under considerable obligation to Mr. Gallie's article "Is the Self a Substance?" *Mind* (1936).

This article is reprinted from *Mind,* vol. 50 (October 1941), by courtesy of the editor and Professor Grice.

(2) Sentences such as "I played cricket yesterday," "I shall be fighting soon."

(3) Sentences such as "I was hit by a golfball," "I fell down the cellar steps."

Now in the sentences of my class (3) I can substitute, for the word "I," the words "my body" without loss or change of meaning. If I tell you that my body was hit by a golfball, I tell you neither more nor less than if I tell you that I was hit by a golfball; moreover, my use of words in the former case is quite a natural one, though perhaps less frequent than that in the latter. But in the case of sentences of my classes (1) and (2), no such substitution is possible. It is clearly unnatural to say "my body is hearing a noise"; and I think it is unnatural to say "my body played cricket" or "my body will be fighting soon." But though sentences of classes (1) and (2) have it in common that no such substitution can be made in them, they do, I think, differ from one another in respect of the use of the word "I" in them. I am inclined to think that the difference consists in the fact that any sentence of my class (2) is analysable, at some stage of analysis, into a sentence or sentences belonging to my class (3), together with a sentence or sentences belonging to my class (1). Thus the sentence "I played cricket yesterday" is analysable into a sentence or sentences stating something about the sort of movements I made (where "I" = "my body"), together with a sentence or sentences stating something about the sort of thoughts and intentions and decisions I had (where "I" does not equal "my body"). Of course these sentences into which sentences of my class (2) are analysable may well be themselves further analysable. The conclusion I draw, then, is that "I" sentences are of at least three kinds: one in which "I" can be replaced by "my body" without loss or change of meaning (3); another in which the sentence as a whole is equivalent to a sentence or sentences of the previous kind together with a sentence or sentences containing "I" used in a different sense from the previous sense (2); and, finally, sentences containing "I" used in this different sense first referred to (1).

Now I think it has been with sentences of the last mentioned kind (1), or with what has been stated by such sentences that most philosophers have been concerned, when dealing with the problem of Personal Identity. And I think that one way of putting the question that most of them have been endeavouring to answer, whether they have been aware of it or not, is to say that they have been trying to answer the question "What is the analysis of sentences of this kind?" Now I think this is not a bad way of putting the question, but I think there is a still better way. For every sentence of my class (1) there will be another sentence differing from the first in that where the first contains the word "I", the second contains the word "someone" (e.g. "I heard a noise": "someone heard a noise"). I will call these sentences "class (1) 'someone' sentences." (There will I think be as many different senses of "someone" as there are different senses of "I.") Now I think the clearest thing to say is that there are really two questions at issue: (*a*) What is the analysis of class (1) "someone" sentences? (*b*) What is the analysis of class (1) "I" sentences? (These two questions will of course be connected: and the sort of answer I give to one may affect the question what sort of answer I can give to the other.) I think this clearer for two reasons: (1) it enables one to make clearer the relations between what Broad calls "The Proper Name Theory," "The Disguised Description Theory," and "The Logical Construction Theory." The P.N.T. and the D.D.T. both give one and the same answer to question (*a*): ("What is the analysis of class (1) 'someone' sentences?"), while the Logical Construction theory gives a different answer to question (*a*). But the P.N.T. and the D.D.T. differ from one another in the answers they give to question (*b*): ("What is the analysis of class (1) 'I' sentences"); (2) it reveals a paradox in an asymmetrical view about the analysis of sentences about other people. For the asymmetricalist will have to maintain that any class (1) 'someone' sentence, e.g. "someone heard a noise" is ambiguous, or else that it is equivalent to a disjunctive sentence of the form '*p* or *q*' where *p* is true when the speaker heard a noise, and *q* when someone else heard a noise: both alternatives being at the least surprising. I shall then maintain that the questions at issue are (*a*) What is the analysis of class (1) "someone" sentences? (*b*) What is the analysis of class (1) "I" sentences; and I hope the next section of my paper will do something to justify this contention.

B.–*The Pure Ego Theory.*

People who have held or discussed forms of what, following Broad, I shall call a Pure Ego theory, have not usually formulated their statements as if they constituted answers to the questions I have enumerated. I propose to take as a sample the statement that "The Self is a Substance." The meaning of this statement has been discussed by Mr. Gallie, and I shall base what I have to say on his account. He suggests that people who have said that the Self is a Substance have meant what he would mean by saying that the Self is an ultimate particular (together with the assertion that the Self is the subject of mental but not of physical attributes, which I shall ignore, as irrelevant to my present purpose); and to say that the self is an ultimate particular is to say that the Self "has qualities and stands in relations, without either being or containing qualities and relations." This definition of "ultimate particular" is taken by Mr. Gallie to exclude from the class of ultimate particulars "all entities which are complex in the way in which the fact that 'This is red' or the event consisting in 'That noise being heard' are complex"; for such entities, though they may be particulars, contain qualities or relations as elements, and are not, therefore, ultimate particulars. In this way Mr. Gallie is able to maintain that the assertion that the Self is a Substance is an assertion which is *really* about the properties of things, and not about the properties of symbols.

I cannot regard this as a satisfactory formulation of a P.E. theory. The words "contain" and "element" are not defined, and I do not think it is possible to give them a sense which will allow to be true *all* of the things Mr. Gallie would want to maintain. In particular, whatever sense we give to "contain," I don't think Mr. Gallie is entitled to maintain *both* that it is impossible for something to be both an ultimate particular and a logical construction (which I am sure he would want to maintain) *and* that the proposition "The Self is a Substance" is *really* about the properties of things. Suppose first that "contain" bears the sense Mr. Gallie seems explicitly to attribute to it, and that X may be said to contain Y when X has to Y the relation which the fact *"This is red"* has to *red* or *redness* or the event *this noise being heard* to *being heard*. Then the Self will be an ultimate particular, even if it is a Logical Construction; for the sense of "contain" in which a Self, if it is a logical construction, could be said to contain, say, a relation which holds between two experiences of that self, or a quality of an experience of that self, will be a very different sense of "contain" from that in which the fact that *this is red* contains *redness;* and if this is so it is possible that the Self might be both a logical construction and an ultimate particular.

Suppose, on the other hand, we give "contain" the only sense which could possibly claim to fit Mr. Gallie's use of the word, and say that "X contains Y" is to be defined in the following kind of way "X has R_1 to Y (where R_1 = the relation which the fact *this is red* has to *redness*) or . . . or X has R_n to Y (when R_n is the relation which a logical construction has to some quality or relation)." But what can it mean to say "X has R_n to Y"? It seems to me it can only mean: X is a logical construction out of things of a certain kind, and one of these things has a relation R to a quality or relation Y (such as the relation which holds between the event *this noise being heard* and *being heard).* But to say that something is a logical construction out of something else is to assert a proposition about words: therefore a proposition of the form "X contains Y" is at least in part *really* about words; and therefore a proposition of the form "X is an ultimate particular" is at least in part about words; moreover, it is verbal in just that part of itself in which we are going to be interested if we are considering whether the Self is an ultimate particular.

What I wish to suggest is that either of two things may be meant by the assertion that the Self is a Substance. (1) To say the Self is a substance is to say some such thing as that selves persist and are capable of change and (perhaps) have causal properties, and so forth; and even in saying this sort of thing I think we shall be asserting something about the use of words; for something something will be said about the way in which words like "someone," "I," etc., can be used significantly. For instance, "selves persist" might mean something like "If it makes sense to say 'someone has ϕ' then it makes sense to say 'someone has ϕ both at t_1 and t_2.'" (I don't make any claims on behalf of this analysis of "selves persist"; it is only intended as an illustration of what is probably the sort of thing asserted by such a proposition.) In this sense of the sentence, "The Self is a Substance," the Self might be both a substance and a logical construction. (2) "The Self is a Substance" may mean (1) plus "the Self is not a logical construction"; and to say that the Self is not a logical construction is to say that sentences such as "someone is hearing a noise" (i.e. class (1) "someone" sentences) are unanalysable in a certain respect. This will not mean that the sentence as a whole is unanalysable; "hearing a noise" might be definable even if a P.E. theory is true; and "someone" may mean "some person," and "person," too, may be definable even on a P.E. theory. What the P.E. theory does assert, I think, is that no final analysis of the sentence "someone is hearing a noise" can be given, which does not contain a variable (e.g. ('someone' or 'something'), such that any proper name or description which can be significantly substituted for "someone" in the sentence "someone is hearing a noise," can be significantly substituted for the variable in the sentence which constitutes a final analysis of the sentence "someone is hearing a noise." For instance, if the final analysis of "someone is hearing a noise" were "something is a mental event and is related by R to the hearing of a noise," then what the P.E. theory asserts about the analysis of "someone is hearing a noise" would not be true; for in the sentence "someone is hearing a noise" I can significantly substitute the word "I" for the word "someone"; but in the sentence "something is a mental event and is related by R to the hearing of a noise" I cannot substitute the word "I" for the word "something" without reducing the sentence to nonsense; so the sentence "someone is hearing a noise" would not be unanalysable in the respect in which the P.E. theory asserts that it is unanalysable. For brevity I shall describe the sort of unanalysability which the P.E. theory attributes to class (1) "someone" sentences by saying that what the P.E. theory asserts is that there is no new level analysis of class (1) "someone" sentences in respect of "someone." And what the L.C.T. asserts is that there is a new level analysis of class (1) "someone" sentences in respect of "someone."

It will I hope be seen that if the P.E. theory is formulated in this way, it avoids some of the objections which have been brought against it. For instance it will not be a valid objection to say that the P.E. theory introduces metaphysical entities, i.e. substrata. To say that substrata are metaphysical entities is to say, I suppose, that the proposition "there are substrata" is unverifiable. But if the P.E. theory is formulated in my way, either it does not follow, given the truth of the P.E. theory *plus* the truth of the proposition "there are selves," that there are substrata, or else, if it does follow, then to assert that there are substrata is to assert (1) that there are selves or people, (2) a proposition about the use of words, which may not be verifiable, but then, why should it be?

A much more serious objection to which the P.E. theory has been exposed is the following. Anyone who maintains a P.E. theory about the analysis of class (1) "someone" sentences, will also have to give an answer to my question (2); namely, "What is the analysis of class (1) "I" sentences?" Now it will be open to him to say either that when I use the symbol "I" in such sentences I use it as a logically proper name, in which case I shall be an object of acquaintance to myself; or that when I use the symbol "I" I use it as the equivalent of a descriptive phrase, in which case presumably, though not necessarily, I shall not be an object of acquaintance to myself. Now the argument against the P.E. theory will be that I am not acquainted with myself, so the P.N. theory of the analysis of "I" sentences cannot be right. But if the P.E. theory were right, the D.D.T. of the analysis of "I" sentences could only be right if I were in fact sometimes acquainted with myself. But I am not acquainted with myself: therefore if the P.E. theory were right neither the P.N. theory nor the D.D.T. could be right. But one must be. Therefore the P.E. theory is not true. I must now produce the arguments for this contention.

First, it may be said: That I am not acquainted with myself is shown by Hume. "When I enter most intimately into what I call myself, I always stumble on some particular perception or other, of heat or cold, light or shade, love or hatred, pain or pleasure. I never can catch myself at any time without a perception, and never can observe anything but the perception." To put the point more conveniently for the argument, we must admit that when we introspect, we are acquainted with experiences of various kinds, but never with anything other than experiences: and so with nothing of which "I" could be the proper name or description.

On the other hand, it will be urged, if we try to combine the P.E. theory with the D.D.T., we must allow that I am sometimes acquainted with myself. What sort of descriptive phrase will it be with which "I" will be synonymous in a class (1) "I" sentence? I don't think it matters much for the purposes of the argument what it is, so I will assume that it is the phrase "the self owning this experience," where "this" is a logically proper name. Thus "I heard a noise" will mean "the self owning this experience heard a noise"; and, in general, any class (1) "I" sentence will assert that the self which owns one experience owns another. But here two observations become relevant. (1) We couldn't possibly know that any experience was owned by any self unless we were acquainted with the self that owned it, just as we couldn't know that anything was red unless we were acquainted with something which was red. We couldn't therefore know any facts such as that someone heard a noise unless we were acquainted with selves. But we do in fact know many such facts; therefore we are acquainted with at least one self. (2) Even if objection (1) is not valid, and we could know, e.g., that someone heard a noise without being acquainted with any self that did hear a noise, we still could not know that two different experiences were owned by the same self unless we were acquainted with a self which owned them both. But many class (1) "I" sentences state that two experiences are owned by the same self; therefore unless we were acquainted with at least one self we could not know what is stated by any of these class (1) "I" sentences. But these class (1) "I" sentences include first those sentences which do state the sort of things we all of us from time to time know, such as "I heard a noise," "I am seeing a red patch." Therefore we have acquaintance with at least our own self, if the P.E. theory and D.D.T. are both true. But we have not acquaintance with our own self (shown above). Therefore not both the P.E. theory and the D.D.T. are true. But since the P.N.T. is false (shown above) the D.D.T. is true. Therefore the P.E. theory is false.

If, on the other hand, we reject the P.E. theory, it is easy to see how both the D.D.T. and the proposition that we sometimes know the truth of what is stated by class (1) "I" sentences such as "I heard a noise" may be true. If, for example, to say that a self owns two experiences is to say that a relation of such and such a kind holds between the experiences, the relation might be of such a kind that I could sometimes know that it held between two experiences; and if so then I might sometimes know such things as that I heard a noise.

The argument which I have just expounded may seem strong, but I do not think it refutes the P.E. theory. I do not propose to question the second part of the argument, the part that concerns the D.D.T. It is the first part of the argument which seems to me unsound, namely, the contention that when we introspect we are acquainted with experiences and nothing but experiences; and therefore I am not an object of acquaintance to myself. The fault in this part of the argument seems to me due to an over-carefree use of the word "acquaintance"; for I think "acquaintance" must be definable. (I am only concerned with "acquaintance" in the sense in which I can be said to be acquainted with particulars, and not in any sense in which I can be said to be acquainted with universals. Indeed, I have always found it difficult to see how to start to answer the question, "Am I acquainted with universals?"; and I think my difficulty is due to the fact that "acquaintance" is a technical term which has been given a use only in sentences which state something about acquaintance with particulars.) My reasons for thinking that "acquaintance", as used by philosophers, must be definable are: (1) It is a technical term; in ordinary life I just don't say "I am acquainted with a loud noise" or "I am acquainted with a thought of dough-nuts," or, for that matter, "I am acquainted with myself." In fact the only people with whom I am acquainted in any ordinary sense of "acquaintance" are people other than myself; but very few philosophers think that, in the philosopher's sense of "acquaintance," I am acquainted with other people. Not only is "acquaintance" in this sense not a word in ordinary use, but there is no word synonymous with it which is in ordinary use; "awareness" is the only candidate: and that has far too wide a meaning; for instance, there are circumstances in which I can say quite truly that I am aware of a table, but (according to most philosophers) I cannot even say truly that I am acquainted with a table. (2) The apparent occurrence of both acquaintance with particulars and knowledge of facts about them seems to invite the attention of Occam's razor; and it is much easier to define "acquaintance" in terms of "knowledge of facts" than "knowledge of facts" in terms of "acquaintance."

So I suggest that "I am acquainted with X" (where X is a particular) means "(a) I know some fact about X, (b) X is not a logical construction." Or, I think, I can put the same suggestion another way, which will not involve the somewhat vague phrase "some fact about X"; namely, "I am acquainted with X" means "(a) I know some fact expressible in a sentence S containing 'this' (or some other demonstration word) where 'this' refers to what 'X' refers to, (b) S is unanalysable in respect of 'this' (or the other demonstrative word in question)." (I put in (b) because a demonstrative word is not always used as a logically proper name; that is, it is often equivalent to a descriptive phrase.)

Let us now apply the first form of this definition to the sentence "I am not acquainted with myself"; this will mean "Either it is false that I know some fact about myself, or it is true that I am a logical construction." But I cannot both (a) deny that I know some fact about myself, and (b) claim that the P.E. theory and D.D.T., if both true, presuppose that I am acquainted with myself, on the grounds that if I were not I could not know facts about myself which I in fact do know. If I do I shall be claiming both to know and not to know facts about myself. So if I want to make the claim referred to in (b) above, the only ground on which I can assert that I am not acquainted with myself will be that I am a logical construction. But if this is so, the argument against the P.E. theory uses the proposition "I am a logical construction" as a premiss in order to show that the P.E. theory is false, that is, that the self is a logical construction. But no holder of the P.E. theory would be converted by such an argument. A similar conclusion will follow if I use the second form of definition of "acquaintance."

So far, I think, the P.E. theory is untouched. Can it then be refuted? I think it is not easy, but I will suggest one or two difficulties in it. The first difficulty is not easy to state shortly, but I will do my best. It seems clear that there are occasions when it would be true to say "someone is not now having an experience." Now this proposition must be distinguished from "it is not the case that someone is now having an experience" (viz. "no one is now having an experience"); and in order to do this, in the P.E. theory, I think we must say that "someone is not now having an experience" contains as part of its meaning "someone has now some characteristic ϕ." Now what sort of characteristic could ϕ be?

(1) It might be some non-dispositional, non-relational characteristic. But it seems to me that the only non-dispositional, non-relational characteristics of selves with which we are familiar are characteristics consisting in the having of such and such an experience. But ϕ could not be any such characteristic without making the proposition "someone is not now having an experience" self-contradictory. ϕ will, then, have to be some characteristic with which we are not familiar; and this seems to me highly objectionable: for in order to have, as I'm sure I do sometimes have, evidence justifying a belief in the proposition "someone is not now having an experience" I should have to have evidence for the proposition "someone has ϕ now"; but if I have no idea what ϕ is, how could I? So it does not seem as if ϕ can be a non-dispositional, non-relational characteristic.

(2) ϕ might be some non-dispositional, relational characteristic. But this seems unsatisfactory: for then I think it would be a proper question to ask "What (or what sort of thing) is it which has ϕ"; and I don't think we should think we had received a proper answer until we had been told some non-relational characteristic of the thing having ϕ; and this could only be a non-dispositional, non-relational characteristic (and so we get back to (1)), *or*

(3) a dispositional characteristic. It doesn't matter to my argument what dispositional characteristic ϕ might be, so let me take for the sake of the argument the characteristic "capacity for thinking." It seems quite clear to me that when I assert "X is now capable of thinking," part at least of what I am asserting is a hypothetical proposition about X to the effect that X would now be thinking if so and so were the case (this proposition not

being intended to exclude the possibility that X is now thinking). So I think "someone is now capable of thinking" must mean one of two things. It might mean (a) "someone would now be thinking, if so and so were the case." But this won't do; for suppose Adam had existed, but Eve had not: then it might be true that someone would now be thinking, if so and so were the case; for it might be true that Adam would now be thinking, if (*inter alia*) he were still alive. But since Adam would have died childless, it would not be true that someone is now capable of thinking. Or (*b*) "someone is now capable of thinking" might mean "someone has now some characteristic ψ, and would now be thinking if so and so were the case." But we now have to start all over again asking the same question about ψ as I have just been asking about ϕ; and we either have to say the ψ is a non-dispositional characteristic, which is open to all the objections which I brought in (1) and (2) above against ϕ's being a non-dispositional characteristic; or that ψ is a dispositional characteristic, in which case there will be yet another characteristic χ which I assert something to have when I assert it to have ψ, and the trouble begins yet again.

I do not see any way out of this difficulty if the P.E. theory is true; but if a Logical Construction theory is true the difficulty may not arise. For to say "someone is not now having an experience" may be to say something like "there have occurred and or will occur some experiences having relation R to one another, and there would be now occurring an experience having R to each of these experiences, if certain conditions were realised; but no such experience is now occurring." And to say "It is not the case that someone is now having an experience" may be to say something like "No experience is now occurring which has relation R to any other experience." (Of course the forms of analysis I have just given may not fit all types of L.C.T.)

My second difficulty is roughly this. Suppose the P.E. theory to be true; and suppose I know that I had a headache yesterday, and that I had a toothache this morning. Now suppose that I am asked how I know that it is one self which had both experiences, and not two exactly similar selves. On the P.E. theory plus the P.N. theory, I don't see that I could give any true answer, except "I just do know." This is, I think, rather unsatisfactory. But on a L.C.T., on the other hand, if I am asked this question, I can answer truly "Because the experiences have to one another the relation R which constitutes 'belonging to the same self as.'" For instance *I* should answer "Because I remember (or know to have occurred) both experiences, and any experiences I remember (or know to have occurred) must be co-personal." This answer would imply, I think, that the self is a logical construction, and is to be defined in terms of memory.

These objections are the only ones I can find against the P.E. theory, so I will now pass on to my third section.

C.—An Alternative Theory.

The theory which I am going to suggest is, I think, mainly a modification of Locke's theory of Personal Identity. Exactly what Locke's answer to my first question (i.e. (*a*) What is the analysis of my class (1) "someone" sentences) would have been is not clear; but I think it would have been that, for example, "someone heard a noise" means "the hearing of a noise (in the past) is the object of some consciousness"; and "someone heard a noise and smelt a smell" means "the (past) hearing of a noise and the (past) smelling of a smell are objects of the same consciousness." This, I think, is borne out by Locke's words: "As far as any intelligent being can repeat the idea of any past action with the same consciousness it had of it at first, and with the same consciousness as it has of any present action, so far it is the same personal self." (Consciousness, at any rate officially, for Locke means "consciousness of . . . as one's own.")

To this theory the following objections may be made.

(1) It is circular in so far as it defines x belonging to a self in terms of "consciousness of x as belonging to a self."

(2) Reid's puzzle about the officer, who was beaten for robbing an orchard as a boy, captured a standard when a young officer, and became a general; when he captured the standard he was conscious of having been beaten as a boy; when he became a general he was conscious of having captured a standard, but not of having been beaten as a boy. Therefore, according to Locke, the person who became a general was the same person as

the person who captured a standard, and the person who captured a standard was the same person as the person who was beaten as a boy; but the general and the person who was beaten as a boy were not the same person. But this is absurd.

(3) If "consciousness of" involves knowledge of, very few experiences separated in time by a long interval could be copersonal (because memories are short).

(4) It is circular in a different respect from (1), in so far as it seems impossible to define "same consciousness" except in terms of "consciousness of (= belonging to) one person."

Difficulty (1) can be avoided by interpreting "consciousness" as meaning "memory," or "memory or introspection." The other difficulties require much more fundamental modification of the theory. This I shall undertake by stages, as my theory is somewhat complicated.

First of all I propose to introduce as a technical term the phrase "total temporary state." This term I shall define later; but I can indicate what I am talking about when I use the term by saying that a total temporary state is composed of all the experiences any one person is having at any given time. Thus, if I am now thinking of Hitler and feeling a pain, and having no other experiences, there will be occurring now a total temporary state containing as elements a thought of Hitler and a feeling of pain. Now since total temporary states may be said to occur at various times, they may be said to form temporal series. (Such series may of course contain gaps: there may be times at which no member of a series is occurring, though members have occurred before these times and will occur after them.) What we want to do is to find something which will be true of any series of total temporary states all the members of which are total temporary states of one and the same person; but false of any series of t.t.s., *not* all the members of which are t.t.s.'s of one and the same person.

As a preliminary shot I suggest the following: in a series of total temporary states belonging to one person, every t.t.s. which is a member of that series will contain as an element a memory of some experience which is an element in the temporally preceding member of the series; in a series of total temporary states not belonging to one person this will not be the case.

We can now give a provisional analysis of a class (1) "someone" sentence, e.g. "someone heard a noise." This will mean "a (past) hearing of a noise is an element in a t.t.s. which is a member of a series of t.t.s.'s such that every member of the series contains as an element a memory of some experience which is an element in the preceding member." This analysis will avoid the difficulties to which Locke's analysis is subject: the paradox about the officer will not arise, nor will the objection that few remotely past experiences could be co-personal with present experiences; and as far as I can see the analysis will not be circular unless it proves impossible to define "t.t.s." except in terms of "person" or "someone." But of that later.

Nevertheless, I do not think the analysis will do as it stands. It seems to me an unwarrantably violent assumption that every t.t.s. of mine (except the first) contains as an element a memory of some immediately preceding experience, indeed of any experience at all; and that every t.t.s. contains at least one experience which is remembered immediately subsequently, indeed remembered at all. So I must amend the analysis to meet this objection. I propose to reconstruct it in terms not merely of actual memory but also of possible memory. The analysis of "someone heard a noise" will now run "a (past) hearing of a noise is an element in a t.t.s., which is a member of a series of t.t.s.'s, such that every member of the series *would, given certain conditions, contain* as an element a memory of some experience which is an element in the preceding member." (For brevity I use "x would, given certain conditions, contain y" in such a way that it is true if x does contain y.)

A little further emendation is required, I think, to reach a satisfactory analysis. For, first of all, there is a difficulty about the first t.t.s. of the kind of series I have been considering; since it is the first t.t.s., there can be no preceding t.t.s. in the series; so the first t.t.s. would not, given *any* conditions, contain a memory of a previous experience. Second, I don't think we should assume that every t.t.s. contains some experience which would, given certain conditions, be remembered in the immediately subsequent t.t.s.; it might, for instance, be the case that even a prolonged process of psycho-analysis would not bring

about the occurrence of a memory of any experience contained
in some t.t.s.'s. To avoid these difficulties I will restate the
analysis of "someone heard a noise" thus: "a (past) hearing of
a noise is an element in a t.t.s. which is a member of a series of
t.t.s.'s such that every member of the series *either* would, given
certain conditions, contain as an element a memory of some
experience which is an element in some previous member, *or*
contains as an element some experience a memory of which
would, given certain conditions, occur as an element in some
subsequent member; there being no subset of members which is
independent of all the rest." (By denying that there is, within
such a series, a subset of members which is independent of all
the set, I mean to assert that any subset of t.t.s.'s includes at
least one t.t.s. which *either* would, given conditions, contain as
an element a memory of some experience contained as an element in some t.t.s. which is not included in the subset, *or* contains as an element some experience a memory of which would,
given certain conditions, occur as an element in some t.t.s. not
included in the subset. This proviso is obviously necessary in
order to prevent the t.t.s.'s of a man who dies at t, and of
another whose first experience occurs at t, from being by definition all t.t.s. of one person.) I can put the analysis more briefly
if I introduce the term "memorative t.t.s." to mean "t.t.s. which
would, given certain conditions, contain as an element a memory
of some experience contained in a previous t.t.s.," and the term
"memorable t.t.s." to mean "t.t.s. which contains as an element
some experience, a memory of which would, given certain conditions, occur as an element in some subsequent t.t.s.," and the
term "interlocking series" to mean "a series in which no subset
of members is independent of all the rest" (in the sense of "independent of" I have just defined). Then "someone heard a
noise" can be analysed "a (past) hearing of a noise is an element
in a member of an interlocking series of memorative and memorable t.t.s.'s."

It now remains for me to define "total temporary state."
"A t.t.s. occurs at t" means "experiences occur at t which belong to the same t.t.s."; and "experiences E and E′ belong to
the same t.t.s." means "E and E′ would, given certain conditions, be known, by memory or introspection, to be simulta-

neous." (I use "simultaneous" to mean whatever would be meant in ordinary speech by "occurring at the same time.")

One final point must be emphasised before I discuss arguments for and against the theory I have propounded. By "memory" I must be understood to mean what is often referred to as "memory-knowledge." I cannot interpret "memory" as, e.g., "true belief about the past." For clearly I can have a true belief that such and such an experience occurred, without the experience having been my experience. I should have to substitute for "true belief about the past" "true belief about *my* past," and then my analysis would contain an obvious circularity. For I should have to analyse "someone" sentences in terms of "true beliefs about someone's past." I think I must further maintain that not merely memory-knowledge, but also memory-acquaintance is possible; that is to say it must be possible, given certain conditions, to know not merely that such and such an experience occurred, but also that *that* experience occurred. I do not however propose to argue this point.

I must now consider what there is to be said for my theory.

(1) It is a form of logical construction theory; and since there seem to me to be grounds for rejecting the P.E. theory and also for rejecting all other forms of logical construction theory which I have encountered, there seems to me reason at any rate to investigate the theory I have suggested.

(2) On my theory it will be possible for some propositions about selves to be known. For two experiences can be known to be co-personal, if, e.g., it can be known that memories of them occur within the same t.t.s., i.e. if it can be known that two memories occur simultaneously. But this can be known. Thus the theory has an advantage over theories of the self which do not allow knowledge of propositions about selves; and there are several such theories.

(3) The theory, if true, enables us to see why such a proposition as "One can only remember one's own experiences" is analytic, and analytic in a way which is not trivial, as it would be trivial if "memory" were to be defined in terms of "having knowledge of one's own past experiences." For even if we were to define "memory" in this sort of way, we should still be left with a question about the proposition, "one can only have

knowledge of one's own past experiences," which seems to me a necessary proposition; and on the theory I suggest it will be analytic.

(4) The theory will recommend itself to those who feel an absurdity in saying "there have been experiences of mine which I could never, given any circumstances, be aware of." For if there were such experiences, they could not be elements in a t.t.s., since "E is an element in t.t.s." is defined in terms of the possibility of knowledge of E. But if they were elements in no t.t.s. they would belong to no self.

I shall conclude by discussing some objections which might be brought against the theory I have suggested. First of all, it may be said, the analysis I have suggested of a sentence like "someone heard a noise" is much too complicated to be the right analysis. I am far too uncertain how far, if at all, the fact that a proposed analysis of an apparently simple sentence is complicated is a good reason for rejecting the analysis, to discuss this objection at length. I will confine myself to the observation that my analysis of "self"-sentences is probably far less complicated than would be the phenomenalist's analysis of any material object-sentence, if indeed a phenomenalist were ever to offer an analysis of such a sentence, and not merely tell us what sort of an analysis it would be if he did give it.

The second objection which I may encounter is that my analysis of class (1) "someone" sentences is circular in a way something like that in which it has been said that phenomenalistic analyses of material object-sentences are circular. To quote Braithwaite (*Propositions about Material Objects,* P.A.S., 1937-38, p. 275): "Now the most serious criticism to which such a theory (i.e. Phenomenalism) lays itself open is that the analysis proposed is circular: it is impossible to state the conditions under which a person will have a sense-datum of a clock on the mantelpiece without specifying a lot of things about the position of the person's body, the integrity of his visual and central nervous system, that he is not dreaming nor hypnotised—in fact a set of propositions which are, I think, equivalent to what I have called the perception in question being reliable." Now it might be urged that a similar criticism can be directed against my theory: for I have analysed "someone" sentences in terms of memories which would occur given certain conditions; but, it may be said, the conditions would have to include the occurrence of certain experiences other than the memories in question; and for the occurrence of such experiences to lead to the occurrence of the memories, it would be necessary that they should be experiences of the person to whom the memories would belong. But this involves a circle.

My answer to this objection is that my analysis of "someone" sentences does not have to say what the conditions would be, given which a memory would occur: while a phenomenalistic analysis of material-object-sentences may have to state what the conditions would be, given which a person will have a sense-datum belonging to a material object. If a phenomenalistic analysis does have to state what the conditions are, one reason why it does have to do so may be the following: suppose I am in a room which does not contain a clock; now the analysis of the sentence "There is a clock in the room" cannot be of the form "There are conditions given which I (or other people) would have sense-data of such and such a kind." For if there is another room exactly similar to the first except that it does contain a clock: it will be true that there are conditions given which I (or other people) would have sense-data of such and such a kind (i.e. the kind I would have if there were a clock in the first room); for I should have such sense-data if (*inter alia*) I were in the second room. But it would still be false that there is a clock in the room (where the room meant is the first room). Now once the Phenomenalist has to state the conditions he is faced with the difficulty mentioned by Braithwaite. But I do not have to state what the conditions are given which a memory would occur; for an experience, a memory of which would, given certain conditions, occur as an element in some t.t.s., belongs to the self of which that t.t.s. is a t.t.s., *whatever* the conditions in question are. Consequently, I think, my analysis is not open to a charge of circularity on this score.

The last possible objection to my theory which I shall consider is that my theory presupposes the occurrence of memory-knowledge; but memory-knowledge never occurs; so my theory is false. Strictly speaking, this is not an accurate way of putting the objection; what actually is the case is that if my theory is true, and if any proposition expressible in class (1) "someone" sentences is true, then it is presupposed that memory-knowledge is *causally possible,* i.e. would occur given certain conditions. But I do not think my theory would be in the least plausible if memory-knowledge never did in fact occur; and if my theory is true it certainly would not be possible ever to *know* that anyone had an experience, unless memory-knowledge sometimes occurred. So I think I am really committed to maintaining that memory-knowledge does occur.

Now most of the objections to the occurrence of memory-knowledge which seem to me at all serious seem to be serious only because they are directed against views concerning the nature of memory which maintain very odd things about the mental images which are reputed to occur in memory situations; they maintain, for instance, that in a memory-knowledge situation there is a mental image which is identical with a past event. But if we refrain from saying such odd things about mental images, and maintain that the function of a mental image in a memory-knowledge situation, if it has any function at all, is, to use Professor Price's word, merely "directive," we escape these objections. And, indeed, it seems to me perfectly clear that when I have memory-knowledge of something, it is not a mental image which I know, or about which I know something, nor does the proposition "I remembered something" entail the proposition "I had a mental image."

If this sort of objection is ruled out, what can the opponent of memory-knowledge say? He may just say that he has never had memory-knowledge of anything. If so I cannot really argue with him, I can only ask him whether he claims to know that he has never had memory-knowledge, or only to believe it; and if he says he knows, ask him how he knows except by means of memory-knowledge; or if he says he believes, ask him what his evidence is and how he acquired it.

But he might produce some further argument against the view that memory-knowledge does occur. Now the only argument I can think of which seems to me at all formidable is a causal argument, which might be stated thus. Suppose that memory-knowings do occur; then, being events, they must be caused. What then is the cause? One view might be, the past experience, which is remembered, together with a stimulus which immediately preceded the remembering. But this involves the possibility of causation at a distance, which (it will be said) is very difficult to maintain. Another view might involve a persistent mental trace (the formation of which was caused by the past experience which is remembered) together with the present stimulus. But again, it will be said, the notion of a "mental trace" is a very difficult one. We are left then with the possibility that it is a persistent physical trace, caused by the past experience, in the body of the person who remembers, together with the present stimulus. Since this trace is usually supposed to be in the brain, I shall refer to it as a "brain-trace." For lack of an alternative, then, we must accept the view that the knowing is caused by existence of the brain-trace plus the occurrence of the stimulus. Now it is possible that the formation of the brain-trace might be caused, not by the past experience, but by, say, an operation by a clever surgeon. If this is so, it is possible that a brain-trace, exactly like that which would be produced by a past experience of such and such a kind, might exist without any such experience having occurred. It will further be possible that both the brain-trace might exist and the stimulus might occur, without the past experience having occurred. But if both the brain-trace existed and the stimulus occurred, the memory-knowing would occur. Therefore the memory-knowing might occur without the remembered experience having occurred. But that is logically impossible. Therefore unless the argument is unsound one of the premisses must be rejected; and the easiest premiss to reject is that memory-knowledge occurs.

Now I think the argument is unsound; but in order to show that it is I must distinguish more closely what the argument asserts, for I think there is an ambiguity in it, due to an ambiguity in the word "possible," which may mean either "logically possible" or "causally possible." Suppose, first, that "possible" means "logically possible." Then the bare bones of the argument will be:

(1) The existence of a brain-trace of kind A *plus* the occurrence of a stimulus of kind B is logically compatible with the non-occurrence of any experience of kind E.

(2) The existence of a brain-trace of kind A *plus* the occur-

rence of a stimulus of kind B causally involves the occurrence of a memory-knowing of an experience of kind E.

Therefore the occurrence of a memory-knowing of an experience of kind E is logically compatible with the non-occurrence of any experience of kind E.

But this is absurd; therefore either (1) is false, which is very, very improbable; or (2) is false, and the falsity of (2) will involve the falsity of the proposition that if these memory-knowings occur they are caused by the existence of a brain-trace *plus* the occurrence of a stimulus; or there are no memory-knowings, which seems the easiest alternative to accept.

But there is a suppressed premiss in the argument which is false. (Perhaps it is rather a principle than a premiss.) The argument should run:

(1) The existence of a brain-trace of kind A *plus* the occurrence of a stimulus of kind B is logically compatible with the non-occurrence of any experience of kind E.

(2) The existence of a brain-trace of kind A *plus* the occurrence of a stimulus of kind B causally involves the occurrence of a memory-knowing of an experience of kind E.

(3) For any propositions p, q, r, if p is logically compatible with q, and p causally implies r, then r is logically compatible with q.

Therefore the occurrence of a memory-knowing of an experience of kind E is logically compatible with the non-occurrence of any experience of kind E.

But (3) only has to be considered to be seen to be false. Let p = it has been raining, q = the ground is not wet, r = the ground is wet. Then p will be logically compatible with q, for it is logically possible that it should have been raining without the ground being wet; and p will causally imply r, for whenever it rains the ground does get wet; but q is clearly not logically compatible with r; for it cannot be true both that the ground is wet and that it is not wet.

I conclude then that the argument in this form is unsound; but before I pass on to the second form the argument might take, I ought to remark that it must not be supposed that I accept the views about the causes of memory-knowledge involved by the argument.

Suppose now that "possible" means "causally possible." The argument (including the suppressed premiss or principle) will now run:

(1) The existence of a brain-trace of kind A *plus* the occurrence of a stimulus of kind B is causally compatible with the non-occurrence of any experience of kind E.

(2) The existence of a brain-trace of kind A *plus* the occurrence of a stimulus of kind B causally involves the occurrence of a memory-knowing of an experience of kind E.

(3) For any *p, q, r*, if *p* is causally compatible with *q*, and *p* causally implies *r*, then *r* is logically compatible with *q*.

Therefore the occurrence of a memory-knowing of an experience of kind E is logically compatible with the non-occurrence of any experience of kind E.

But this is absurd; therefore (as before) we must reject memory-knowledge.

(3) is now, I think, true; but its gain is (1)'s loss. For the supporter of the argument is now committed to maintaining not that it is logically possible that a brain-trace of kind A should exist without the occurrence of an experience of kind E, but that it is causally possible that it should so exist. That means, I think, that he has got to maintain that there are conditions given which there *would* be a brain-trace of kind E without any experience of kind E having occurred; and in order to support this contention he must maintain, for example, that if a surgeon operated in a certain way he *would* produce the brain-trace, or give some other explanation how the brain-trace could be produced. But to maintain any such thing as this is something, I should have thought, that no reasonable man would be prepared to do. For I cannot see what evidence in favour of it *he* could possibly have.

I do not then think that any real doubt has been cast on the occurrence of memory-knowledge; and it seems to me, therefore, that my theory is untouched by objections of the kind I have just discussed.

PART III

CRITICISMS OF
THE MEMORY THEORY

Joseph Butler

5

Of Personal Identity

Whether we are to live in a future state, as it is the most important question which can possibly be asked, so it is the most intelligible one which can be expressed in language. Yet strange
perplexities have been raised about the meaning of that identity,
or sameness of person, which is implied in the notion of our
living now and hereafter, or in any two successive moments.
And the solution of these difficulties hath been stranger than
the difficulties themselves. For, personal identity has been explained so by some, as to render the inquiry concerning a future
life of no consequence at all to us, the persons who are making
it. And though few men can be misled by such subtleties, yet it
may be proper a little to consider them.

   Now, when it is asked wherein personal identity consists,
the answer should be the same as if it were asked, wherein consists similitude or equality; that all attempts to define, would
but perplex it. Yet there is no difficulty at all in ascertaining
the idea. For as, upon two triangles being compared or viewed
together, there arises to the mind the idea of similitude; or upon
twice two and four, the idea of equality; so likewise, upon comparing the consciousness of one's self, or one's own existence
in any two moments, there as immediately arises to the mind
the idea of personal identity. And as the two former comparisons not only give the idea of similitude and equality, but also

This selection is the first appendix to Butler's *The Analogy of Religion*,
first published in 1736.

shows us, that two triangles are like, and twice two and four are equal; so the latter comparison not only gives us the idea of personal identity but also shows us the identity of ourselves in those two moments; the present, suppose, and that immediately past; or the present, and that a month, a year, or twenty years past. Or, in other words, by reflecting upon that which is myself now, and that which was myself twenty years ago, I discern they are not two, but one and the same self.

But though consciousness of what is past does thus ascertain our personal identity to ourselves, yet, to say that it makes personal identity, or is necessary to our being the same persons, is to say, that a person has not existed a single moment, nor done one action, but what he can remember; indeed none but what he reflects upon. And one should really think it self-evident, that consciousness of personal identity presupposes, and therefore cannot constitute, personal identity, any more than knowledge, in any other case, can constitute truth, which it presupposes.

This wonderful mistake may possibly have arisen from hence, that to be endued with consciousness, is inseparable from the idea of a person, or intelligent being. For, this might be expressed inaccurately thus—that consciousness makes personality; and from hence it might be concluded to make personal identity. But though present consciousness of what we at present do and feel, is necessary to our being the persons we now are; yet present consciousness of past actions, or feelings, is not necessary to our being the same persons who performed those actions, or had those feelings.

The inquiry, what makes vegetables the same in the common acceptation of the word, does not appear to have any relation to this of personal identity; because the word *same,* when applied to them and to persons, is not only applied to different subjects, but it is also used in different senses. For when a man swears to the same tree, as having stood fifty years in the same place, he means only the same as to all the purposes of property and uses of common life, and not that the tree has been all that time the same in the strict philosophical sense of the word. For he does not know whether any one particle of the present tree be the same with any one particle of the tree which stood in the same place fifty years ago. And if they have not one common particle of matter, they cannot be the same tree, in the proper philosophic sense of the word *same;* it being evidently a contradiction in terms, to say they are, when no part of their substance, and no one of their properties, is the same; no part of their substance, by the supposition; no one of their properties, because it is allowed that the same property cannot be transferred from one substance to another. And therefore, when we say the identity or sameness of a plant consists in a continuation of the same life communicated under the same organization, to a number of particles of matter, whether the same or not, the word *same,* when applied to life and to organization, cannot possibly be understood to signify, what it signifies in this very sentence, when applied to matter. In a loose and popular sense, then, the life, and the organization, and the plant, are justly said to be the same, notwithstanding the perpetual change of the parts. But in a strict and philosophical manner of speech, no man, no being, no mode of being, nor any thing, can be the same with that, with which it hath indeed nothing the same. Now, sameness is used in this latter sense when applied to persons. The identity of these, therefore, cannot subsist with diversity of substance.

The thing here considered, and demonstratively, as I think, determined, is proposed by Mr. Locke in these words, *Whether it,* i.e., the same self or person, *be the same identical substance?* And he has suggested what is a much better answer to the question than that which he give it in form. For he defines person, *a thinking intelligent being,* etc. and personal identity *the sameness of a rational being.*[1] The question then is, whether the same rational being is the same substance; which needs no answer, because being and substance, in this place, stand for the same idea. The ground of the doubt, whether the same person be the same substance, is said to be this; that the consciousness of our own existence in youth and in old age, or in any two joint successive moments, is not *the same individual action,*[2] i.e., not the same consciousness, but different successive consciousnesses. Now it is strange that this should have occasioned such perplexities. For it is surely conceivable, that a person may have a capacity of knowing some object or other to be the same now, which it was when he contemplated it formerly; yet, in this case, where, by the supposition, the object is perceived to be the same, the perception of it in any two moments cannot be one and the same perception. And thus, though the successive consciousnesses which we have of our own existence are not the same, yet are they consciousnesses of one and the same thing or object; of the same person, self, or living agent. The person, of whose existence the consciousness is felt now, and was felt an hour or a year ago, is discerned to be, not two persons, but one and the same person; and therefore is one and the same.

Mr. Locke's observations upon this subject appear hasty; and he seems to profess himself dissatisfied with suppositions, which he has made relating to it.[3] But some of those hasty observations have been carried to a strange length by others; whose notion, when traced and examined to the bottom, amounts, I think, to this:[4] "That personality is not a permanent, but a transient thing: that it lives and dies, begins and ends, continually: that no one can any more remain one and the same person two moments together, than two successive moments can be one and the same moment: that our substance is indeed continually changing; but whether this be so or not, is, it seems, nothing to the purpose; since it is not substance, but consciousness alone, which constitutes personality; which consciousness, being successive, cannot be the same in any two moments, nor consequently the personality constituted by it." And from hence it must follow, that it is a fallacy upon ourselves, to charge our present selves with any thing we did, or to imagine our present selves interested in any thing which befell us yesterday, or that our present self will be interested in what will befall us to-morrow; since our present self is not, in reality, the same with the self of yesterday, but another like self or person coming in its room, and mistaken for it; to which another self will succeed tomorrow. This, I say, must follow: for if the self or person of today, and that of tomorrow, are not the same, but only like persons, the person of today is really no more interested in what will befall the person of tomorrow, than in what will befall any other person. It may be thought, perhaps, that this is not a just representation of the opinion we are speaking of; because those who maintain it allow, that a person is the same as far back as his remembrance reaches. And, indeed, they do use the words, *identity* and *same* person. Nor will language permit these words to be laid aside: since if they were, there must be, I know not what, ridiculous periphrasis substituted in the room of them. But they cannot, consistently with themselves, mean, that the person is really the same. For it is self-evident, that the personality cannot be really the same, if, as they expressly assert, that in which it consists is not the same. And as, consistently with themselves, they cannot, so, I think, it appears they do not, mean, that the person is *really* the same, but only that he is so in a fictitious sense: in such a sense only as they assert; for this they do assert, that any number of persons whatever may be the same person. The bare unfolding this notion, and laying it thus naked and open, seems the best confutation of it. However, since great stress is said to be put upon it, I add the following things:

First, This notion is absolutely contradictory to that certain conviction, which necessarily, and every moment, rises within us, when we turn our thoughts upon ourselves; when we reflect upon what is past, and look forward upon what is to come. All imagination of a daily change of that living agent which each man calls himself, for another, or of any such change throughout our whole present life, is entirely borne down by our natural sense of things. Nor is it possible for a person in his wits to alter his conduct, with regard to his health or affairs, from a suspicion, that though he should live tomorrow, he should not, however, be the same person he is today. And yet, if it be reasonable to act, with respect to a future life, upon this notion, that personality is transient; it is reasonable to act upon it, with respect to the present. Here then is a notion equally applicable to religion and to our temporal concerns; and every one sees and feels the inexpressible absurdity of it in the latter case. If, therefore, any can take up with it in the former, this cannot proceed from the reason of the thing, but must be owing to an inward unfairness, and secret corruption of heart.

Secondly, It is not an idea, or abstract notion, or quality, but a being only which is capable of life and action, of happiness and misery. Now all beings confessedly continue the same, during the whole time of their existence. Consider then a living being now existing, and which has existed for any time alive: this living being must have done and suffered and enjoyed, what it has done and suffered and enjoyed formerly (this living being, I say, and not another), as really as it does and suffers and enjoys, what it does and suffers and enjoys this instant. All these successive actions, enjoyments, and sufferings, are actions, enjoyments, and sufferings, of the same living being. And they are so, prior to all consideration of its remembering or forgetting; since remembering or forgetting can make no alteration in the truth of past matter of fact. And suppose this being endued with limited powers of knowledge and memory, there is no more difficulty in conceiving it to have a power of knowing itself to be the same living being which it was some time ago, of remembering some of its actions, sufferings, and enjoyments, and forgetting others, than in conceiving it to know, or remember, or forget any thing else.

Thirdly, Every person is conscious, that he is now the same person or self he was, as far back as his remembrance reaches; since, when any one reflects upon a past action of his own, he is just as certain of the person who did that action, namely himself, the person who now reflects upon it, as he is certain that the action was at all done. Nay, very often a person's assurance of an action having been done, of which he is absolutely assured, arises wholly from the consciousness that he himself did it. And this he, person, or self, must either be a substance, or the property of some substance. If he, if person, be a substance; then consciousness that he is the same person, is consciousness that he is the same substance. If the person, or he, be the property of a substance; still consciousness that he is the same property, is as certain a proof that his substance remains the same, as consciousness the he remains the same substance would be; since the same property cannot be transferred from one substance to another.

But though we are thus certain that we are the same agents, living beings, or substances, now, which we were as far back as our remembrance reaches; yet it is asked, whether we may not possibly be deceived in it? And this question may be asked at the end of any demonstration whatever; because it is a question concerning the truth of perception by memory. And he who can doubt, whether perception by memory can in this case be depended upon, may doubt also, whether perception by deduction and reasoning, which also include memory, or, indeed, whether intuitive perception can. Here then we can go no farther. For it is ridiculous to attempt to prove the truth of those perceptions, whose truth we can no otherwise prove, than by other perceptions of exactly the same kind with them, and which there is just the same ground to suspect; or to attempt to prove the truth of our faculties, which can no otherwise be proved, than by the use or means of those very suspected faculties themselves.

NOTES

1. Locke's Works, vol. i. p. 146.
2. Ibid., pp. 146, 147.
3. Ibid., p. 152.
4. See an answer to Dr. Clarke's third defence of his letter to Mr. Dodwell, 2d edit. pp. 44, 56, etc.

Thomas Reid

6

Of Identity

The conviction which every man has of his identity, as far back as his memory reaches, needs no aid of philosophy to strengthen it; and no philosophy can weaken it, without first producing some degree of insanity.

The philosopher, however, may very properly consider this conviction as a phenomenon of human nature worthy of his attention. If he can discover its cause, an addition is made to his stock of knowledge; if not, it must be held as a part of our original constitution, or an effect of that constitution produced in a manner unknown to us.

We may observe, first of all, that this conviction is indispensably necessary to all exercise of reason. The operations of reason, whether in action or in speculation, are made up of successive parts. The antecedent are the foundation of the consequent, and, without the conviction that the antecedent have been seen or done by me, I could have no reason to proceed to the consequent, in any speculation, or in any active project whatever.

There can be no memory of what is past without the conviction that we existed at the time remembered. There may be good arguments to convince me that I existed before the earliest thing I can remember; but to suppose that my memory

This selection is chapter 4 of "Of Memory," which is the third essay in Reid's *Essays on the Intellectual Powers of Man,* first published in 1785.

reaches a moment farther back than my belief and conviction of my existence, is a contradiction.

The moment a man loses this conviction, as if he had drunk the water of Lethe, past things are done away; and, in his own belief, he then begins to exist. Whatever was thought, or said, or done, or suffered before that period, may belong to some other person; but he can never impute it to himself, or take any subsequent step that supposes it to be his doing.

From this it is evident that we must have the conviction of our own continued existence and identity, as soon as we are capable of thinking or doing anything, on account of what we have thought, or done, or suffered before; that is, as soon as we are reasonable creatures.

That we may form as distinct a notion as we are able of this phenomenon of the human mind, it is proper to consider what is meant by identity in general, what by our own personal identity, and how we are led into that invincible belief and conviction which every man has of his own personal identity, as far as his memory reaches.

Identity in general I take to be a relation between a thing which is known to exist at one time, and a thing which is known to have existed at another time. If you ask whether they are one and the same, or two different things, every man of common sense understands the meaning of your question perfectly. Whence we may infer with certainty, that every man of common sense has a clear and distinct notion of identity.

If you ask a definition of identity, I confess I can give none; it is too simple a notion to admit of logical definition: I can say it is a relation, but I cannot find words to express the specific difference between this and other relations, though I am in no danger of confounding it with any other. I can say that diversity is a contrary relation, and that similitude and dissimilitude are another couple of contrary relations, which every man easily distinguishes in his conception from identity and diversity.

I see evidently that identity supposes an uninterrupted continuance of existence. That which has ceased to exist cannot be the same with that which afterwards begins to exist; for this would be to suppose a being to exist after it ceased to exist, and to have had existence before it was produced, which are mani-

fest contradictions. Continued uninterrupted existence is therefore necessarily implied in identity.

Hence we may infer, that identity cannot, in its proper
sense, be applied to our pains, our pleasures, our thoughts, or
any operation of our minds. The pain felt this day is not the
same individual pain which I felt yesterday, though they may
be *similar* in kind and degree, and have the same cause. The
same may be said of every feeling, and of every operation of
mind. They are all successive in their nature, like time itself, no
two moments of which can be the same moment.

It is otherwise with the parts of absolute space. They always are, and were, and will be the same. So far, I think, we
proceed upon clear ground in fixing the notion of identity in
general.

It is perhaps more difficult to ascertain with precision the
meaning of personality; but it is not necessary in the present
subject: it is sufficient for our purpose to observe, that all mankind place their personality in something that cannot be divided,
or consist of parts.

A part of a person is a manifest absurdity. When a man
loses his estate, his health, his strength, he is still the same person, and has lost nothing of his personality. If he has a leg or
an arm cut off, he is the same person he was before. The am-
putated member is no part of his person, otherwise it would
have a right to a part of his estate, and be liable for a part of
his engagements. It would be entitled to a share of his merit
and demerit, which is manifestly absurd. A person is something
indivisible, and is what Leibnitz calls a *monad.*

My personal identity, therefore, implies the continued existence of that indivisible thing which I call *myself.* Whatever
this self may be, it is something which thinks, and deliberates,
and resolves, and acts, and suffers. I am not thought, I am not
action, I am not feeling; I am something that thinks, and acts,
and suffers. My thoughts, and actions, and feelings, change
every moment; they have no continued, but a successive, existence; but that *self,* or *I,* to which they belong, is permanent,
and has the same relation to all the succeeding thoughts, actions,
and feelings which I call mine.

Such are the notions that I have of my personal identity.

But perhaps it may be said, this may all be fancy without reality. How do you know—what evidence have you—that there is such a permanent self which has a claim to all the thoughts, actions, and feelings which you call yours?

To this I answer, that the proper evidence I have of all this is remembrance. I remember that twenty years ago I conversed with such a person; I remember several things that passed in that conversation: my memory testifies, not only that this was done, but that it was done by me who now remember it. If it was done by me, I must have existed at that time, and continued to exist from that time to the present: if the identical person whom I call myself had not a part in that conversation, my memory is fallacious; it gives a distinct and positive testimony of what is not true. Every man in his senses believes what he distinctly remembers, and every thing he remembers convinces him that he existed at the time remembered.

Although memory gives the most irresistible evidence of my being the identical person that did such a thing, at such a time, I may have other good evidence of things which befell me, and which I do not remember: I know who bare me, and suckled me, but I do not remember these events.

It may here be observed (though the observation would have been unnecessary, if some great philosophers had not contradicted it), that it is not my remembering any action of mine that makes me to be the person who did it. This remembrance makes me to know assuredly that I did it; but I might have done it, though I did not remember it. That relation to me, which is expressed by saying that I did it, would be the same, though I had not the least remembrance of it. To say that my remembering that I did such a thing, or, as some choose to express it, my being conscious that I did it, makes me to have done it, appears to me as great an absurdity as it would be to say, that my belief that the world was created made it to be created.

When we pass judgment on the identity of other persons than ourselves, we proceed upon other grounds, and determine from a variety of circumstances, which sometimes produce the firmest assurance, and sometimes leave room for doubt. The identity of persons has often furnished matter of serious litigation before tribunals of justice. But no man of a sound mind ever doubted of his own identity, as far as he distinctly remembered.

The identity of a person is a perfect identity: wherever it is real, it admits of no degrees; and it is impossible that a person should be in part the same, and in part different; because a person is a *monad,* and is not divisible into parts. The evidence of identity in other persons than ourselves does indeed admit of all degrees, from what we account certainty, to the least degree of probability. But still it is true, that the same person is perfectly the same, and cannot be so in part, or in some degree only.

For this cause, I have first considered personal identity, as that which is perfect in its kind, and the natural measure of that which is imperfect.

We probably at first derive our notion of identity from that natural conviction which every man has from the dawn of reason of his own identity and continued existence. The operations of our minds are all successive, and have no continued existence. But the thinking being has a continued existence, and we have an invincible belief, that it remains the same when all its thoughts and operations change.

Our judgments of the identity of objects of sense seem to be formed much upon the same grounds as our judgments of the identity of other persons than ourselves.

Wherever we observe great similarity, we are apt to presume identity, if no reason appears to the contrary. Two objects ever so like, when they are perceived at the same time, cannot be the same; but if they are presented to our senses at different times, we are apt to think them the same, merely from their similarity.

Whether this be a natural prejudice, or from whatever cause it proceeds, it certainly appears in children from infancy; and when we grow up, it is confirmed in most instances by experience: for we rarely find two individuals of the same species that are not distinguishable by obvious differences.

A man challenges a thief whom he finds in possession of his horse or his watch, only on similarity. When the watchmaker swears that he sold this watch to such a person, his testimony is grounded on similarity. The testimony of witnesses to the identity of a person is commonly grounded on no other evidence.

Thus it appears, that the evidence we have of our own identity, as far back as we remember, is totally of a different kind from the evidence we have of the identity of other persons, or of objects of sense. The first is grounded on memory, and gives undoubted certainty. The last is grounded on similarity, and on other circumstances, which in many cases are not so decisive as to leave no room for doubt.

It may likewise be observed, that the identity of objects of sense is never perfect. All bodies, as they consist of innumerable parts that may be disjoined from them by a great variety of causes, are subject to continual changes of their substance, increasing, diminishing, changing insensibly. When such alterations are gradual, because language could not afford a different name for every different state of such a changeable being, it retains the same name, and is considered as the same thing. Thus we say of an old regiment, that it did such a thing a century ago, though there now is not a man alive who then belonged to it. We say a tree is the same in the seed-bed and in the forest. A ship of war, which has successively changed her anchors, her tackle, her sails, her masts, her planks, and her timbers, while she keeps the same name, is the same.

The identity, therefore, which we ascribe to bodies, whether natural or artificial, is not perfect identity; it is rather something which, for the conveniency of speech, we call identity. It admits of a great change of the subject, providing the change be gradual; sometimes, even of a total change. And the changes which in common language are made consistent with identity differ from those that are thought to destroy it, not in kind, but in number and degree. It has no fixed nature when applied to bodies; and questions about the identity of a body are very often questions about words. But identity, when applied to persons, has no ambiguity, and admits not of degrees, or of more and less. It is the foundation of all rights and obligations, and of all accountableness; and the notion of it is fixed and precise.

Thomas Reid

7

Of Mr. Locke's Account
of Our Personal Identity

In a long chapter upon Identity and Diversity, Mr. Locke has made many ingenious and just observations, and some which I think cannot be defended. I shall only take notice of the account he gives of our own personal identity. His doctrine upon this subject has been censured by Bishop Butler, in a short essay subjoined to his *Analogy,* with whose sentiments I perfectly agree.

Identity, as was observed (Chap. 4 of this Essay), supposes the continued existence of the being of which it is affirmed, and therefore can be applied only to things which have a continued existence. While any being continues to exist, it is the same being; but two beings which have a different beginning or a different ending of their existence cannot possibly be the same. To this, I think, Mr. Locke agrees.

He observes, very justly, that, to know what is meant by the same person, we must consider what the word *person* stands for; and he defines a person to be an intelligent being, endowed with reason and with consciousness, which last he thinks inseparable from thought.

From this definition of a person, it must necessarily follow, that, while the intelligent being continues to exist and to be intelligent, it must be the same person. To say that the intelligent being is the person, and yet that the person ceases to exist

This selection is chapter 6 of "Of Memory," which is the third essay in Reid's *Essays on the Intellectual Powers of Man,* first published in 1785.

while the intelligent being continues, or that the person continues while the intelligent being ceases to exist, is to my apprehension a manifest contradiction.

One would think that the definition of a person should perfectly ascertain the nature of personal identity, or wherein it consists, though it might still be a question how we come to know and be assured of our personal identity.

Mr. Locke tells us, however, "that personal identity, that is, the sameness of a rational being, consists in consciousness alone, and, as far as this consciousness can be extended backwards to any past action or thought, so far reaches the identity of that person. So that whatever has the consciousness of present and past actions is the same person to whom they belong."

This doctrine has some strange consequences, which the author was aware of. Such as, that if the same consciousness can be transferred from one intelligent being to another, which he thinks we cannot show to be impossible, *then two or twenty intelligent beings may be the same person.* And if the intelligent being may lose the consciousness of the actions done by him, which surely is possible, then he is not the person that did those actions; so that *one intelligent being may be two or twenty different persons,* if he shall so often lose the consciousness of his former actions.

There is another consequence of this doctrine, which follows no less necessarily, though Mr. Locke probably did not see it. It is, *that a man may be, and at the same time not be, the person that did a particular action.*

Suppose a brave officer to have been flogged when a boy at school for robbing an orchard, to have taken a standard from the enemy in his first campaign, and to have been made a general in advanced life; suppose, also, which must be admitted to be possible, that, when he took the standard, he was conscious of his having been flogged at school, and that, when made a general, he was conscious of his taking the standard, but had absolutely lost the consciousness of his flogging.

These things being supposed, it follows, from Mr. Locke's doctrine, that he who was flogged at school is the same person who took the standard, and that he who took the standard is the same person who was made a general. Whence it follows, if there be any truth in logic, that the general is the same person with him who was flogged at school. But the general's consciousness does not reach so far back as his flogging; therefore, according to Mr. Locke's doctrine, he is not the person who was flogged. Therefore the general is, and at the same time is not, the same person with him who was flogged at school.

Leaving the consequences of this doctrine to those who have leisure to trace them, we may observe, with regard to the doctrine itself,

First, that Mr. Locke attributes to consciousness the conviction we have of our past actions, as if a man may now be conscious of what he did twenty years ago. It is impossible to understand the meaning of this, unless by consciousness be meant memory, the only faculty by which we have an immediate knowledge of our past actions.

Sometimes, in popular discourse, a man says he is conscious that he did such a thing, meaning that he distinctly remembers that he did it. It is unnecessary, in common discourse, to fix accurately the limits between consciousness and memory. This was formerly shown to be the case with regard to sense and memory: and therefore distinct remembrance is sometimes called sense, sometimes consciousness, without any inconvenience.

But this ought to be avoided in philosophy, otherwise we confound the different powers of the mind, and ascribe to one what really belongs to another. If a man can be conscious of what he did twenty years or twenty minutes ago, there is no use for memory, nor ought we to allow that there is any such faculty. The faculties of consciousness and memory are chiefly distinguished by this, that the first is an immediate knowledge of the present, the second an immediate knowledge of the past.

When, therefore, Mr. Locke's notion of personal identity is properly expressed, it is, that personal identity consists in distinct remembrance: for, even in the popular sense, to say that I am conscious of a past action means nothing else than that I distinctly remember that I did it.

Secondly, it may be observed, that, in this doctrine, not only is consciousness confounded with memory, but, which is still more strange, personal identity is confounded with the evidence which we have of our personal identity.

It is very true, that my remembrance that I did such a thing is the evidence I have that I am the identical person who did it. And this, I am apt to think, Mr. Locke meant. But to say that my remembrance that I did such a thing, or my consciousness, makes me the person who did it, is, in my apprehension, an absurdity too gross to be entertained by any man who attends to the meaning of it; for it is to attribute to memory or consciousness a strange magical power of producing its object, though that object must have existed before the memory or consciousness which produced it.

Consciousness is the testimony of one faculty; memory is the testimony of another faculty; and to say that the testimony is the cause of the thing testified, this surely is absurd, if any thing be, and could not have been said by Mr. Locke, if he had not confounded the testimony with the thing testified.

When a horse that was stolen is found and claimed by the owner, the only evidence he can have, or that a judge or witnesses can have, that this is the very identical horse which was his property, is similitude. But would it not be ridiculous from this to infer that the identity of a horse consists in similitude only? The only evidence I have that I am the identical person who did such actions is, that I remember distinctly I did them; or, as Mr. Locke expresses it, I am conscious I did them. To infer from this, that personal identity consists in consciousness, is an argument which, if it had any force, would prove the identity of a stolen horse to consist solely in similitude.

Thirdly, is it not strange that the sameness or identity of a person should consist in a thing which is continually changing, and is not any two minutes the same?

Our consciousness, our memory, and every operation of the mind, are still flowing like the water of a river, or like time itself. The consciousness I have this moment can no more be the same consciousness I had last moment, than this moment can be the last moment. Identity can only be affirmed of things which have a continued existence. Consciousness, and every kind of thought, are transient and momentary, and have no continued existence; and, therefore, if personal identity consisted in consciousness, it would certainly follow, that no man is the same person any two moments of his life; and as the right and justice of reward and punishment are founded on personal identity, no man could be responsible for his actions.

But though I take this to be the unavoidable consequence of Mr. Locke's doctrine concerning personal identity, and though some persons may have liked the doctrine the better on this account, I am far from imputing any thing of this kind to Mr. Locke. He was too good a man not to have rejected with abhorrence a doctrine which he believed to draw this consequence after it.

Fourthly, there are many expressions used by Mr. Locke, in speaking of personal identity, which to me are altogether unintelligible, unless we suppose that he confounded that sameness or identity which we ascribe to an individual with the identity which, in common discourse, is often ascribed to many individuals of the same species.

When we say that pain and pleasure, consciousness and memory, are the same in all men, this sameness can only mean similarity, or sameness of kind. That the pain of one man can be the same individual pain with that of another man is no less impossible, than that one man should be another man: the pain felt by me yesterday can no more be the pain I feel to-day, than yesterday can be this day; and the same thing may be said of every passion and of every operation of the mind. The same kind or species of operation may be in different men, or in the same man at different times; but it is impossible that the same individual operation should be in different men, or in the same man at different times.

When Mr. Locke, therefore, speaks of "the same consciousness being continued through a succession of different substances"; when he speaks of "repeating the idea of a past action, with the same consciousness we had of it at the first," and of "the same consciousness extending to actions past and to come"; these expressions are to me unintelligible, unless he means not the same individual consciousness, but a consciousness that is similar, or of the same kind.

If our personal identity consists in consciousness, as this consciousness cannot be the same individually any two moments, but only of the same kind, it would follow, that we are not for any two moments the same individual persons, but the same kind of persons.

As our consciousness sometimes ceases to exist, as in sound sleep, our personal identity must cease with it. Mr. Locke allows, that the same thing cannot have two beginnings of existence, so that our identity would be irrecoverably gone every time we ceased to think, if it was but for a moment.

Sydney Shoemaker

8

Personal Identity and Memory *

Persons, unlike other things, make statements about their own pasts, and can be said to know these statements to be true. This fact would be of little importance, as far as the problem of personal identity is concerned, if these statements were always grounded in the ways in which people's statements about the past histories of things other than themselves are grounded. But while our statements about our own pasts are sometimes based on diaries, photographs, fingerprints, and the like, normally they are not. Normally they are based on our own memories, and the way in which one's memory provides one with knowledge concerning one's own past is quite unlike the way in which it provides one with knowledge concerning the past history of another person or thing. It is largely for this reason, I believe, that in addition to whatever problems there are about the notion of identity in general there has always been felt to be a special problem about *personal* identity. It is, for example, the way in which one knows one's own past that has led some philosophers to hold that personal identity is the only *real* identity that we have any knowledge of, the identity we ascribe to ships and stones being only, as Thomas Reid expressed it, "something which, for convenience of speech, we call identity."[1] What I wish to do in this paper is to consider how the concept of memory and the concept of personal identity are related. In particular, I want to consider the view that memory provides a criterion of personal identity, or, as H. P. Grice expressed it some years ago, that "the self is a logical construction and is to be defined in terms of memory."[2]

1. Clearly the concepts of memory and personal identity are not logically independent. As has often been pointed out, it is a logical truth that, if a person remembers[3] a past event, then he, the very person who remembers, must have been a witness to that event. It is partly this logical truth that has led some philosophers to hold that personal identity can be wholly or partially defined in terms of memory. And this view may seem to be supported by the fact that we sometimes use, as grounds for saying that a person was present when an event occurred, the fact that he apparently remembers the event, i.e., is able to give a correct and detailed account of it and does not appear to have anything other than his own memory on the basis of which he could know of it.

But it does not seem, offhand, that these considerations force us to accept this view. For it might be held that while there is a logical relationship between the concepts of memory and personal identity, this is because the former is definable or analyzable in terms of the latter and not vice versa. The assertion that a person A remembers an event X can plausibly be analyzed as meaning (1) that A now has knowledge of X, (2) that A's knowledge is not grounded inductively or based on the testimony of other persons, and (3) that A witnessed X when it occurred. To know with certainty that A remembers X, it might be held, we would have to know all three of these conditions were satisfied, and we could know that (3) is satisfied only if we had a criterion of personal identity by which we could judge that A, the person who now has knowledge of X, is identical with one of the persons who witnessed X. Obviously our criterion of identity here could not be the fact that A remembers X, for we could know this fact only if we had already established that such an identity holds.

The view just described, I think, must be the view of any philosopher who thinks that the identity of a human body is the sole criterion of personal identity. And this view seems compatible with the fact that sometimes, when we do not have independent grounds for saying that a person witnessed an event, we accept his being able to describe the event as evidence that he was a witness to it. For it might be held that in such cases we are reasoning inductively. We have, it might be said, found out empirically (using bodily identity as our criterion of personal identity) that when someone claims to remember a past event it is generally the case that such an event did occur and that he was a witness to it. On this view it is an inductively established correlation, and not any logical relationship between memory and personal identity, that justifies us in using the memory claims of persons as evidence for identity judgments about them.

2. On the view just described the criteria of personal identity are simply the criteria of bodily identity (i.e., I suppose, spatiotemporal continuity). But it is often argued that bodily identity is not even a necessary condition of personal identity, let alone a sufficient condition, and the same arguments have been alleged to show that memory is a criterion of personal identity. We must now consider some of these arguments.

Considerable attention has been paid, in discussions of personal identity, to so-called "puzzle cases," ostensible cases of what I will call "bodily transfer." It has been argued that if certain imaginable events were to occur we would be obliged to say, or at least would have good grounds for saying, that someone had changed bodies, i.e., had come to have a body that is numerically different from the body that had been his in the past. Locke, it may be recalled, thought it conceivable that the soul of a prince might "enter and inform" the body of a cobbler, "carrying with it the consciousness of the prince's past life," and said that if this happened the cobbler would become "the same person with the prince, accountable only for the prince's actions."[4] And it is certainly imaginable that a cobbler, living somewhere in the Bronx, might awake some morning and show great surprise at the appearance of his body, that he might claim to find his surroundings, and the persons who claim to know him, totally unfamiliar, that he might exhibit a detailed knowledge of the past life of Prince Philip, reporting the Prince's actions as his own, and that he might, in his subsequent behavior, exhibit all of the mannerisms, interests, and personality and character traits that Prince Philip had displayed in the past. Let us imagine this happening immediately after the death of the man now known as Prince Philip.

What we say about such cases is clearly relevant to the question whether memory is a criterion of personal identity. If the above case inclines us to say that bodily transfer is possible, this is largely because the cobbler is imagined to be able to describe in detail, thereby giving evidence of being able to remember, the past life of Prince Philip. That this so much inclines us to admit the possibility of bodily transfer, whether or not we do admit it, seems to be grounds for saying that bodily identity is not our sole criterion of personal identity, and that memory, and perhaps also sameness of personality, has a place among our criteria.

Many philosophers have held that personal identity and bodily identity are logically quite distinct. This view is implied by the Cartesian conception of the mind (or soul) as a substance distinct from the body, and it also seems to be implied by the view of Locke, that it is "same consciousness" that "makes" the same person, and by the views of those philosophers, such as Hume and (at one time) Russell, who have held that the persistence of a person through time consists simply in the occurrence of a series of mental events ("perceptions," "experiences") that are bound together by a non-physical relationship of "co-personality" (perhaps the relation "being the memory of"). in short, it is implied by any view according to which the identity of a person is essentially the identity of a mind, and according to which a mind (whether regarded as a Cartesian "spiritual substance" or a Humeian "bundle" of mental events) is something logically distinct from a human body. To hold such a view is to admit the possibility of bodily transfer, and it is partly the prevalence of such views that accounts for the attention that philosophers have paid to "puzzle cases" such as the one I have described. But it is hardly plausible to suppose that those who have held such views have come to hold them because they have been persuaded by such cases that bodily transfer is possible. For even if it is admitted that such cases would be cases of bodily transfer, it by no means follows that personal identity and bodily identity are logically independent. It does not follow that bodily transfer could become the rule rather than the exception, and it certainly does not follow that a person could exist without having a body at all. Indeed, the view that bodily transfer is possible is quite compatible with a completely behavioristic view concerning the nature of mind and a completely materialistic conception of the nature of a person. After all, in the case I have imagined it is bodily and behavioral facts (the behavior of the cobbler and the past behavior of Prince Philip) that incline one to say that a bodily transfer has occurred.

So while such cases provide some grounds for thinking that memory is among the criteria of personal identity, we must look further if we wish to account for the plausibility of the view that the criteria of personal identity are "mental" or "psychological," one version of which being the view that memory is, to the exclusion of bodily identity, the sole criterion of personal identity. But we need not look much further; all that we have to do, in fact, is to describe such cases in the first person rather than in the third person. For it is when one considers the way in which one knows, or seems to know, one's *own* identity that it becomes plausible to regard personal identity as something logically independent of bodily identity. One does not have to observe, or (it seems) know anything about, the present state of one's body in order to make past tense statements about oneself on the basis of memory. But such statements imply the persistence of a person through time, and it is natural to regard them as expressing knowledge of one's own identity, knowledge that a "present self" (that to which the word "I" refers) is identical with a "past self" (the person who did such and such in the past). One is inclined to suppose that the real criteria of personal identity must be criteria that one uses in making statements about one's own identity. And since it appears that one can make such statements, and know them to be true, without first knowing the facts that would justify an assertion about the identity of one's body, the conclusion would seem to be that bodily identity cannot be a criterion of personal identity. The real criteria of personal identity, it seems, cannot be bodily or behavioral criteria of any sort, but must be criteria that one can know to be satisfied in one's own case without knowing anything about one's body. For similar reasons one is inclined to reject the view that the notion of memory is definable or analyzable in terms of the notion of personal identity. For when

one says that one remembers a past event it is surely not the
case that one has first established that one is the same as someone who witnessed the event, and then concluded, on the basis
of this fact and others, that one remembers the event. That one
remembers an event seems, from one's own point of view, a
brute, unanalyzable fact. But if there is a logical relationship
between the concepts of memory and personal identity, and if
the former is not definable or analyzable in terms of the latter,
what seems to follow is that the latter is somehow definable in
terms of the former, and that memory provides the criterion of
personal identity.

3. Whether or not memory is *a* criterion of personal identity, it is not *the* criterion. As I will argue later, it cannot be
the sole criterion that we use in making identity statements
about other persons. And while it is true that one does not use
bodily identity as a criterion of personal identity when one says
on the basis of memory that one did something in the past, this
is not because one uses something else as a criterion, but is
rather because one uses no criterion at all.

Suppose that I make the statement "I broke the front window yesterday." If this statement is based on a criterion of personal identity it must be the case that I know that someone
broke the front window yesterday, and that I have found out,
by use of my criterion, that that person was myself. And my
statement must be based, at least in part, on what I know about
that person as he was at the time at which he broke the window. Let us suppose that my own memory is my only source of
knowledge concerning the past event in question, for that is the
sort of case that we are interested in. Then my statement must
be a conclusion from what I remember about the person who
broke the window yesterday, and perhaps from other facts as
well (facts about my "present self"), and my criterion of identity must be what justifies me in drawing this conclusion from
these facts. Presumably, if I had remembered different facts
about that person I would have drawn a different conclusion,
namely that he was not myself. It should be noted that, if all of
this were so, then, strictly speaking, it would be incorrect for
me to say "*I remember* that I broke the front window yesterday." For if my statement "I broke the front window yester-

day" expresses a conclusion *from* what I remember it is not itself a memory statement, i.e., is not simply a description or report of what I actually remember. We must distinguish statements that are "based" on memory simply in the sense of being memory statements from those that are "based" on memory in the sense of being conclusions drawn from remembered facts.[5] If one thinks that one cannot make a first person past tense statement except on the basis of a criterion of identity, one must accept the consequence that no such statement can be a memory statement. In the case at hand, if my statement is grounded on a criterion of identity then what I actually remember cannot be that *I* broke the window yesterday, but must be that someone of such and such a description broke the window, the assertion that it was myself being a conclusion from what I remember about the person.

Now it is a logical truth, as I have already said, that if a person remembers a past event then he, that same person, must have been a witness to the event, i.e., must have been present when it occurred and in a position to know of its occurrence. So if I remember someone breaking the front window yesterday it follows that I was present at the time. And since, if I remember this, I am entitled to say "I remember someone breaking the front window yesterday," I am also entitled to say "I was present yesterday when the front window was broken." But this last statement is a first person past tense statement, so let us see whether it can be grounded on any criterion of personal identity. Clearly it cannot be. It is not, as it would have to be if based on a criterion of identity, a conclusion from what I know about someone who existed in the past. What I know about the past, in the case we are considering, is what I remember, but this statement is not a conclusion from *what* I remember at all; it is a conclusion from the fact *that I remember something,* not from any of the facts that I remember.

But if I can know that I was present when an action was done without using a criterion of identity, why can't I know in this way that I did the action? Is it that I must employ a criterion in order to know *which* of the persons present was myself? In that case, presumably, I would not need to employ my criterion if I remembered that only one person was present, for that person would obviously have to be myself. But the trouble is that he would have to be myself *no matter what* I remembered about him. i.e., even if the remembered facts were such that I would have to conclude, in accordance with my criterion, that he was *not* myself. If I had a criterion of identity that I could use in such cases, it seems to me, it would be possible for me to remember someone doing a certain action, discover by the use of my criterion that he was not myself, and then find, by consulting my memory of the event, that he was the only person present when the action was done. And clearly this is not possible.

It is sometimes suggested that one is able to identify a remembered "past self" as one's own self by the fact that one is able to remember the private thoughts, feelings, sensations, etc., of that self. There does seem to be a sense in which my own thoughts and feelings are the only ones that I can remember. Certainly they are the only ones that I can remember *having*. But it is a mistake to conclude from this that memory is used as a first person criterion of personal identity. The sentence "I remember having a headache yesterday" does not differ in meaning from the sentence "I remember my having a headache yesterday." But if what I remember when I remember a past headache is *my having* a headache, or that *I* had a headache, my statement "I had a headache" is a memory statement, not a conclusion from what I remember, and cannot be grounded on any criterion of identity. If, however, what I remember is that someone had a headache, or that a headache occurred, it is clear that the remembered facts provide no grounds for the conclusion that *I* had a headache. Nor can we say, as some have said, that the relation "being the memory of" is the relation of "co-personality" between mental events, and that I know that a past sensation was mine because I have established that one of my present mental states is a memory of it and therefore co-personal with it. For, contrary to what Hume and others seem to have supposed, in the sort of case we are considering it makes no sense to speak of comparing one's present memory with a past sensation and finding that the one is the memory of (on Hume's theory, that it resembles) the other. One could make such a comparison only if one knew of the past sensation on some grounds other than one's memory of it, and our concern here is with cases in which one's memory is one's only source of knowledge concerning the past events in question. In such a case, comparing a past sensation with one's memory of it could only be comparing one's memory with itself—and comparing something with itself (if that means anything) is certainly not a way of discovering whether two events are related in a certain way. One can raise the question whether two events are related in a particular way (in *any* given way) only if one knows of the occurrence of both events. And if one knows of one of the events on the basis of memory, one must, in inquiring whether it is related in some way to the other event, be relying on one's memory of it, and clearly cannot be raising any question as to whether one does remember it (or whether one of one's present mental states is a memory of it). Indeed, if one's knowledge of a past sensation is memory knowledge it is misleading to say that one knows that one remembers a particular past sensation. It makes sense to speak of knowing that one remembers a particular event (knowing of an event that one remembers it) only where it would also make sense to speak of knowing of that event that one does not remember it (as is the case if one's knowledge of an event is based on something other than, or in addition to, one's memory). When I say that I have a headache I am not mentioning some particular headache and reporting, as a fact that I know about it, that it is experienced by me; likewise, when I say that I remember a headache I am not, in most cases, saying of some particular headache that I remember it. Normally I can identify a past sensation only as one that I remember (or, as I should prefer to say, one that I remember having). And when this is so there cannot arise any question concerning the ownership of the sensation, and there is no room for the employment of criteria of ownership or criteria of personal identity.

4. If, as I have argued, one does not use criteria of identity in making statements about one's own past on the basis of memory, the criteria of personal identity must be third person criteria. And if memory were the sole criterion of personal identity it would have to be the sole criterion that we use in making identity statements about persons other than ourselves. It is

easily shown, however, that if we did not have some criterion other than memory that we could use in making statements of personal identity we could not use what others remember, or claim to remember, as evidence of any sort (criteriological or otherwise) for identity statements about them.

To begin with, if the word "remember" is to have any meaning it must be possible to establish whether someone is using it using it correctly. If some of the utterances that persons make are to count as memory claims, and therefore as evidence of what they remember or seem to remember, it must be possible to establish what a person means by the words he utters. But establishing what a person means by a term, or whether he is using it correctly, involves observing his use of it in various circumstances and over a period of time. This, of course, involves being able to know that it was one and the same person who uttered a given word on two different occasions, and to be able to know this one must have a criterion of identity. What could this criterion be if not bodily identity? It could not be any "psychological" criterion (such as memory or sameness of personality), for the use of such criteria (if criteria they are) involves accepting what a person says as indicating what his psychological state is (e.g., that he seems to remember doing a certain thing), and one could not do this if one were trying to establish what he means by, or whether he understands, the expressions he is using. In *some* circumstances, at least, bodily identity must be a criterion of personal identity.

Moreover, memory claims can be mistaken, and there must, accordingly, be such a thing as checking on the truth of a memory claim, i.e., establishing whether a person remembers something without taking his word for it that he does. And this, if he claims to have done a certain thing in the past, would involve establishing whether he, the person who claims this, is the same as someone who did do such an action in the past. In establishing this we could not use memory as our criterion of personal identity, and it is difficult to see what we could use if not bodily identity. And if, in such cases, we could not use bodily identity (or something other than memory) as a criterion of identity, it would not be possible to establish whether someone understands the use of the term "remember," and that term could not so much as have a meaning. It is, I believe, a logical or conceptual truth, not a contingent truth, that memory beliefs, and therefore honest memory claims, are generally true.[6] If someone frequently prefaced past tense statements with the words "I remember that," and these statements generally turned out to be false, this would be grounds for saying that he did not understand the use of these words. We would not think that we had succeeded in teaching a child the use of the word "remember" if he commonly said "I remember doing such and such" when he had not done the thing in question. Again, suppose that we had discovered a new people whose language we did not know, and that someone had proposed a way of translating their language that involved regarding a certain class of statements (or utterances) as memory statements. Clearly, if all or most of those statements turned out to be false if translated as proposed, there could be no reason for accepting that way of translating them as correct, and there would be every reason for rejecting it as mistaken. But if it is a conceptual truth that memory claims are generally true, establishing that someone understands the use of the term "remember" must surely involve establishing whether his memory claims (or what appear to be his memory claims) are true or false. And to be able to do this we must have something other than memory that we can use as a criterion of personal identity.

5. The arguments of the last section may seem to give support to the view that bodily identity is, to the exclusion of memory, the sole criterion of personal identity. But this view seems to me to be mistaken. Bodily identity is certainly *a* criterion of personal identity, and if it were not, I have argued, nothing else could be so much as evidence of personal identity. But I do not think that it can be the sole criterion, and I think that there is an important sense in which memory, though certainly not the sole criterion, is one of the criteria.

Let us consider one consequence of the view that bodily identity is the sole criterion of personal identity. As I said in section 1, if this view were correct it would have to be the case that we are reasoning inductively when we use the fact that someone claims to remember something as grounds for a statement about his past. It would be a contingent fact, one that we have discovered empirically, that most memory claims are true, or that people generally remember what they claim to remember. This would, indeed, be nothing other than the fact that the memory claims that issue from the mouth of a certain body generally correspond to events in the past history of that same body. But I have argued that it is a logical fact, not a contingent fact, that memory claims are generally true. If this is so, inferences of the form "He claims to remember doing X, so he probably did X" are not simply inductive inferences, for they are warranted by a generalization that is logically rather than empirically true.[7]

Now let us return briefly to the case of the cobbler and the prince. If one is inclined to use the memory claims of the cobbler as grounds that he is (has become) the prince, the inference one is inclined to make is not of the form "He claims to remember doing X, so he probably did do X," but is of a more complex sort. Roughly, it is of the form "He claims to remember doing X, Y, and Z under such and such circumstances and at such and such times and places, and X, Y, and Z were done by someone under precisely those circumstances and at those times and places, so there is reason to believe that he is the person who did those actions." But it seems to me that if inferences of the first sort are not inductive, neither are inferences of the second sort. And I think that to say that inferences of the second sort are legitimate (as they certainly are, at least under certain circumstances), and that they are non-inductive, is tantamount to saying that memory is a criterion of personal identity.

It should be noted that if such inferences were merely inductive, and if bodily identity were the sole criterion of personal identity, it would be patently absurd to make such an inference in a case in which the body of the person making a memory claim is known not to be identical with the body of the person who did the action that he claims to remember. The absurdity would be that of asserting something to be true, or probably true, on the basis of indirect evidence, when one has direct and conclusive evidence that it is false. But in the imaginary case I have described, the claim that the cobbler is (has become) the prince does not, I think, strike us as having *this* sort of absurdity.

I have not attempted to say whether, if the events I have described were to occur, it would be correct to say that the cobbler had become the prince, and I do not know how this question could be settled. But this in itself seems to me significant. The fact that such cases so much as incline us to admit the possibility of bodily transfer, or leave us in doubt as to what to say, seems to me *prima facie* evidence that memory is a criterion of personal identity. It is not as if our doubts were due to ignorance of empirical facts that, if known, would settle the issue. Doubts of that sort are easily removed, for we need only add further details to the description of the case. But if, knowing all of the relevant facts, we are in doubt as to how we should answer a question of identity, this is surely an indication that the case is such that the question is not unambiguously decidable by our criterion of identity. This, in turn, suggests that there is a conflict of criteria. In the case at hand, our doubts are evidence that one criterion of personal identity, namely bodily identity, is in conflict with another, namely memory.

But now I must try to meet an objection. It might be argued that while the inference "He claims to remember doing X, so he probably did X" is not inductive, we are nevertheless reasoning inductively when we take what a person says as evidence for a statement about his past history. For what justifies us in taking the sounds that a person utters as expressing a memory claim? As was argued earlier, if a question arises as to whether a person understands the use of the word "remember," or is using it to mean what we mean by it, the question can be settled only by establishing, independently of what he says, whether the things that he claims (or apparently claims) to remember are things he actually did, endured, or witnessed in the past. If in a number of cases it turns out that the actions that he apparently claims to remember having done are actions that he actually did, this is evidence that he does understand the use of such words as "remember," and that his apparent memory claims are really memory claims and can generally be relied upon upon. Must it not be much the same sort of considerations, i.e., our having observed certain correlations between the sounds that people utter and what they have done in the past, that justifies our general reliance on people's memory claims, or rather our acceptance of people's utterances as memory claims? If so, it would seem that our use of people's memory claims as evidence for statements about their own pasts, including identity statements about them, is, in the end, inductively based. Though it is a logical fact that memory claims are generally true, what does this come to except the fact that if there did not exist correlations of the sort mentioned none of the utterance of persons would be memory claims? But the existence of such correlations is a contingent fact, and it is on this contingent fact, it might be argued, that inferences of the sort "He claims to remember doing X, so he probably did X" are ultimately based. As for the case of the cobbler and the prince, it might be argued that if what I said in section 4 is correct then the facts that I have imagined would be evidence, not that the cobbler had become the prince, but rather that his utterances were not memory claims at all, and that he did not understand the use of the term "remember."

To take the last point first, suppose that we were in doubt as to whether the cobbler really understood the words that he was using. Could we not satisfy ourselves that he did by observing his subsequent behavior, and by establishing (using bodily identity as our criterion of personal identity) that when he claims to have done an action that occurred *after* the alleged bodily transfer it is generally the case that he did do that action? When we are trying to establish whether a person understands the words he utters we must, I have argued, use bodily identity as a criterion of identity, but it does not follow from this that there cannot, in exceptional cases, be personal identity in the absence of bodily identity.

As for the rest of the objection, it is certainly true that unless there existed certain correlations between the sounds people utter and events in the past histories of those who utter them it would be impossible to have knowledge of the past that is based on the memory claims of other persons. These correlations are those that must exist if any of the utterances that people make are to be memory claims. But it cannot be the case, I believe, that we regard certain of the utterances of other persons as memory claims *because* we have established, inductively, that such correlations hold. To be sure, from the fact that a person utters the sounds that I would utter if making a certain memory claim it does not necessarily follow that he speaks the language that I speak and means by those sounds what I would mean by them. Under exceptional circumstances I might raise a question as to whether what sounds to me like a memory claim is really one, and such a question could be settled empirically, by observing the behavior of the person who made the claim. But except when we have definite grounds for supposing the contrary, we must, I believe, regard other persons as speaking a language, our own if the words sound familiar, without having any general empirical justification for doing so. Let us consider whether it would be possible for me to question whether there is anyone at all (other than myself) who speaks the language that I speak, and then to discover empirically, by observing correlations between the sounds people utter and their present and past behavior, that those around me do speak the language that I speak and that certain of their utterances are memory claims and can generally be relied upon. In carrying on such an investigation I would, of course, have to rely on my own memory. But one's memory can be mistaken. It is essential to the very notion of memory that there be a distinction between remembering something and merely seeming to remember something. And for there to be such a distinction there must be such a thing as checking up on one's own memory and finding that one does, or does not, remember what one seems to remember. As Wittgenstein pointed out,[8] there are and must be circumstances in which we would accept other sorts of evidence concerning the past as more authoritative than our own memories. But an important—I think essential—check on one's own memory is the testimony of other persons. And this sort of check would not be available to me if I could not even regard the utterances of other persons as testimony until I had completed my investigation and established the required set of correlations. Unless there were some persons whose utterances I would be willing to accept as memory claims without having conducted such an investigation I would in effect be admitting no distinction between finding the correlations and merely seeming to have found them.

It is, I should like to say, part of the concept of a person that persons are capable of making memory statements about their own pasts. Since it is a conceptual truth that memory statements are generally true, it is a conceptual truth that persons are capable of knowing their own pasts in a special way, a way that does not involve the use of criteria of personal identity, and it is a conceptual truth (or a logical fact) that the memory claims that a person makes can be used by others as grounds for statements about the past history of that person. This, I think, is the kernel of truth that is embodied in the view that personal identity can be defined in terms of memory.

NOTES

*This article is reprinted from *The Journal of Philosophy*, Vol. 56, No. 22 (October 22, 1959), by courtesy of the editor and Professor Shoemaker.

1. Thomas Reid, *Essays on the Intellectual Powers of Man,* ed. by A. D. Woozley (London: Macmillan, 1941), p. 206.

2. H. P. Grice, "Personal Identity," *Mind,* (October, 1941), 340.

3. I use "remember" in its most common sense, in which "I remember that P" entails "P," and "I remember X occurring" entails "X occurred."

4. John Locke, *An Essay Concerning Human Understanding,* I, ed. by Fraser (Oxford: The Clarendon Press, 1894), 457.

5. Roughly speaking, a statement is a memory statement if (supposing it to be an honest assertion) it cannot be false unless the speaker has misremembered. A conclusion from what is remembered, on the other hand, can be false without there being a mistaken memory. E.g., I mistakenly identify the man I saw as John when in fact it was his identical twin.

6. The word "generally" is vague, but I doubt if this can be made much more precise. This statement should perhaps be qualified so as to apply only to memory beliefs concerning the *recent* past.

7. We can, of course, have inductive grounds for believing that one person's memory claims are exceptionally reliable and that another's are exceptionally unreliable.

8. Ludwig Wittgenstein, *Philosophical Investigations* (Oxford: Basil Blackwell, 1953), I, paras. 56 and 265.

John Perry

9

Personal Identity, Memory,
and the Problem of Circularity

When it is asked wherein personal identity consists, the answer should be . . . that all attempts to define would but perplex it."[1] When he said this, Butler was thinking of Locke's[2] attempt to define personal identity in terms of memory; if his opinion about a future state, which motivated his interest in personal identity, proved correct, he has doubtless since had similar thoughts about more recent "memory theorists," such as H. P. Grice[3] and Anthony Quinton.[4] For in spite of such perceptive critics as Butler and Reid,[5] the thought that personal identity is analyzable, and analyzable in terms of memory, has been periodically revived.

In this essay, I try to discover the strengths and weaknesses of the memory theory, by defending the best version of it against arguments that could be raised by those, who feel as Butler did that the concept of personal identity is primitive. The memory theory emerges from this defense with its letter intact but its spirit scathed.

GRICE'S THEORY

Locke suggested that A is the same person as B if and only if A can remember having an experience of B's.[6] The sufficient condition implied is plausible: if I really can remember going to the store yesterday, then I must have gone to the store. That is, I must be the same person as someone who went to the store. But the implied necessary condition is much too strong,

as Reid and other critics have pointed out. That I cannot remember going to the store yesterday does not mean that I did
not go. Forgetting, even beyond the possibility of recall, is
possible.

Later memory theorists have concentrated on weakening
the necessary condition to the point of plausibility. Grice,
whose account is, in my opinion, the most subtle and successful, in essence takes Locke's relation, disjoins it with its converse, and takes the ancestral of the result. Grice adopts the notion
of a total temporary state, or t.t.s., which is a set of simultaneous
experiences of a single person, and conceives of his task as finding
the relation that must obtain between t.t.s.'s that belong to one
person. In Grice's terms, with A and B now being t.t.s.'s and not
persons, the relation Locke uses in his analysis is this:

R_L: A contains, or would contain given certain conditions,
a memory of an experience contained in B.

The relation that results from Grice's weakening maneuvers we
can express this way:

R_G: There is a sequence of t.t.s.'s (not necessarily in the
order they occur in time, and not excluding repetitions),
the first of which is A and the last of which is B, such that
each t.t.s. in the sequence either (i) contains, or would
contain given certain conditions, a memory of an experience contained in the next, or (ii) contains an experience
of which the next contains a memory, or would contain
a memory given certain conditions.[7]

A set of t.t.s.'s which can be formed into a sequence of this
sort, and to which no more t.t.s.'s can be added (which I shall
call a "Grice-set"), is a person or self.

Grice's account avoids the Brave Officer Paradox[8] and
other stock counterexamples to memory theories of personal
identity, to which his predecessors and successors have fallen
prey. But it is not at all obvious that he avoids objections of
another sort, in the spirit of Butler's criticism of Locke: "memory presupposes, and so cannot constitute, personal identity."[9]
In this essay I will examine three charges of circularity, each
maintaining for a different reason that Grice implicitly uses the
concept of personal identity in his analysis of it.

I shall not examine every interesting objection of this sort
that could be made against Grice; in particular, I shall not ex-

amine the objection that experiences themselves, the ultimate
building blocks in Grice's constructions of persons, must be
individuated in terms of persons. I do not believe this objection
is fatal, but discussion of it would lead us away from the topics
I wish to discuss, into the difficult problem of the individuation
of events.

CIRCLES AND LOGICAL CONSTRUCTIONS

Before settling down to specifics, we must satisfy ourselves
that Grice's enterprise is of a sort for which circularity is a vice.
He explicitly defends the view that persons are logical constructions from experiences. Whether he held this view as a part of
a generally phenomenalistic philosophy is not disclosed in the
article on personal identity, and Grice may well have had special
views about the nature of the logical constructor's enterprise,
and special motivation for holding persons to be so construct-
able. But it will be helpful and only fair, given lack of contrary
evidence, to suppose Grice involved in a logical construction of
a "standard" sort.

The logical constructor attempts to analyze sentences
about objects of some category, into sentences about objects of
some other category. Examples of such analyzed and analyzing
categories are numbers and classes, material objects and sense-
data, persons and t.t.s.'s. The analyzing sentences may themselves be thought analyzable—for example, sentences about
classes into sentences about propositional functions, or sentences
about t.t.s.'s into sentences about experiences. At the bottom
of the structure are sentences with a favored epistemological
status, as, for example, that they can be directly known, because the objects they are about can be directly inspected.
Through analysis, this favored status, or at least some status
more favorable than was originally apparent, is transmitted up
the structure to the analyzed sentences. Talk about persons
might have seemed to involve us in talk about pure egos, or substances of some other obscure sort, but when we see that talk
of persons is, really, just talk of t.t.s.'s and ultimately, of experiences, our knowledge is revealed as more secure than it
seemed.

Sentences about experiences seem to be directly knowable, by the people who have the experiences, at the time they occur. Now a present tense sentence about persons, or material objects, cannot plausibly be regarded as merely a remark about present experiences. But it has been thought that they could be plausibly regarded as asserting no more than would be asserted by a string of sentences about past, present, and future experiences. While not all these sentences could be directly known at one time, each of them could be directly known at some time. The complex of assertions, into which a sentence about persons or material objects can be analyzed, will not have as favored an epistemological status as a sentence about a present experience. But it will have a more favored status than a sentence that asserted things never directly knowable by anyone at any time.

(In both the construction of material objects and of persons, it soon becomes clear that past, present, and future experiences do not provide sufficient materials: possible experiences, the experiences someone would have had, had things been different than they were, are also needed. And it is not clear that sentences about possible experiences have much favored epistemological status to transmit upward.)

On Grice's conception of logical constructions, if all goes well, the analyzed sentence (say, "Someone heard a noise") and the analyzing sentence (say, "A past hearing of a noise is contained in a t.t.s. which is a member of a Grice set") will have just the same truth conditions.[10] If this were the only condition of a successful analysis, the analyzed sentence could serve as the analysis of the analyzing sentence, for "has the same truth conditions" expresses a symmetrical relation. It is the favored status of the analyzing sentence which gives the logical construction its noncircular structure.

A charge of circularity against Grice, then, will consist of two claims. First, that the analyzing sentence does not seem to have the favored status, and so must itself be analyzed. Second, that its analysis will have to employ sentences about objects of the category constructed, that is, sentences about persons. This would show that even if Grice has produced an analysis free from counterexample, it is a failure: the mystery of personal identity is transmitted downward to memory, rather than the clarity of memory being transmitted upward to personal identity.

THREE CHARGES OF CIRCULARITY

The core of Grice's analysis is R_L. R_L is in itself a disjunction; the first charge of circularity will concern the first, simpler, disjunct:

A contains a memory of an experience contained in *B.*
The second and third counts of circularity concern the second disjunct:

A would contain, given certain conditions, a memory of
an experience contained in *B.*
For simplicity, I explain these charges in an assertive tone, but the reader should keep in mind that ultimately I shall reject them.

(i) Smith examines a green cube, and later vividly describes his examination of it. Jones has never examined a green cube; he is hypnotized, and told that when he awakes he will remember examining one. Jones later vividly describes examining a green cube. To observers who do not know the whole story, Smith and Jones both seem to be remembering, in vivid detail, a past examination of a green cube.

Smith is really remembering, Jones is not. Their present experiences, the occurrence of which they know directly through introspection, are indiscernible. Jones cannot discover he is mistaken through careful attention to his own mind. Their outward behavior, the sentences they use, their facial expression, etc., is also indiscernible. And yet Smith's experience is a memory of a past experience, and Jones's is not. Saying of an experience, that it is a memory, is thus a complex attribution, and not just a report of what is directly observed through introspection. That a person is really remembering at a given time, and not just seeming to, cannot always be determined solely on the basis of observations of the person made at that time, whether by that person or others.

That we are *seeming* to remember a past experience, can be known directly; that we are really remembering involves more. And this more is not just the occurrence of a past experience of the appropriate sort directly knowable when it occurred.

For there was a past experience of the sort Jones *seems* to remember—Smith's experience of examining the cube. What further must be added? The example suggests that one further necessary condition is that the same person who is seeming to remember have had, in the past, the experience in question. But then, spelled out, with the full analysis of memory incorporated into the condition, the first disjunct of R_L would look like this:

A contains an apparent memory of an experience contained in B, and A is a t.t.s. *of the same person of whom B is a t.t.s.,* and . . .

The ". . ." represents whatever further conditions may be found necessary for an analysis of memory. But we need go no further. The italicized condition is sufficient to doom Grice's analysis to circularity.

(ii) Even if the last objection is somehow overcome, Grice's analysis would still be circular, in virtue of the subjunctive conditional, "would, given certain conditions," contained in the second disjunct of R_L.

Let us look at the kind of example that makes this disjunct necessary. Wilson is asleep. His present t.t.s. contains only a vague blissful feeling, which he will never remember after awakening. Thus there are no actual memory links between Wilson's present t.t.s. and his past (because his present t.t.s. contains no memories), and there never will be any actual memory links between Wilson's future t.t.s.'s and his present one. So the analysis cannot rely solely on the first disjunct of R_L.

Had we shaken Wilson a moment ago and asked, "What thrilling things did you do today?" he would now be telling us about seeing Wynn hit a home run at Dodger Stadium earlier in the day. Although his t.t.s. contains no memory of this past experience, given certain conditions (our having shaken him and asked him the question) it would now contain such memories. It contains, we might say, only *possible* memories of the past t.t.s. The second disjunct asserts that there will always be at least a chain of possible memory links where there is personal identity.

Now, the problem with this conditional is not simply that its truth cannot be known through any sort of direct observation, but that, taken literally, the sentence "t.t.s. *A* would, under certain circumstances, contain a memory of seeing Wynn hit a home run," makes no sense. To make sense of it we will have to use the concept of personal identity.

It makes no sense, taken literally, because the identity of a t.t.s. must be determined by the experiences it contains. A t.t.s. is a set of experiences, and a set's whole identity is wrapped up in its membership.[11] The t.t.s. or set of experiences Smith would have had, if he had been awakened and questioned, and the t.t.s. he actually has, while asleep, are different t.t.s.'s. When we say, "The t.t.s. would have contained a memory . . ." we can only mean something like "The person would have had a different t.t.s. than he did have, and that different t.t.s. would have contained a memory." And in making sense of the conditional, we have had to talk about persons.

An analogy may help to make this point clear. When we say, "If the meeting had been advertised, the number of people in the hall would have been greater," we don't mean to imply that there is a certain number, say 50, which would have been greater if the meeting had been advertised. The number 50 will always be a little greater than 49 and a little less than 51, no matter how well advertised meetings are. Rather, we mean that a different number, say 101, would have fit the description, "number of people in the room," had the advertising been more thorough. So with the t.t.s. Wilson had and the t.t.s. Wilson would have had. They are not the same t.t.s., but different t.t.s.'s, one which deserves, and one which would have deserved, the description, "Wilson's t.t.s."

In order to state a conditional like the one about the meeting or the one about Wilson fully and explicitly, we need some "anchor"—some entity that retains its identity under the imagined change in circumstances, and in terms of which the number or t.t.s. is identified. In the case of the meeting, the meeting itself is the anchor: the *same* meeting would have drawn a different number of people. And in the case of Wilson, Wilson himself seems the natural anchor: the *same* person would have had a t.t.s. that contained a memory . . . had he been awakened and questioned. But then, fully spelled out, the second disjunct of R_L is:

> Given certain conditions, the same person of whom *A* is
> the t.t.s. would have had a t.t.s. that contained a memory
> of an experience of *B*'s.

But this uses the concept of personal identity, and so the analysis is circular.

(iii) Even if charges (i) and (ii) are somehow circumvented,
the phrase "given certain conditions" leads to a third problem.

Should Grice tell us which conditions it is, under which
t.t.s. *A* would contain a memory of an experience contained in
t.t.s. *B*? If he simply means "There is at least one condition
such that, if it obtained, t.t.s. ·*A* would contain memories of an
experience contained in t.t.s. *B*" then he owes us no such list,
the analysis is complete as it stands. But if not just any condition will do, he should tell us which ones will.

But it seems quite clear that Grice cannot mean simply
"There is at least one condition such that . . ." by the phrase
"under certain conditions." For if he does mean this, "Under
certain conditions, t.t.s. *A* could contain a memory of an experience of t.t.s. *B*'s" would not mean anything like what it is
supposed to mean, viz., "The person, of whom *A* is a t.t.s., can
remember an experience of *B*'s." Consider this example. Johnson saw a flash of lightning in the sky last Thursday; immediately afterward he received a serious head injury. As a result he
cannot remember seeing the flash—the injury, we may suppose,
interfered with the consolidation of short term memory which
makes memory of such events for more than a few seconds possible. In this case, we would not say "Johnson can remember
seeing the flash of lightning." No amount of reminding or
prompting will bring it about that Johnson remembers. But we
can state a condition such that, if it had obtained, Johnson
would now be remembering the flash of lightning: that he didn't
receive an injury, and was just asked if he had ever seen lightning. (We may suppose Johnson had never seen lightning before,
and would surely have remembered it, if not for the injury.)
But the fact that the conditional, "If Johnson had not been in-
jured, and had just been asked about it, he would now be remembering seeing the flash of lightning" is true, does not show
that Johnson *can remember* seeing the lightning, even though
the truth of some other conditional like "If Johnson were not

asleep, and had just been asked about it, he would remember . . ." would show that he can remember seeing it. So some conditionals of the form, "If C, then Johnson would remember . . ." are relevant to the claim that he can remember, and some are not. So the words "t.t.s. A would, given certain conditions . . ." must mean "there are certain conditions, C_1, C_2 . . ., and under one of these conditions t.t.s. A would . . ." Grice owes us a list, or some other specification, of these conditions.

I wish to make, but not press here, the point that it is unlikely this could be done. The point essential to this charge is that, even if the conditions were exhaustively listed, it seems inevitable that the concept of personal identity would be required. The only example we have discussed so far of such a condition is that the person with t.t.s. A was awakened a few moments ago and questioned; if, under those conditions, the person would remember, then, under actual conditions, he *can* remember. Now it is hard to see how this condition, or any of the conditions involving prompting, reminding, threatening, all of which typically occur somewhat before the occurrence of the t.t.s. in question, could be expressed without requiring that it be the *same* person who is prompted, etc., who is later to remember. If the phrase "given certain condition" were cashed in, as it must be, for a list of conditions, the second disjunct of R_L would look like this:

> t.t.s. A would contain, if *the same person* who has A had been awakened and asked, or if *the same person* who has A had not just taken a powerful drug, or . . . a memory of an experience contained in B.

And so, again, we see that Grice's analysis makes implicit use of the concept of personal identity and is circular.

MEMORY

Memory can be analyzed without use of the concept of personal identity, and Grice thus cleared of these charges of circularity. I sketch such an analysis here, focusing first on the ordinary way of expressing event memory, as in "MacKenzie remembers Wilbur's marriage," or "Sandy remembers seeing her high marks," and later considering Grice's rather specialized locution, "t.t.s. *A* contains a memory of an experience contained in t.t.s. *B*."

Event memory must be distinguished from memory *that* or factual memory, particularly from factual memory that an event occurred. Most of us remember *that* Columbus discovered America in 1492. We wouldn't miss that question on an exam. But no one now alive remembers *Columbus discovering America*. Most of us remember that we were born; few of us remember our birth. We can remember *that* events occurred which we never witnessed, and no plausible account of personal identity could be built on factual memory. But we can only have memories *of* events that we witnessed or in which we consciously took part. (This last is added because of the peculiarity of saying that I "witnessed" the event of my drinking my coffee; I didn't witness that event, I was a part of it. Having noticed this peculiarity, I shall go on to use "witness" in this extended and peculiar way, to cover both witnessing of and participation in an event.) This last fact, which I shall call the Witnessing Condition, was appealed to in the discussion of Smith, Jones, and the green cube. The issue between the memory theorist and his critic is not whether the Witnessing Condition is true, but whether it is a part of the analysis of memory, as the critic maintains, or a consequence of the analysis of personal identity, as the memory theorist does.

Events are commonly designated by nominalizations of sentences: "John's hitting of Mary," "the sinking of the Titanic," etc. Event memory is commonly expressed by prefacing such an event designation with words of the form "X remembers." But such event designations do not usually completely identify the event that they are being used to designate. Thomson and Robinson might both truly say, "I remember Zimbalist's becoming confused," though they remember different events; Zimbalist is easily confused. Most event designations completely identify only an event *type*. I shall use the letter "*E*" as a dummy event designation and as a variable ranging over event types, and "*e*" as a variable ranging over specific events. "*X* remembers *E*" I take as making the claim that (i) there is an event *e* which *X* remembers, such that (ii) *e* is of type *E*. I rely on the intuitive feel for what it is for an event to be of a type, in order to concentrate on (i).[12]

The analysis of memory requires three sorts of conditions, having to do, in turn, with what must happen at the time of the remembering, what must have happened at the time of the remembered event, and what the link between the remembered event and the event of remembering must be.

The first condition I call the Representation Condition. Representation is a notion I borrow from Martin and Deutscher's excellent discussion of memory.[13] It has been thought, for example by Locke,[14] Hume,[15] and Russell,[16] that mental imagery is required for memory of an event. This is a mistake. Someone giving a vivid verbal description of a past event, or painting a picture of it, could be said to be remembering that event, whether or not he was having, or could produce, mental imagery of the event. But something separates the rememberer and the apparent rememberer from the common run of mankind. Martin and Deutscher introduced the term "represent" to cover the many ways a person can indicate the past occurrence of an event of a certain type, and I follow them not only in adopting this notion, but in apologizing for not giving a fuller account of it.

The first step in our analysis of "A remembers e," then, is

(1) A represents the past occurrence of an event of some type E.

What sort of thing is A? A is to be a live human body, or a human being. The difference between this concept and that of a person has been emphasized by many writers on personal identity, and is a point of agreement between memory theorists and Butler and other critics who think personal identity an unanalyzable concept. So I shall feel free to use the concept of a live human body, and of bodily identity, in the analysis of memory, without fear of circularity.

Condition (1) is satisfied by both the real and apparent rememberer, as well as others who comment on the past: factual rememberers, liars, historians, and the like.

The second condition is a detoxified version of the Witnessing Condition:

(2) B witnessed event e.

I shall call this the Weak Witnessing Condition. It makes no claim of identity between A and B.

Now suppose we had added, as held necessary in the first charge of circularity, the (strong) Witnessing Condition. This would have disqualified Jones as a rememberer, but the analysis would still be deficient. Hennig examined the green cube, then received an electrical shock that wiped out his memory. The Electrical Company, in compensation, had him hypnotized, and given the same posthypnotic suggestion as Jones. Hennig satisfies (1) and the Witnessing Condition, but is not a rememberer. So, even if we had the Witnessing Condition in the analysis, we would still need a third condition, a Linking Condition, to rule out Hennig. It seems clear that what would be further required is some condition to the effect that the past witnessing *bring about* the present representing. My strategy, in what follows, is to beef up the Linking Condition in such a way that the Witnessing Condition is not needed.

With or without the Witnessing Condition, it is not easy to see what exactly the Linking Condition should be. I believe that the view Martin and Deutscher defend, that the link is a causal one, is correct.[17] But, as they point out, merely requiring that if the witnessing had not occurred, the representing would not be occurring, will not do. If Hennig had not examined a green cube, the Electrical Company would not have underwritten his hypnosis, and he would not be representing. (And Smith, the rememberer, would be representing, even if he had not examined the cube, for in that case I would have had him hypnotized and treated like Jones.) The witnessing must not just cause the representing, it must cause it *in a certain way*.

Scientists are trying to discover the causal mechanisms involved in memory. Suppose they discover that a certain process is involved in memory. Could our linking condition simply be that *that* process led from B's witnessing to A's representing? No, for in analyzing the concept of memory we seek beliefs common to all who use with understanding the formula "X remembers E," and knowledge of, or even specific beliefs about, the processes involved in memory are not at all common.

But we may believe that memory involves some characteristic process, without having a belief about which process, or what kind of process, that might be. In fact, I think we do believe this. Some who have the concept of memory may be sure the process is not, or not merely, a material one; this was apparently Bergson's view.[18] Others may believe it certainly is a material process, an electrochemical process of the central nervous system. Perhaps most have no opinions on the matter. But in accepting, as we all do, that "He remembers it" is an explanation of representing; in predicting, as we all do, that in certain circumstances people are likely to remember the past, and in other circumstances unlikely to; in seeking, as we all do, alternative explanations for representing of the past when circumstances make memory unlikely ("He can't have remembered, he was too young—his mother must have told him."), we indicate that we do believe there are certain processes involved in memory, which can be expected to occur in some circumstances, and not in others. This is a hypothesis, a speculation if you will, for no such process can be observed by the ordinary man, introspectively or otherwise. But it is an irresistible hypothesis.

Let us say that a witnessing and a representing are M-related when they are the beginning and end of such a process. Then our analysis is simply:

A remembers e if and only if

(1) A represents the past occurrence of an event of type E;

(2) B witnessed e;

(3) B's witnessing of e is M-related to A's representation of the past occurrence of an event of type E.

But is it fair to use, in the analysis, a relation the nature of which we haven't disclosed? It is fair only if we can identify the relation, independently of the concept analyzed. This I have not done, for all I have said about the M-relation is that it is the relation involved in memory. But I shall now try to provide such an independent identification of the M-relation.

"Recollection" I shall use purely as a technical term, for which I stipulate this definition:

A recollects e if and only if

(1) A represents the past occurrence of an event of type E;

(2) B witnessed e, and e is of type E;

(3) B and A are the same live human body.

Recollection, so defined, occurs often. One of the things we all know about live human bodies is that they are quite likely to recollect, and we know the conditions that make recollection more and less likely. But recollection is a significantly different notion from memory. Returning to the case of the green cube, both Smith and Hennig recollect examining the cube, though only Smith remembers. With regard to cases that actually occur, memory is a more restrictive concept than recollection. Oddly enough, with regard to cases produced in the imagination of man, memory seems less restrictive. Philosophers thinking about personal identity, seeing no contradiction in trans-bodily memory, have produced many characters who remember what they do not recollect: Locke's prince,[19] Shoemaker's Brownson,[20] Quinton's no longer fat but still apolaustic Pole.[21] And the occupants of the Hereafter are regularly conceived as remembering earthly events, although the "resurrected" bodies of those occupants must not be the very same bodies as were buried and rotted away on earth. So the concept of memory is not simply more restrictive and not simply less restrictive than recollection, but sits askew of it.

An *unaided* case of recollection is one in which the representing of A is not explained by provision of information about e other than B's witnessing of it. Now any ordinary human is drawn to the belief that there is an explanation for the frequent occurrence of unaided cases of recollection, that there is some process, material or immaterial, gross or sublime, complex or simple, which frequently occurs when a human being witnesses an event and leads to that same human's later représentation of it. When the witnessing of an event leads by this process to a later representation of it, the witnessing and the representation are M-related.

I now have identified the M-relation not just as the relation that links the witnessing and representing in memory, but, noncircularly, as the relation that explains the great bulk of cases of recollection. And, of course, it is not an accident that the M-relation plays both roles.

My view is that the key to understanding memory is seeing it as an explanatory concept, not merely in that individual cases of past-representing are explained by memory, but that a generalization about human behavior, the frequency of recollection, is explained by an hypothesized process, and that this process is incorporated into the very concept of memory. This conception of memory explains its skewed relation to recollection. Memory is a more restrictive concept, in that more is required, the witness and the representor must not just be the same human being, but a certain process must have occurred. But by distinguishing between the M-relation and the relation of being or belonging to the same human body, and by virtue of our lack of knowledge of the nature of the M-relation, it becomes possible to think of the two as separate; we are able to imagine the possibility that certain witnessings and representings might be M-related, though not experiences of the same human body. It does not follow, after all, from the fact that the M-relation is regularly associated with sameness of human body, that it must always be so associated. And indeed we can, through use of the M-relation, extend the class of remembers. We can let A and B in our analysis stand for, not just human bodies but human bodies and any other sorts of things, ghosts or even gorse-bushes, that might, for all we know, become M-related to them.

There is another dissimilarity between memory and recollection. In a case of recollection, the representation must be accurate, the event recollected must be of the type represented, but no such condition has been placed on memory. We do not require a person's memory of an event to be accurate. Smith may be rattling on about the time he met the Prince of Wales in London; Jones may quite correctly observe that Smith never met the Prince of Wales, and has never been in London, but is really remembering the time when, as a part of a hoax that defies summary, he met Stanky in Philadelphia. The point is not that Smith speaks truly when he says "I remember meeting the Prince of Wales in London." His claim, remember, is twofold, that he remembered a certain event, and that it has a certain type, that it was a meeting of a Prince of Wales in London. The point is rather that Jones speaks truly when he says Smith is remembering meeting Stanky in Philadelphia, even though Smith is not representing the past occurrence of an event of *that* type. The event remembered need not be of the type represented. This too is explained by the suggested relation between recollection and memory. We build the concept of memory on a relation, the M-relation, in which we are interested largely because it so often leads to accurate past-representing. But we allow that the processes involved, when conditions are less than ideal, may not inevitably lead to accuracy.

If we add to the three conditions of memory these two:

(4) e is of type E;

(5) A believes (1)-(4);

we shall have what I call a *paradigm* case of memory. Paradigm cases explain our interest in memory as a source of knowledge about the past; only when a person is remembering accurately, and knows he is remembering, and not, say, imagining, can he derive knowledge of the past from his own tendency to represent it.

What is the relation between "A remembers e," the concept just analyzed, and "t.t.s. A contains a memory of an experience of t.t.s. B," the expression Grice uses? I take it that experiences are a species of events. But it will not do simply to say, as an explication of Grice's notion, "A remembers e, and e is an experience." For suppose Wilson remembers Wynn watching the ball go over the fence. Then Wilson is remembering an experience, but Wilson's present t.t.s. does not contain a memory of an experience contained in Wynn's earlier t.t.s., in Grice's intended sense, or else Grice's analysis is in more serious trouble than contemplated so far. The experience we are after is not the event remembered, even if it is an experience, but the witnessing of it. Now given our peculiar use of "witnessing," the witnessing may be the event remembered. Wynn remembers watching the ball go over the fence, and it is this very watching of the ball which, in virtue of our extended use of witnessing" as including participation in the past event, is, in his case, the witnessing of the remembered event. But when the witnessing and the event remembered are distinct, it is the witnessing, and not the event witnessed, that belongs in the rememberer's biography. So I shall take "t.t.s. A contains a memory of an experience contained in t.t.s. B" to mean "A is representing the past occurrence of an event of some type E, and this representing is M-related to B's witnessing of some event e."

Now we must turn to the charges of circularity, to see if Grice has been cleared.

(i) This charge rested on the claim that the Witnessing Condition must be incorporated into the analysis of memory. But

I have argued that with a properly formulated Linking Condition, the Weak Witnessing Condition is sufficient. The Witnessing Condition is not rejected. I remains true, a consequence of the analysis of memory plus Grice's analysis of personal identity.

(ii) This charge was that in order to make sense of the conditional used in the expression of possible memory, we had to take the person as the "anchor," the entity that stayed the same under the imagined change of conditions. We could, I think, answer this by simply taking the human being involved to be the anchor. But in replying to the third charge, we shall eliminate the use of subjunctive conditional in the expression of possible memory, making the present charge irrelevant.

(iii) We certainly have a concept of possible memory, of persons who could remember a certain event, although they are not in fact doing so. And there are certainly conditions such that, if their obtaining would lead a person to remember, then it is true of him that he can remember. But it would be a mistake to approach the concept of possible memory by trying to list these conditions.

A better approach to the problem begins with the notion of an inclination to believe that an event of type E occurred. Someone who is inclined to believe that an event of type E occurred will be disposed to represent that such an event occurred at that time. We do not need to have an exhaustive list of the conditions under which this disposition will be triggered in order to understand what it is to be so disposed, any more than we need to have an exhaustive list of the conditions under which a belief will be expressed, in order to know what it is to believe. Now, just as we believe that humans often represent the occurrence of past events of a certain type as a result of a certain process set in motion by a past witnessing, we also, I think, believe that a person may have such a disposition to represent, as a result of such a process. Indeed, we believe that having such a disposition is a part of the process that eventually leads, in some cases, to representation. Thus we can introduce the M' relation, which obtains when the processes that lead from witnessings to dispositions to represent occur, and analyze *A has a possible memory of e* as follows:

(1) A is disposed to represent the past occurrence of an event of type E;

(2) B witnessed e;

(3) B's witnessing of e is M'-related to A's being disposed to represent the past occurrence of an event of type E.

For this analysis to be legitimate, we should provide an independent identification of the M' relation; this could be done along the lines used before, by first constructing a notion of possible recollection, and introducing the M'-relation in terms of the processes that explain the frequency of unaided possible recollection.

LOGICAL CONSTRUCTIONS AND INFERRED ENTITIES

Although I have defended Grice against the charges of circularity, the concept of memory I have used does not fit well with his conception of a person as a logical construction from experiences.

If a person is a logical construction from experiences, the existence of a person should follow, as a matter of logic, from the occurrence of the experiences of which the person is composed. The existence of a person entails nothing more than the existence of those experiences, related in a certain way, a way that itself could be immediately read off from experience. Thus Russell contrasts logical constructions with "inferred entities," where the word "inference" carries the implication of a nondemonstrative inference, incorporating some element of probability, or some explanatory hypothesis, that goes beyond the directly known facts.[22]

But when I say that my toothache this morning, and my headache of last night, belong to the same person, because my toothache belongs to the same t.t.s. as a memory of the headache, we are saying, according to the concept of memory just defended, that a certain process, the nature of which we do not know, led from the headache to this morning's toothache-accompanied memory impression. The occurrence of this process does not follow from the occurrence of the headache, the toothache, and the memory impression. The occurrence of the process, and so of the person who both had the headache and has the toothache, is in fact an inference, not something directly known at all. We believe that there is such a process at all since that seems the most likely explanation of the frequency of recollection; we believe such a process was involved in this case because of a lack of alternative explanations, and because it seems very likely that such a process should have occurred, given the other things we believe, including things believed on the basis of memory; for example, that given last night's other activities, a headache was to be expected; that given last night's sleep, with no evidence of interruption by electrical shock, mad scientist, brain transplanter, or hypnotist, a memory of it was to be expected.

Also in the explanation of possible memory, that which might be directly knowable was sacrificed for what can only be inferred. A memory impression, an "occurrent" belief, a representing, may perhaps be objects of direct observation, but beliefs in the ordinary sense, in which I have many beliefs with which my mind is not now occupied, a disposition to represent, a possible memory,—these are all states we ascribe to persons, including ourselves, as a way of systematizing and explaining the conditions under which more directly observable phenomena occur. Indeed, in using subjunctive conditionals in his formulation, Grice had already left the realm of what, in any reasonable sense, can be directly known.

So neither the primitiveness of memory nor the primitiveness of personal identity is suggested by our investigation, but only the derivative nature of both concepts. And they are derivative, not from the conception of a world of atomistic experiences, but from our scheme of a material world of which human beings are a part. And the nature of the derivation is not logical construction, but generalization and theory building in the service of explanation and prediction. And if such theories as the belief in a process that explains recollection lead us to speculations and even convictions that carry us well beyond the material world that forms their evidential base, that is a danger of the natural human bent for such theory building against which must be weighed its utility in the mundane tasks from which these speculations provide an occasional relief.

I end with two disclaimers. I do not think Grice's theory, even freed from its origins in the project of logical construction, and incorporating the concept of memory defended here, is fully satisfactory. As Quinton saw, ways in which a person's past are expected to influence his future other than just event memory, should be incorporated into our account of personal identity. The pattern used in doing this, however, could be one suggested by our investigation of Grice, first elaborating generalizations about human behavior after the pattern of our concept of recollection, and then introducing the relation which is believed to underlie them, and forms the basis of our concept of a person. But this is a large project.

Secondly, the approach that has emerged from our investigation of Grice is not inimical to Locke's original scheme, for Locke was not a logical constructor and had a place, in his version of the memory theory, for unknown processes and inferred states. This fact has often been sighted as a sign of his faintheartedness, in not banishing from his philosophy the last traces of the notion of substance, but I think it is rather a sign of his levelheadedness. And Locke would also, I think, be sympathetic with the point made above, for it is only by generalizing from the memory theory, and incorporating somehow into our account of personal identity the sort of character development, stability of ideals and values, influence of past intentions, and the like, which we normally expect to find in humans, that the forensic and moral importance of personal identity, which Locke so rightly emphasized, can be explained.

NOTES

1. Joseph Butler, "Of Personal Identity," originally an appendix to *The Analogy of Religion* (1736); reprinted in this anthology.

2. John Locke, "Of Identity and Diversity," chap. 27 of *An Essay Concerning Human Understanding,* 2d ed. (1694); reprinted in this anthology.

3. H. P. Grice, "Personal Identity," *Mind,* vol. 50 (October, 1941); reprinted in this anthology.

4. Anthony Quinton, "The Soul," *Journal of Philosophy,* vol. 59 (July, 1962); reprinted in this anthology.

5. Thomas Reid, "Of Mr. Locke's Account of Our Personal Identity," from chap. 6 of *Essays on the Intellectual Powers of Man* (1985); reprinted in this anthology.

6. Locke's actual words are, "as far as this consciousness can be ex-

tended backwards to any past action or thought, so far reaches the identity of that person . . ." ("Of Identity and Diversity," sect. 9).

7. Grice actually describes the series, co-membership in which is required of *A* and *B,* as follows, "every member of the series either would, given certain conditions, contain as an element a member of some experience which is an element in some previous member, or contains as an element some experience a memory of which would, given certain conditions, occur as an element in some subsequent member; there being no subset of members which is independent of all the rest." ("Personal Identity," sect. C.) The condition imposed on *A* and *B* by R_G is equivalent to this; a series of the sort Grice describes would result from the R_G sequence by putting the members in chronological order and eliminating repetitions; an R_G sequence can be obtained from a series of the sort Grice describes by starting with any t.t.s. and building an appropriately linked sequence, repeating a multiply linked t.t.s. when necessary in order to continue until all the t.t.s.'s are used. For a comparison of Grice, Quinton, and Locke, see the introduction to this anthology.

8. See Reid, "Of Mr. Locke's Account of Our Personal Identity."

9. Butler, "Of Personal Identity."

10. This seems to be a difference between Grice and Russell, the pioneer logical constructor. In Russell's view, the logical construction was the philosopher's contribution to an improved conception of, say, a material object, free of the epistemological problems inherent in the ordinary conception. So analysis, for Russell, does not preserve exact meaning. But Grice intends to be making explicit, through analysis, the concept we already have. (See Bertrand Russell, *Our Knowledge of the External World* [New York: W. W. Norton, 1929]).

11. Grice does not say explicitly that a t.t.s. is a set. But it seems clear that if a t.t.s. is not a set, it is nevertheless some other sort of entity the identity of which is determined by the experiences contained in it.

12. Our "intuitive feel," of course, won't take us far when the difficult cases of event individuation and classification arise.

13. C. B. Martin and Max Deutscher, "Remembering," *Philosophical Review* (1966).

14. John Locke, "On Retention," chap. 10 of Book II of his *Essay Concerning Human Understanding.*

15. David Hume, "Of the Ideas of Memory and Imagination," Sect. III of Pt I, Book I, *A Treatise of Human Nature.*

16. Bertrand Russell, "Memory," chap. 9 of *An Analysis of Mind* (London: Allen and Unwin, 1921).

17. But I do not accept their final version of this condition.

18. Henri Bergson, *Matter and Memory* (London: Allen and Unwin, 1912).

19. See Locke, "Of Identity and Diversity," sect. 15.

20. Sydney Shoemaker, *Self-Knowledge and Self-Identity* (Ithaca: Cornell University Press, 1963) p. 23.

21. See Quinton, "The Soul," sect. 3.

22. See *Mysticism and Logic* (New York, 1929), pp. 155 ff.

PART IV

THE ABANDONMENT OF
PERSONAL IDENTITY

David Hume

10

Our Idea of Identity

First, as to the principle of individuation; we may observe, that the view of any one object is not sufficient to convey the idea of identity. For in that proposition, *an object is the same with itself,* if the idea express'd by the word, *object,* were no ways distinguish'd from that meant by *itself;* we really shou'd mean nothing, nor wou'd the proposition contain a predicate and a subject, which however are imply'd in this affirmation. One single object conveys the idea of unity, not that of identity.

On the other hand, a multiplicity of objects can never convey this idea, however resembling they may be suppos'd. The mind always pronounces the one not to be the other, and considers them as forming two, three, or any determinate number of objects, whose existences are entirely distinct and independent.

Since then both number and unity are incompatible with the relation of identity, it must lie in something that is neither of them. But to tell the truth, at first sight this seems utterly impossible. Betwixt unity and number there can be no medium; no more than betwixt existence and non-existence. After one object is suppos'd to exist, we must either suppose another also to exist; in which case we have the idea of number: Or we must suppose it not to exist; in which case the first object remains at unity.

This selection is a part of "Of Skepticism With Regard to The Senses," which is section 2 of Part IV of Book I of Hume's *Treatise of Human Nature,* first published in 1739. The title, "Our Idea of Identity," is not in the original.

To remove this difficulty, let us have recourse to the idea of time or duration. I have already observ'd,* that time, in a strict sense, implies succession, and that when we apply its idea to any unchangeable object, 'tis only by a fiction of the imagination, by which the unchangeable object is suppos'd to participate of the changes of the co-existent objects, and in particular of that of our perceptions. The fiction of the imagination almost universally takes place; and 'tis by means of it, that a single object, plac'd before us, and survey'd for any time without our discovering in it any interruption or variation, is able to give us a notion of identity. For when we consider any two points of this time, we may place them in different lights: We may either survey them at the very same instant; in which case they give us the idea of number, both by themselves and by the object; which must be multiply'd, in order to be conceiv'd at once, as existent in these two different points of time: Or on the other hand, we may trace the succession of time by a like succession of ideas, and conceiving first one moment, along with the object then existent, imagine afterwards a change in the time without any *variation* or *interruption* in the object; in which case it gives us the idea of unity. Here then is an idea, which is a medium betwixt unity and number; or more properly speaking, is either of them, according to the view, in which we take it: And this idea we call that of identity. We cannot, in any propriety of speech, say, that an object is the same with itself, unless we mean, that the object existent at one time is the same with itself existent at another. By this means we make a difference, betwixt the idea meant by the word, *object,* and that meant by *itself,* without going the length of number, and at the same time without restraining ourselves to a strict and absolute unity.

Thus the principle of individuation is nothing but the *invariableness* and *uninterruptedness* of any object, thro' a suppos'd variation of time, by which the mind can trace it in the different periods of its existence, without any break of the view, and without being oblig'd to form the idea of multiplicity or number.

---

*Sect. 5, Part II, Book I, *Treatise of Human Nature.*

David Hume

11

Of Personal Identity

There are some philosophers, who imagine we are every moment intimately conscious of what we call our *self;* that we feel its existence and its continuance in existence; and are certain, beyond the evidence of a demonstration, both of its perfect identity and simplicity. The strongest sensation, the most violent passion, say they, instead of distracting us from this view, only fix it the more intensely, and make us consider their influence on *self* either by their pain or pleasure. To attempt a farther proof of this were to weaken its evidence; since no proof can be derived from any fact of which we are so intimately conscious; nor is there any thing, of which we can be certain, if we doubt of this.

Unluckily all these positive assertions are contrary to that very experience which is pleaded for them; nor have we any idea of *self,* after the manner it is here explained. For, from what impression could this idea be derived? This question 'tis impossible to answer without a manifest contradiction and absurdity; and yet 'tis a question which must necessarily be answered, if we would have the idea of self pass for clear and intelligible. It must be some one impression that gives rise to every real idea. But self or person is not any one impression, but that to which our several impressions and ideas are supposed to have

This selection is section 6 of Part IV of Book I of Hume's *Treatise of Human Nature,* first published in 1739.

a reference. If any impression gives rise to the idea of self, that impression must continue invariably the same, through the whole course of our lives; since self is supposed to exist after that manner. But there is no impression constant and invariable. Pain and pleasure, grief and joy, passions and sensations succeed each other, and never all exist at the same time. It cannot therefore be from any of these impressions, or from any other, that the idea of self is derived; and consequently there is no such idea.

But farther, what must become of all our particular perceptions upon this hypothesis? All these are different, and distinguishable, and separable from each other, and may be separately considered, and may exist separately, and have no need of any thing to support their existence. After what manner therefore do they belong to self, and how are they connected with it? For my part, when I enter most intimately into what I call *myself,* I always stumble on some particular perception or other, of heat or cold, light or shade, love or hatred, pain or pleasure. I never can catch *myself* at any time without a perception, and never can observe any thing but the perception. When my perceptions are removed for any time, as by sound sleep, so long am I insensible of *myself,* and may truly be said not to exist. And were all my perceptions removed by death, and could I neither think, nor feel, nor see, nor love, nor hate, after the dissolution of my body, I should be entirely annihilated, nor do I conceive what is farther requisite to make me a perfect nonentity. If any one, upon serious and unprejudiced reflection, thinks he has a different notion of *himself,* I must confess I can reason no longer with him. All I can allow him is, that he may be in the right as well as I, and that we are essentially different in this particular. He may, perhaps, perceive something simple and continued, which he calls *himself;* though I am certain there is no such principle in me.

But setting aside some metaphysicians of this kind, I may venture to affirm of the rest of mankind, that they are nothing but a bundle or collection of different perceptions, which succeed each other with an inconceivable rapidity, and are in a perpetual flux and movement. Our eyes cannot turn in their sockets without varying our perceptions. Our thought is still

more variable than our sight; and all our other senses and faculties contribute to this change; nor is there any single power of
the soul, which remains unalterably the same, perhaps for one
moment. The mind is a kind of theatre, where several perceptions successively make their appearance; pass, repass, glide
away, and mingle in an infinite variety of postures and situations. There is properly no *simplicity* in it at one time, nor
identity in different, whatever natural propension we may have
to imagine that simplicity and identity. The comparison of the
theatre must not mislead us. They are the successive perceptions
only, that constitute the mind; nor have we the most distant
notion of the place where these scenes are represented, or of the
materials of which it is composed.

What then gives us so great a propension to ascribe an
identity to these successive perceptions, and to suppose ourselves possessed of an invariable and uninterrupted existence
through the whole course of our lives? In order to answer this
question, we must distinguish betwixt personal identity, as it
regards our thought or imagination, and as it regards our passions or the concern we take in ourselves. The first is our present subject; and to explain it perfectly we must take the matter
pretty deep, and account for that identity, which we attribute
to plants and animals; there being a great analogy betwixt it
and the identity of a self or person.

We have a distinct idea of an object that remains invariable
and uninterrupted through a supposed variation of time; and
this idea we call that of *identity* or *sameness.* We have also a
distinct idea of several different objects existing in succession,
and connected together by a close relation; and this to an accurate view affords as perfect a notion of *diversity,* as if there
was no manner of relation among the objects. But though these
two ideas of identity, and a succession of related objects, be in
themselves perfectly distinct, and even contrary, yet 'tis certain
that, in our common way of thinking, they are generally confounded with each other. That action of the imagination, by
which we consider the uninterrupted and invariable object, and
that by which we reflect on the succession of related objects,
are almost the same to the feeling; nor is there much more effort of thought required in the latter case than in the former.

The relation facilitates the transition of the mind from one object to another, and renders its passage as smooth as if it contemplated one continued object. This resemblance is the cause of the confusion and mistake, and makes us substitute the notion of identity, instead of that of related objects. However at one instant we may consider the related succession as variable or interrupted, we are sure the next to ascribe to it a perfect identity, and regard it as invariable and uninterrupted. Our propensity to this mistake is so great from the resemblance above mentioned, that we fall into it before we are aware; and though we incessantly correct ourselves by reflection, and return to a more accurate method of thinking, yet we cannot long sustain our philosophy, or take off this bias from the imagination. Our last resource is to yield to it, and boldly assert that these different related objects are in effect the same, however interrupted and variable. In order to justify to ourselves this absurdity, we often feign some new and unintelligible principle, that connects the objects together, and prevents their interruption or variation. Thus, we feign the continued existence of the perceptions of our senses, to remove the interruption; and run into the notion of a *soul,* and *self,* and *substance,* to disguise the variation. But, we may farther observe, that where we do not give rise to such a fiction, our propension to confound identity with relation is so great, that we are apt to imagine something unknown and mysterious,* connecting the parts, beside their relation; and this I take to be the case with regard to the identity we ascribe to plants and vegetables. And even when this does not take place, we still feel a propensity to confound these ideas, though we are not able fully to satisfy ourselves in that particular, nor find any thing invariable and uninterrupted to justify our notion of identity.

Thus, the controversy concerning identity is not merely a dispute of words. For, when we attribute identity, in an improper sense, to variable or interrupted objects, our mistake is

---

*If the reader is desirous to see how a great genius may be influenced by these seemingly trivial principles of the imagination, as well as the mere vulgar, let him read my Lord Shaftsbury's reasonings concerning the uniting principle of the universe, and the identity of plants and animals. See his *Moralists,* or *Philosophical Rhapsody.*

not confined to the expression, but is commonly attended with
a fiction, either of something invariable and uninterrupted, or
of something mysterious and inexplicable, or at least with a
propensity to such fictions. What will suffice to prove this hypothesis to the satisfaction of every fair inquirer, is to show,
from daily experience and observation, that the objects which
are variable or interrupted, and yet are supposed to continue
the same, are such only as consist of a succession of parts, connected together by resemblance, contiguity, or causation. For as
such a succession answers evidently to our notion of diversity,
it can only be by mistake we ascribe to it an identity; and as
the relation of parts, which leads us into this mistake, is really
nothing but a quality, which produces an association of ideas,
and an easy transition of the imagination from one to another,
it can only be from the resemblance, which this act of the mind
bears to that by which we contemplate one continued object,
that the error arises. Our chief business, then, must be to prove,
that all objects, to which we ascribe identity, without observing
their invariableness and uninterruptedness, are such as consist of
a succession of related objects.

In order to this, suppose any mass of matter, of which the
parts are contiguous and connected, to be placed before us; 'tis
plain we must attribute a perfect identity to this mass, provided
all the parts continue uninterruptedly and invariably the same,
whatever motion or change of place we may observe either in
the whole or in any of the parts. But supposing some very *small*
or *inconsiderable* part to be added to the mass, or subtracted
from it; though this absolutely destroys the identity of the
whole, strictly speaking, yet as we seldom think so accurately,
we scruple not to pronounce a mass of matter the same, where
we find so trivial an alteration. The passage of the thought from
the object before the change to the object after it, is so smooth
and easy, that we scarce perceive the transition, and are apt to
imagine, that 'tis nothing but a continued survey of the same
object.

There is a very remarkable circumstance that attends this
experiment; which is, that though the change of any considerable part in a mass of matter destroys the identity of the whole,
yet we must measure the greatness of the part, not absolutely,

but by its *proportion* to the whole. The addition or diminution of a mountain would not be sufficient to produce a diversity in a planet; though the change of a very few inches would be able to destroy the identity of some bodies. 'Twill be impossible to account for this, but by reflecting that objects operate upon the mind, and break or interrupt the continuity of its actions, not according to their real greatness, but according to their proportion to each other; and therefore, since this interruption makes an object cease to appear the same, it must be the uninterrupted progress of the thought which constitutes the imperfect identity.

This may be confirmed by another phenomenon. A change in any considerable part of a body destroys its identity; but 'tis remarkable, that where the change is produced *gradually* and *insensibly,* we are less apt to ascribe to it the same effect. The reason can plainly be no other, than that the mind, in following the successive changes of the body, feels an easy passage from the surveying its condition in one moment, to the viewing of it in another, and in no particular time perceives any interruption in its actions. From which continued perception, it ascribes a continued existence and identity to the object.

But whatever precaution we may use in introducing the changes gradually, and making them proportionable to the whole, 'tis certain, that where the changes are at last observed to become considerable, we make a scruple of ascribing identity to such different objects. There is, however, another artifice, by which we may induce the imagination to advance a step farther; and that is, by producing a reference of the parts to each other, and a combination to some *common end* or purpose. A ship, of which a considerable part has been changed by frequent reparations, is still considered as the same; nor does the difference of the materials hinder us from ascribing an identity to it. The common end, in which the parts conspire, is the same under all their variations, and affords an easy transition of the imagination from one situation of the body to another.

But this is still more remarkable, when we add a *sympathy* of parts to their *common end,* and suppose that they bear to each other the reciprocal relation of cause and effect in all their actions and operations. This is the case with all animals and vegetables; where not only the several parts have a reference to some general purpose, but also a mutual dependence on, and connexion with, each other. The effect of so strong a relation is, that though every one must allow, that in a very few years both vegetables and animals endure a *total* change, yet we still attribute identity to them, while their form, size and substance, are entirely altered. An oak that grows from a small plant to a large tree is still the same oak, though there be not one particle of matter or figure of its parts the same. An infant becomes a man, and is sometimes fat, sometimes lean, without any change in his identity.

We may also consider the two following phenomena, which are remarkable in their kind. The first is, that though we commonly be able to distinguish pretty exactly betwixt numerical and specific identity, yet it sometimes happens that we confound them, and in our thinking and reasoning employ the one for the other. Thus, a man who hears a noise that is frequently interrupted and renewed, says it is still the same noise, though 'tis evident the sounds have only a specific identity or resemblance, and there is nothing numerically the same but the cause which produced them. In like manner it may be said, without breach of the propriety of language, that such a church, which was formerly of brick, fell to ruin, and that the parish rebuilt the same church of freestone, and according to modern architecture. Here neither the form nor materials are the same, nor is there any thing common to the two objects but their relation to the inhabitants of the parish; and yet this alone is sufficient to make us denominate them the same. But we must observe, that in these cases the first object is in a manner annihilated before the second comes into existence; by which means, we are never presented, in any one point of time, with the idea of difference and multiplicity; and for that reason are less scrupulous in calling them the same.

Secondly, we may remark, that though, in a succession of related objects, it be in a manner requisite that the change of parts be not sudden nor entire, in order to preserve the identity, yet where the objects are in their nature changeable and inconstant, we admit of a more sudden transition than would otherwise be consistent with that relation. Thus, as the nature of a river consists in the motion and change of parts, though in less than four-and-twenty hours these be totally altered, this hinders not the river from continuing the same during several ages. What is natural and essential to any thing is, in a manner, expected; and what is expected makes less impression, and appears of less moment than what is unusual and extraordinary. A considerable change of the former kind seems really less to the imagination than the most trivial alteration of the latter; and by breaking less the continuity of the thought, has less influence in destroying the identity.

We now proceed to explain the nature of *personal identity,* which has become so great a question in philosophy, especially of late years, in England, where all the abstruser sciences are studied with a peculiar ardour and application. And here 'tis evident the same method of reasoning must be continued which has so successfully explained the identity of plants, and animals, and ships, and houses, and of all the compounded and change-able productions either of art or nature. The identity which we ascribe to the mind of man is only a fictitious one, and of a like kind with that which we ascribe to vegetables and animal bodies. It cannot therefore have a different origin, but must proceed from a like operation of the imagination upon like objects.

But lest this argument should not convince the reader, though in my opinion perfectly decisive, let him weigh the following reasoning, which is still closer and more immediate. 'Tis evident that the identity which we attribute to the human mind, however perfect we may imagine it to be, is not able to run the several different perceptions into one, and make them lose their characters of distinction and difference, which are essential to them. 'Tis still true that every distinct perception which enters into the composition of the mind, is a distinct existence, and is different, and distinguishable, and separable from every other perception, either contemporary or successive. But as, notwithstanding this distinction and separability, we suppose the whole train of perceptions to be united by identity, a question naturally arises concerning this relation of identity, whether it be something that really binds our several perceptions together, or only associates their ideas in the imagination; that is, in other words, whether, in pronouncing concerning the identity of a person, we observe some real bond among his perceptions, or only feel one among the ideas we form of them. This question we might easily decide, if we would recollect what has been already proved at large, that the understanding never observes any real connexion among objects, and that even the union of cause and effect, when strictly examined, resolves itself into a customary association of ideas. For from thence it evidently follows, that identity is nothing really belonging to these different perceptions, and uniting them together, but is merely a quality which we attribute to them, because of the union of their ideas in the imagination when we reflect upon them. Now, the only qualities which can give ideas an union in the imagination, are these three relations above mentioned. These are the uniting principles in the ideal world, and without them every distinct object is separable by the mind, and may be separately considered, and appears not to have any more connexion with any other object than if disjoined by the greatest difference and remoteness. 'Tis therefore on some of these three relations of resemblance, contiguity and causation, that identity depends; and as the very essence of these relations consists in their producing an easy transition of ideas, it follows, that our notions of personal identity proceed entirely from the smooth and uninterrupted progress of the thought along a train of connected ideas, according to the principles above explained.

The only question, therefore, which remains is, by what relations this uninterrupted progress of our thought is produced, when we consider the successive existence of a mind or thinking person. And here 'tis evident we must confine ourselves to resemblance and causation, and must drop contiguity, which has little or no influence in the present case.

To begin with *resemblance;* suppose we could see clearly into the breast of another, and observe that succession of perceptions which constitutes his mind or thinking principle, and suppose that he always preserves the memory of a considerable part of past perceptions, 'tis evident that nothing could more contribute to the bestowing a relation on this succession amidst all its variations. For what is the memory but a faculty, by which we raise up the images of past perceptions? And as an

image necessarily resembles its object, must not the frequent
placing of these resembling perceptions in the chain of thought,
convey the imagination more easily from one link to another,
and make the whole seem like the continuance of one object?
In this particular, then, the memory not only discovers the identity, but also contributes to its production, by producing the
relation of resemblance among the perceptions. The case is the
same, whether we consider ourselves or others.

As to *causation;* we may observe, that the true idea of the
human mind, is to consider it as a system of different perceptions or different existences, which are linked together by the
relation of cause and effect, and mutually produce, destroy, influence, and modify each other. Our impressions give rise to
their correspondent idea; and these ideas, in their turn, produce
other impressions. One thought chases another, and draws after
it a third, by which it is expelled in its turn. In this respect, I
cannot compare the soul more properly to any thing than to a
republic or commonwealth, in which the several members are
united by the reciprocal ties of government and subordination,
and give rise to other persons who propagate the same republic
in the incessant changes of its parts. And as the same individual
republic may not only change its members, but also its laws and
constitutions; in like manner the same person may vary his
character and disposition, as well as his impressions and ideas,
without losing his identity. Whatever changes he endures, his
several parts are still connected by the relation of causation.
And in this view our identity with regard to the passions serves
to corroborate that with regard to the imagination, by the
making our distant perceptions influence each other, and by
giving us a present concern for our past or future pains or pleasures.

As memory alone acquaints us with the continuance and
extent of this succession of perceptions, 'tis to be considered,
upon that account chiefly, as the source of personal identity.
Had we no memory, we never should have any notion of causation, nor consequently of that chain of causes and effects, which
constitute our self or person. But having once acquired this notion of causation from the memory, we can extend the same
chain of causes, and consequently the identity of our persons

beyond our memory, and can comprehend times, and circumstances, and actions, which we have entirely forgot, but suppose in general to have existed. For how few of our past actions are there, of which we have any memory? Who can tell me, for instance, what were his thoughts and actions on the first of January 1715, the eleventh of March 1719, and the third of August 1733? Or will he affirm, because he has entirely forgot the incidents of these days, that the present self is not the same person with the self of that time; and by that means overturn all the most established notions of personal identity? In this view, therefore, memory does not so much *produce* as *discover* personal identity, by showing us the relation of cause and effect among our different perceptions. 'Twill be incumbent on those who affirm that memory produces entirely our personal identity, to give a reason why we can thus extend our identity beyond our memory.

The whole of this doctrine leads us to a conclusion, which is of great importance in the present affair, viz. that all the nice and subtile questions concerning personal identity can never possibly be decided, and are to be regarded rather as grammatical than as philosophical difficulties. Identity depends on the relations of ideas; and these relations produce identity, by means of that easy transition they occasion. But as the relations, and the easiness of the transition may diminish by insensible degrees, we have no just standard by which we can decide any dispute concerning the time when they acquire or lose a title to the name of identity. All the disputes concerning the identity of connected objects are merely verbal, except so far as the relation of parts gives rise to some fiction or imaginary principle of union, as we have already observed.

What I have said concerning the first origin and uncertainty of our notion of identity, as applied to the human mind, may be extended with little or no variation to that of *simplicity*. An object, whose different coexistent parts are bound together by a close relation, operates upon the imagination after much the same manner as one perfectly simple and indivisible, and requires not a much greater stretch of thought in order to its conception. From this similarity of operation we attribute a simplicity to it, and feign a principle of union as the support of this simplicity, and the centre of all the different parts and qualities of the object.

Thus we have finished our examination of the several systems of philosophy, both of the intellectual and moral world; and, in our miscellaneous way of reasoning, have been led into several topics, which will either illustrate and confirm some preceding part of this discourse, or prepare the way for our following opinions. 'Tis now time to return to a more close examination of our subject, and to proceed in the accurate anatomy of human nature, having fully explained the nature of our judgment and understanding.

David Hume

12

Second Thoughts

I had entertain'd some hopes, that however deficient our theory
of the intellectual world might be, it wou'd be free from those
contradictions, and absurdities, which seem to attend every explication, that human reason can give of the material world. But
upon a more strict review of the section concerning *personal
identity,* I find myself involv'd in such a labyrinth, that, I must
confess, I neither know how to correct my former opinions, nor
how to render them consistent. If this be not a good *general*
reason for scepticism, 'tis at least a sufficient one (if I were not
already abundantly supplied) for me to entertain a diffidence
and modesty in all my decisions. I shall propose the arguments
on both sides, beginning with those that induc'd me to deny the
strict and proper identity and simplicity of a self or thinking
being.

When we talk of *self* or *substance,* we must have an idea
annex'd to these terms, otherwise they are altogether unintelligible. Every idea is deriv'd from preceding impressions; and we
have no impression of self or substance, as something simple and
individual. We have, therefore, no idea of them in that sense.

The same imperfection attends our ideas of the Deity; but this can
have no effect either on religion or morals. The order of the universe
proves an omnipotent mind; that is, a mind whose will is *constantly attended* with the obedience of every creature and being. Nothing more is

This selection is from the appendix Hume attached to the first edition of
the third book of his *Treatise of Human Nature,* which was first published
in 1740. The title "Second Thoughts" has been supplied by the editor.

requisite to give a foundation to all the articles of religion, nor is it necessary we shou'd form a distinct idea of the force and energy of the supreme Being.

Whatever is distinct, is distinguishable; and whatever is distinguishable, is separable by the thought or imagination. All perceptions are distinct. They are, therefore, distinguishable, and separable, and may be conceiv'd as separately existent, and may exist separately, without any contradiction or absurdity.

When I view this table and that chimney, nothing is present to me but particular perception, which are of a like nature with all the other perceptions. This is the doctrine of philosophers. But this table, which is present to me, and that chimney, may and do exist separately. This is the doctrine of the vulgar, and implies no contradiction. There is no contradiction, therefore, in extending the same doctrine to all the perceptions.

In general, the following reasoning seems satisfactory. All ideas are borrow'd from preceding perceptions. Our ideas of objects, therefore, are deriv'd from that source. Consequently no proposition can be intelligible or consistent with regard to objects, which is not so with regard to perceptions. But 'tis intelligible and consistent to say, that objects exist distinct and independent, without any common *simple* substance or subject of inhesion. This proposition, therefore, can never be absurd with regard to perceptions.

When I turn my reflexion on *myself,* I never can perceive this *self* without some one or more perceptions; nor can I ever perceive any thing but the perceptions. 'Tis the composition of these, therefore, which forms the self.

We can conceive a thinking being to have either many or few perceptions. Suppose the mind to be reduc'd even below the life of an oyster. Suppose it to have only one perception, as of thirst or hunger. Consider it in that situation. Do you conceive any thing but merely that perception? Have you any notion of *self* or *substance*? If not, the addition of other perceptions can never give you that notion.

The annihilation, which some people suppose to follow upon death, and which entirely destroys this self, is nothing but an extinction of all particular perceptions; love and hatred, pain and pleasure, thought and sensation. These therefore must be the same with self; since the one cannot survive the other.

Is *self* the same with *substance*? If it be, how can that question have place, concerning the subsistence of self, under a change of substance? If they be distinct, what is the difference betwixt them? For my part, I have a notion of neither, when conceiv'd distinct from particular perceptions.

Philosophers begin to be reconcil'd to the principle, *that we have no idea of external substance, distinct from the ideas of particular qualities.* This must pave the way for a like principle with regard to the mind, *that we have no notion of it, distinct from the particular perceptions.*

So far I seem to be attended with sufficient evidence. But having thus loosen'd all our particular perceptions, when* I proceed to explain the principle of connexion, which binds them together, and makes us attribute to them a real simplicity and identity; I am sensible, that my account is very defective, and that nothing but the seeming evidence of the precedent reasonings cou'd have induc'd me to receive it. If perceptions are distinct existences, they form a whole only by being connected together. But no connexions among distinct existences are ever discoverable by human understanding. We only *feel* a connexion or determination of the thought, to pass from one object to another. It follows, therefore, that the thought alone finds personal identity, when reflecting on the train of past perceptions, that compose a mind, the ideas of them are felt to be connected together, and naturally introduce each other. However extraordinary this conclusion may seem, it need not surprize us. Most philosophers seem inclin'd to think, that personal identity *arises* from consciousness; and consciousness is nothing but a reflected thought or perception. The present philosophy, therefore, has so far a promising aspect. But all my hopes vanish, when I come to explain the principles, that unite our successive perceptions in our thought or consciousness. I cannot discover any theory, which gives me satisfaction on this head.

In short there are two principles, which I cannot render consistent; nor is it in my power to renounce either of them, viz. *that all our distinct perceptions are distinct existences,* and

* Book I.

that the mind never perceives any real connexion among distinct existences. Did our perceptions either inhere in something simple and individual, or did the mind perceive some real connexion among them, there wou'd be no difficulty in the case. For my part, I must plead the privilege of a sceptic, and confess, that this difficulty is too hard for my understanding. I pretend not, however, to pronounce it absolutely insuperable. Others, perhaps, or myself, upon more mature reflexions, may discover some hypothesis, that will reconcile those contradictions.

PART V

PERSONAL IDENTITY AND SURVIVAL

Bernard Williams

13

The Self and the Future

Suppose that there were some process to which two persons, *A*
and *B*, could be subjected as a result of which they might be said
—question-beggingly—to have *exchanged bodies.* That is to say—
less question-beggingly—there is a certain human body which is
such that when previously we were confronted with it, we were
confronted with person *A*, certain utterances coming from it
were expressive of memories of the past experiences of *A*, certain movements of it partly constituted the actions of *A* and
were taken as expressive of the character of *A*, and so forth;
but now, after the process is completed, utterances coming from
this body are expressive of what seem to be just those memories
which previously we identified as memories of the past experiences of *B*, its movements partly constitute actions expressive of
the character of *B*, and so forth; and conversely with the other
body.

There are certain important philosophical limitations on
how such imaginary cases are to be constructed, and how they
are to be taken when constructed in various ways. I shall mention two principal limitations, not in order to pursue them further here, but precisely in order to get them out of the way.

There are certain limitations, particularly with regard to
character and mannerisms, to our ability to imagine such cases
even in the most restricted sense of our being disposed to take

This article is reprinted from *The Philosophical Review,* vol. 79, no. 2
(April, 1970), by courtesy of the editor and of Professor Williams.

the later performances of that body which was previously A's as expressive of B's character; if the previous A and B were extremely unlike one another both physically and psychologically, and if, say, in addition, they were of different sex, there might be grave difficulties in reading B's dispositions in any possible performances of A's body. Let us forget this, and for the present purpose just take A and B as being sufficiently alike (however alike that has to be) for the difficulty not to arise; after the experiment, persons familiar with A and B are just *overwhelmingly struck* by the B-ish character of the doings associated with what was previously A's body and conversely. Thus the feat of imagining an exchange of bodies is supposed possible in the most restricted sense. But now there is a further limitation which has to be overcome if the feat is to be not merely possible in the most restricted sense but also is to have an outcome which, on serious reflection, we are prepared to describe as A and B having changed bodies—that is, an outcome where, confronted with what was previously A's body, we are prepared seriously to say that we are now confronted with B.

It would seem a necessary condition of so doing that the utternaces coming from that body be taken as genuinely expressive of memories of B's past. But memory is a causal notion; and as we actually use it, it seems a necessary condition on x's present knowledge of x's earlier experiences constituting memory of those experiences that the causal chain linking the experiences and the knowledge should not run outside x's body. Hence if utterances coming from a given body are to be taken as expressive of memories of the experiences of B, there should be some suitable causal link between the appropriate state of that body and the original happening of those experiences to B. One radical way of securing that condition in the imagined exchange case is to suppose, with Shoemaker,[1] that the brains of A and of B are transposed. We may not need so radical a condition. Thus suppose it were possible to extract information from a man's brain and store it in a device while his brain was repaired, or even renewed, the information then being replaced: it would seem exaggerated to insist that the resultant man could not possibly have the memories he had before the operation. With regard to our knowledge of our own past, we draw distinctions between merely recalling, being reminded, and learning again, and those distinctions correspond (roughly) to distinctions between no new input, partial new input, and total new input with regard to the information in question; and it seems clear that the information-parking case just imagined would not count as new input in the sense necessary and sufficient for "learning again." Hence we can imagine the case we are concerned with in terms of information extracted into such devices from *A*'s and *B*'s brains and replaced in the other brain; this is the sort of model which, I think not unfairly for the present argument, I shall have in mind.

We imagine the following. The process considered above exists; two persons can enter some machine, let us say, and emerge changed in the appropriate ways. If *A* and *B* are the persons who enter, let us call the persons who emerge the *A-body-person* and the *B-body-person:* the *A*-body-person is that person (whoever it is) with whom I am confronted when, after the experiment, I am confronted with that body which previously was *A*'s body—that is to say, that person who would naturally be taken for *A* by someone who just saw this person, was familiar with *A*'s appearance before the experiment, and did not know about the happening of the experiment. A non-question-begging description of the experiment will leave it open which (if either) of the persons *A* and *B* the *A*-body-person is; the description of the experiment as "persons changing bodies" of course implies that the *A*-body-person is actually *B*.

We take two persons *A* and *B* who are going to have the process carried out on them. (We can suppose, rather hazily, that they are willing for this to happen; to investigate at all closely at this stage why they might be willing or unwilling, what they would fear, and so forth, would anticipate some later issues.) We further announce that one of the two resultant persons, the *A*-body-person and the *B*-body-person, is going after the experiment to be given $100,000, while the other is going to be tortured. We then ask each *A* and *B* to choose which treatment should be dealt out to which of the persons who will emerge from the experiment, the choice to be made (if it can be) on selfish grounds.

Suppose that *A* chooses that the *B*-body-person should get the pleasant treatment and the A-body-person the unpleasant treatment; and B chooses conversely (this might indicate that they thought that "changing bodies" was indeed a good description of the outcome). The experimenter cannot act in accordance with both these sets of preferences, those expressed by A and those expressed by B. Hence there is one clear sense in which A and B cannot both get what they want: namely, that if the experimenter, before the experiment, announces to A and B that he intends to carry out the alternative (for example), of treating the B-body-person unpleasantly and the A-body-person pleasantly—then A can say rightly, "That's not the outcome I chose to happen," and B can say rightly, "That's just the outcome I chose to happen." So, evidently, A and B before the experiment can each come to know either that the outcome he chose will be that which will happen, or that the one he chose will not happen, and in that sense they can get or fail to get what they wanted. But is it also true that when the experimenter proceeds *after* the experiment to act in accordance with one of the preferences and not the other, then one of A and B will have got what he wanted, and the other not?

There seems very good ground for saying so. For suppose the experimenter, having elicited A's and B's preference, says nothing to A and B about what he will do; conducts the experiment; and then, for example, gives the unpleasant treatment to the B-body-person and the pleasant treatment to the A-body-person. Then the B-body-person will not only complain of the unpleasant treatment as such, but will complain (since he has A's memories) that that was not the outcome he chose, since he chose the the B-body-person should be well treated; and since A made his choice in selfish spirit, he may add that he precisely chose in that way because he did not want the unpleasant things to happen to *him*. The A-body-person meanwhile will express satisfaction both at the receipt of the $100,000, and also at the fact that the experimenter has chosen to act in the way that he, B, so wisely chose. These facts make a strong case for saying that the experimenter has brought it about that B did in the outcome get what he wanted and A did not. It is therefore a strong case for saying that the B-body-person really is A, and the A-body-person really is B; and therefore for saying that the process of the experiment really is that of changing bodies. For the same reasons it would seem that *A* and *B* in our example really did choose wisely, and that it was *A*'s bad luck that the choice he correctly made was not carried out, *B*'s good luck that the choice he correctly made was carried out. This seems to show that to care about what happens to me in the future is not necessarily to care about what happens to *this* body (the one I now have); and this in turn might be taken to show that in some sense of Descartes's obscure phrase, I and my body are "really distinct" (though, of course, nothing in these considerations could support the idea that I could exist without a body at all).

These suggestions seem to be reinforced if we consider the cases where *A* and *B* make other choices with regard to the experiment. Suppose that *A* chooses that the *A*-body-person should get the money, and the *B*-body-person get the pain, and *B* chooses conversely. Here again there can be no outcome which matches the expressed preferences of both of them: they cannot both get what they want. The experimenter announces, before the experiment, that the *A*-body-person will in fact get the money, and the *B*-body-person will get the pain. So *A* at this stage gets what he wants (the announced outcome matches his expressed preference). After the experiment, the distribution is carried out as announced. Both the *A*-body-person and the *B*-body-person will have to agree that what is happening is in accordance with the preference that *A* originally expressed. The *B*-body-person will naturally express this acknowledgment (since he has *A*'s memories) by saying that this is the distribution he chose; he will recall, among other things, the experimenter announcing this outcome, his approving it as what he chose, and so forth. However, he (the *B*-body-person) certainly does not like what is now happening to him, and would much prefer to be receiving what the *A*-body-person is receiving—namely, $100,000. The *A*-body-person will on the other hand recall choosing an outcome other than this one, but will reckon it good luck that the experimenter did not do what he recalls choosing. It looks, then, as though the *A*-body-person had gotten what he wanted, but not what he chose, while the *B*-body-person has gotten what he chose, but not what he wanted. So once more it looks as though they are, respectively, B and A; and that in this case the original choices of both A and B were unwise.

Suppose, lastly, that in the original choice A takes the line of the first case and B of the second: that is A chooses that the B-body-person should get the money and the A-body-person the pain, and B chooses exactly the same thing. In this case, the experimenter would seem to be in the happy situation of giving both persons what they want—or at least, like God, what they have chosen. In this case, the B-body-person likes what he is receiving, recalls choosing it, and congratulates himself on the wisdom of (as he puts it) his choice; while the A-body-person does not like what he is receiving, recalls choosing it, and is forced to acknowledge that (as he puts it) his choice was unwise. So once more we seem to get results to support the suggestions drawn from the first case.

Let us now consider the question, not of A and B choosing certain outcomes to take place after the experiment, but of their willingness to engage in the experiment at all. If they were initially inclined to accept the description of the experiment as "changing bodies" then one thing that would interest them would be the character of the other person's body. In this respect also what would happen after the experiment would seem to suggest that "changing bodies" was a good description of the experiment. If A and B agreed to the experiment, being each not displeased with the appearance, physique, and so forth of the other person's body; after the experiment the B-body-person might well be found saying such things as: "When I agreed to this experiment, I thought that B's face was quite attractive, but now I look at it in the mirror, I am not so sure"; or the A-body-person might say "When I agreed to this experiment I did not know that A had a wooden leg; but now, after it is over, I find that I have this wooden leg, and I want the experiment reversed." It is possible that he might say further that he finds the leg very uncomfortable, and that the B-body-person should say, for instance, that he recalls that he found it very uncomfortable at first, but one gets used to it: but perhaps one would need to know more than at least I do about the physiology of habituation to artificial limbs to know whether the A-body-person would find the leg uncomfortable: that body, after all, has had the leg on it for some time. But apart from this sort of detail, the general line of the outcome regarded from this point of view seems to confirm our previous conclusions about the experiment.

Now let us suppose that when the experiment is proposed (in non-question-begging terms) A and B think rather of their psychological advantages and disadvantages. A's thoughts turn primarily to certain sorts of anxiety to which he is very prone, while B is concerned with the frightful memories he has of past experiences which still distress him. They each hope that the experiment will in some way result in their being able to get away from these things. They may even have been impressed by philosophical arguments to the effect that bodily continuity is at least a necessary condition of personal identity: A, for example, reasons that, granted the experiment comes off, then the person who is bodily continuous with him will not have this anxiety, while the other person will no doubt have some anxiety—perhaps in some sense his anxiety—and at least that person will not be he. The experiment is performed and the experimenter (to whom A and B previously revealed privately their several difficulties and hopes) asks the A-body-person whether he has gotten rid of his anxiety. This person presumably replies that he does not know what the man is talking about; he never had such anxiety, but he did have some very disagreeable memories, and recalls engaging in the experiment to get rid of them, and is disappointed to discover that he still has them. The B-body-person will react in a similar way to questions about his painful memories, pointing out that he still has his anxiety. These results seem to confirm still further the description of the experiment as "changing bodies." And all the results suggest that the only rational thing to do, confronted with such an experiment, would be to identify oneself with one's memories, and so forth, and not with one's body. The philosophical arguments designed to show that bodily continuity was at least a necessary condition of personal identity would seem to be just mistaken.

Let us now consider something apparently different. Someone in whose power I am tells me that I am going to be tortured tomorrow. I am frightened, and look forward to tomorrow in great apprehension. He adds that when the time comes, I shall not remember being told that this was going to happen to me, since shortly before the torture something else will be done to me which will make me forget the announcement. This certainly will not cheer me up, since I know perfectly well that I can forget things, and that there is such a thing as indeed being tortured unexpectedly because I had forgotten or been made to forget a prediction of the torture: that will still be a torture which, so long as I do know about the prediction, I look forward to in fear. He then adds that my forgetting the announcement will be only part of a larger process: when the moment of torture comes, I shall not remember any of the things I am now in a position to remember. This does not cheer me up, either, since I can readily conceive of being involved in an accident, for instance, as a result of which I wake up in a completely amnesiac state and also in great pain; that could certainly happen to me, I should not like it to happen to me, nor to know that it was going to happen to me. He now further adds that at the moment of torture I shall not only not remember the things I am now in a position to remember, but will have a different set of impressions of my past, quite different from the memories I now have. I do not think that this would cheer me up, either. For I can at least conceive the possibility, if not the concrete reality, of going completely mad, and thinking perhaps that I am George IV or somebody; and being told that something like that was going to happen to me would have no tendency to reduce the terror of being told authoritatively that I was going to be tortured, but would merely compound the horror. Nor do I see why I should be put into any better frame of mind by the person in charge adding lastly that the impressions of my past with which I shall be equipped on the eve of torture will exactly fit the past of another person now living, and that indeed I shall acquire these impressions by (for instance) information now in his brain being copied into mine. Fear, surely, would still be the proper reaction: and not because one did not know what was going to happen, but because in one vital respect at least one did know what was going to happen—torture, which one can indeed expect to happen to oneself, and to be preceded by certain mental derangements as well.

If this is right, the whole question seems now to be totally mysterious. For what we have just been through is of course merely one side, differently represented, of the transaction which we considered before; and it represents it as a perfectly hateful prospect, while the previous considerations represented it as something one should rationally, perhaps even cheerfully, choose out of the options there presented. It is differently presented, of course, and in two notable respects; but when we look at these two differences of presentation, can we really convince ourselves that the second presentation is wrong or misleading, thus leaving the road open to the first version which at the time seemed so convincing? Surely not.

The first difference is that in the second version the torture is throughout represented as going to happen to *me*: "you," the man in charge persistently says. Thus he is not very neutral. But should he have been neutral? Or, to put it another way, does his use of the second person have a merely emotional and rhetorical effect on me, making me afraid when further reflection would have shown that I had no reason to be? It is certainly not obviously so. The problem just is that through every step of his predictions I seem to be able to follow him successfully. And if I reflect on whether what he has said gives me grounds for fearing that I shall be tortured, I could consider that behind my fears lies some principle such as this: that my undergoing physical pain in the future is not excluded by any psychological state I may be in at the time, with the platitudinous exception of those psychological states which in themselves exclude experiencing pain, notably (if it is a psychological state) unconsciousness. In particular, what impressions I have about the past will not have any effect on whether I undergo the pain or not. This principle seems sound enough.

It is an important fact that not everything I would, as things are, regard as an evil would be something that I should rationally fear as an evil if it were predicted that it would happen to me in the future and also predicted that I should undergo significant psychological changes in the meantime. For the fact that I regard that happening, things being as they are, as an evil can be dependent on factors of belief or character which might themselves be modified by the psychological changes in question. Thus if I am appallingly subject to acrophobia, and am told that I shall find myself on top of a steep mountain in the near future, I shall to that extent be afraid; but if I am told that I shall be psychologically changed in the meantime in such a way as to rid me of my acrophobia (and as with the other prediction, I believe it), then I have no reason to be afraid of the predicted happening, or at least not the same reason. Again, I might look forward to meeting a certain person again with either alarm or excitement because of my memories of our past relations. In some part, these memories operate in connection with my emotion, not only on the present time, but projectively forward: for it is to a meeting itself affected by the presence of those memories that I look forward. If I am convinced that when the time comes I shall not have those memories, then I shall not have just the same reasons as before for looking forward to that meeting with the one emotion or the other. (Spiritualism, incidentally, appears to involve the belief that I have just the same reasons for a given attitude toward encountering people again after I am dead, as I did before: with the one modification that I can be sure it will all be very nice.)

Physical pain, however, the example which for simplicity (and not for any obsessional reason) I have taken, is absolutely minimally dependent on character or belief. No amount of change in my character or my beliefs would seem to affect substantially the nastiness of tortures applied to me; correspondingly, no degree of predicted change in my character and beliefs can unseat the fear of torture which, together with those changes, is predicted for me.

I am not at all suggesting that the *only* basis, or indeed the only rational basis, for fear in the face of these various predictions is how things will be relative to my psychological state in the eventual outcome. I am merely pointing out that this is one component; it is not the only one. For certainly one will fear and otherwise reject the changes themselves, or in very many cases one would. Thus one of the old paradoxes of hedonistic utilitarianism; if one had assurances that undergoing certain operations and being attached to a machine would provide one for the rest of one's existence with an unending sequence of delicious and varied experiences, one might very well reject the option, and react with fear if someone proposed to apply it compulsorily; and that fear and horror would seem appropriate reactions in the second case may help to discredit the interpretation (if anyone has the nerve to propose it) that one's reason for rejecting the option voluntarily would be a consciousness of duties to others which one in one's hedonic state would leave undone. The prospect of contented madness or vegetableness if found by many (not perhaps by all) appalling in ways which are obviously not a function of how things would then be for them, for things would then be for them not appalling. In the case we are at present discussing, these sorts of considerations seem merely to make it clearer that the predictions of the man in charge provide a double ground of horror: at the prospect of torture, and at the prospect of the change in character and in impressions of the past that will precede it. And certainly, to repeat what has already been said, the prospect of the second certainly seems to provide no ground for rejecting or not fearing the prospect of the first.

I said that there were two notable differences between the second presentation of our situation and the first. The first difference, which we have just said something about, was that the man predicted the torture for *me*, a psychologically very changed "me." We have yet to find a reason for saying that he should not have done this, or that I really should be unable to follow him if he does; I seem to be able to follow him only too well. The second difference is that in this presentation he does not mention the other man, except in the somewhat incidental role of being the provenance of the impressions of the past I end up with. He does not mention him at all as someone who will end up with impressions of the past derived from me (and, incidentally, with $100,000 as well—a consideration which, in the frame of mind appropriate to this version, will merely make me jealous).

But why *should* he mention this man and what is going to happen to him? My selfish concern is to be told what is going to happen to me, and now I know: torture, preceded by changes of character, brain operations, changes in impressions of the past. The knowledge that one other person, or none, or many will be similarly mistreated may affect me in other ways, of sympathy, greater horror at the power of this tyrant, and so forth; but surely it cannot affect my expectations of torture? But—someone will say—this is to leave out exactly the feature which, as the first presentation of the case showed, makes all the difference: for it is to leave out the person who, as the first presentation showed, will be you. It is to leave out not merely a feature which should fundamentally affect your fears, it is to leave out the very person for whom you are fearful. So of course, the objector will say, this makes all the difference.

But can it? Consider the following series of cases. In each case we are to suppose that after what is described, A is, as before, to be tortured; we are also to suppose the person A is informed beforehand that just these things followed by the torture will happen to him:

(i) A is subjected to an operation which produces total amnesia;

(ii) amnesia is produced in A, and other interference leads to certain changes in his character;

(iii) changes in his character are produced, and at the same time certain illusory "memory" beliefs are induced in him; these are of a quite fictitious kind and do not fit the life of any actual person;

(iv) the same as (iii), except that both the character traits and the "memory" impressions are designed to be appropriate to another actual person, B;

(v) the same as (iv), except that the result is produced by putting the information into A from the brain of B, by a method which leaves B the same as he was before;

(vi) the same happens to A as in (v), but B is not left the same, since a similar operation is conducted in the reverse direction.

I take it that no one is going to dispute that A has reasons, and fairly straightforward reasons, for fear of pain when the prospect is that of situation (i); there seems no conceivable reason why this should not extend to situation (ii), and the situation (iii) can surely introduce no difference of principle—it just seems a situation which for more than one reason we should have grounds for fearing, as suggested above. Situation (iv) at least introduces the person B, who was the focus of the objection we are now discussing. But it does not seem to introduce him in any way which makes a material difference; if I can expect pain through a transformation which involves new "memory"-impressions, it would seem a purely external fact, relative to that, that the "memory"-impressions had a model. Nor, in (*iv*), do we satisfy a causal condition which I mentioned at the beginning for the "memories" actually being memories; though notice that if the job were done thoroughly, I might well be able to elicit from the *A*-body-person the kinds of remarks about his previous expectations of the experiment—remarks appropriate to the original *B*—which so impressed us in the first version of the story. I shall have a similar assurance of this being so in situation (*v*), where, moreover, a plausible application of the causal condition is available.

But two things are to be noticed about this situation. First, if we concentrate on *A* and the *A*-body-person, we do not seem to have added anything which from the point of view of his fears makes any material difference; just as, in the move from (*iii*) to (*iv*), it made no relevant difference that the new "memory"-impressions which precede the pain had, as it happened, a model, so in the move from (*iv*) to (*v*) all we have added is that they have a model which is also their cause: and it is still difficult to see why that, to him looking forward, could possibly make the difference between expecting pain and not expecting pain. To illustrate that point from the case of character: if *A* is capable of expecting pain, he is capable of expecting pain preceded by a change in his dispositions—and to that expectation it can make no difference, whether that change in his dispositions is modeled on, or indeed indirectly caused by, the dispositions of some other person. If his fears can, as it were, reach through the change, it seems a mere trimming how the change is in fact induced. The second point about situation (*v*) is that if the crucial question for *A*'s fears with regard to what befalls the *A*-body-person is whether the *A*-body-person is or is not the person *B*,[2] then that condition has not yet been satisfied in situation (*v*): for there we have an undisputed *B* in addition to the *A*-body-person, and certainly those two are not the same person.

But in situation (*vi*), we seemed to think, that is finally what he is. But if A's original fears could reach through the expected changes in (v), as they did in (iv) and (iii), then certainly they can reach through in (vi). Indeed, from the point of view of A's expectations and fears, there is less difference between (vi) and (v) than there is between (v) and (iv) or between (iv) and (iii). In those transitions, there were at least differences —though we could not see that they were really relevant differences—in the content and cause of what happened to him; in the present case there is absolutely no difference at all in what happens to him, the only difference being in what happens to someone else. If he can fear pain when (v) is predicted, why should he cease to when (vi) is?

I can see only one way of relevantly laying great weight on the transition from (v) to (vi); and this involves a considerable difficulty. This is to deny that, as I put it, the transition from (v) to (vi) involves merely the addition of something happening to *somebody else*; what rather it does, it will be said, is to involve the reintroduction of A himself, as the B-body-person; since he has reappeared in this form, it is for this person, and not for the unfortunate A-body-person, that A will have his expectations. This is to reassert, in effect, the viewpoint emphasized in our first presentation of the experiment. But this surely has the consequence that A should not have fears for the A-body-person who appeared in situation (v). For by the present argument, the A-body-person in (vi) is not A; the B-body-person is. But the A-body-person in (v) is, in character, history, everything, exactly the same as the A-body-person in (vi); so if the latter is not A, then neither is the former. (It is this point, no doubt, that encourages one to speak of the difference that goes with [vi] as being, on the present view; the *reintroduction* of A.) But no one else in (v) has any better claim to be A. So in (v), it seems, A just does not exist. This would certainly explain why A should have no fears for the state of things in (v)— though he might well have fears for the path to it. But it rather looked earlier as though he could well have fears for the state of things in (v). Let us grant, however, that that was an illusion, and that A really does not exist in (v); then does he exist in (iv), (iii), (ii), or (i)? It seems very difficult to deny it for (i) and (ii); are we perhaps to draw the line between (iii) and (iv)?

Here someone will say: you must not insist on drawing a line—borderline cases are borderline cases, and you must not push our concepts beyond their limits. But this well-known piece of advice, sensible as it is in many cases, seems in the present case to involve an extraordinary difficulty. It may intellectually comfort observers of A's situation; but what is A supposed to make of it? To be told that a future situation is a borderline one for its being myself that is hurt, that it is conceptually undecidable whether it will be me or not, is something which, it seems, I can do nothing with; because, in particular, it seems to have no comprehensible representation in my expectations and the emotions that go with them.

If I expect that a certain situation, S, will come about in the future, there is of course a wide range of emotions and concerns, directed on S, which I may experience now in relation to my expectation. Unless I am exceptionally egoistic, it is not a condition on my being concerned in relation to this expectation, that I myself will be involved in S—where my being "involved" in S means that I figure in S as someone doing something at that time or having something done to me, or, again, that S will have consequences affecting me at that or some subsequent time. There are some emotions, however, which I will feel only if I will be involved in S, and fear is an obvious example.

Now the description of S under which it figures in my expectations will necessarily be, in various ways, indeterminate; and one way in which it may be indeterminate is that it leave open whether I shall be involved in S or not. Thus I may have good reason to expect that one out of us five is going to get hurt, but no reason to expect it to be me rather than one of the others. My present emotions will be correspondingly affected by this indeterminacy. Thus, sticking to the egoistic concern involved in fear, I shall presumably be somewhat more cheerful than if I knew it was going to be me, somewhat less cheerful than if I had been left out altogether. Fear will be mixed with, and qualified by, apprehension; and so forth. These emotions revolve around the thought of the eventual determination of the indeterminacy; moments of straight fear focus on its really turning out to be me, of hope on its turning out not to be me.

All the emotions are related to the coming about of what I expect: and what I expect in such a case just cannot come about save by coming about in one of the ways or another.

There are other ways in which indeterminate expectations can be related to fear. Thus I may expect (perhaps neurotically) that something nasty is going to happen to me, indeed expect that when it happens it will take some determinate form, but have no range, or no closed range, of candidates for the determinate form to rehearse in my present thought. Different from this would be the fear of something radically indeterminate—the fear (one might say) of a nameless horror. If somebody had such a fear, one could even say that he had, in a sense, a perfectly determinate expectation: if what he expects indeed comes about, there will be nothing more determinate to be said about it after the event than was said in the expectation. Both these cases of course are cases of *fear* because one thing that is fixed amid the indeterminacy is the belief that it is to me to which the things will happen.

Central to the expectation of S is the thought of what it will be like when it happens—thought which may be indeterminate, range over alternatives, and so forth. When S involves me, there can be the possibility of a special form of such thought: the thought of how it will be for me, the imaginative projection of myself as participant in S.[3]

I do not have to think about S in this way, when it involves me; but I may be able to. (It might be suggested that this possibility was even mirrored in the language, in the distinction between "expecting to be hurt" and "expecting that I shall be hurt"; but I am very doubtful about this point, which is in any case of no importance.)

Suppose now that there is an S with regard to which it is for conceptual reasons undecidable whether it involves me or not, as is proposed for the experimental situation by the line we are discussing. It is important that the expectation of S is not *indeterminate* in any of the ways we have just been considering. It is not like the nameless horror, since the fixed point of that case was that it was going to happen to the subject, and that made his state unequivocally fear. Nor is it like the expectation of the man who expects one of the five to be hurt; his fear was indeed equivocal, but its focus, and that of the expectation, was that when S came about, it would certainly come about in one way or the other. In the present case, fear (of the torture, that is to say, not of the initial experiment) seems neither appropriate, nor inappropriate, nor appropriately equivocal. Relatedly, the subject has an incurable difficulty about how he may think about S. If he engages in projective imaginative thinking (about how it will be for him), he implicitly answers the necessarily unanswerable question; if he thinks that he cannot engage in such thinking, it looks very much as if he also answers it, though in the opposite direction. Perhaps he must just refrain from such thinking; but is he just refraining from it, if it is incurably undecidable whether he can or cannot engage in it?

It may be said that all that these considerations can show is that fear, at any rate, does not get its proper footing in this case; but that there could be some other, more ambivalent, form of concern which would indeed be appropriate to this particular expectation, the expectation of the conceptually undecidable situation. There are, perhaps, analogous feelings that actually occur in actual situations. Thus material objects do occasionally undergo puzzling transformations which leave a conceptual shadow over their identity. Suppose I were sentimentally attached to an object to which this sort of thing then happened; then it might be that I could neither feel about it quite as I did originally, nor be totally indifferent to it, but would have some other and rather ambivalent feeling toward it. Similarly, it may be said, toward the prospective sufferer of pain, my identity relations with whom are conceptually shadowed, I can feel neither as I would if he were certainly me, nor as I would if he were certainly not, but rather some such ambivalent concern.

But this analogy does little to remove the most baffling aspect of the present case—an aspect which has already turned up in what was said about the subject's difficulty in thinking either projectively or non-projectively about the situation. For to regard the prospective pain-sufferer *just* like the transmogrified object of sentiment, and to conceive of my ambivalent distress about his future pain as just like ambivalent distress about some future damage to such an object, is of course to leave him and me clearly distinct from one another, and thus to displace the conceptual shadow from its proper place. I have to get nearer to him than that. But is there any nearer that I can get to him without expecting his pain? If there is, the analogy has not shown us it. We can certainly not get nearer by expecting, as it were, *ambivalent* pain; there is no place at all for that. There seems to be an obstinate bafflement to mirroring in my expectations a situation in which it is conceptually undecidable whether I occur.

The bafflement seems, moreover, to turn to plain absurdity if we move from conceptual undecidability to its close friend and neighbor, conventionalist decision. This comes out if we consider another description, overtly conventionalist, of the series of cases which occasioned the present discussion. This description would reject a point I relied on in an earlier argument —namely, that if we deny that the A-body-person in (vi) is A (because the B-body-person is), then we must deny that the A-body-person in (v) is A, since they are exactly the same. "No," it may be said, "this is just to assume that we say the same in different sorts of situations. No doubt when we have the very good candidate for being A—namely, the B-body-person —we call him A; but this does not mean that we should not call the A-body-person A in that other situation when we have no better candidate around. Different situations call for different descriptions." This line of talk is the sort of thing indeed appropriate to lawyers deciding the ownership of some property which has undergone some bewildering set of transformations; they just have to decide, and in each situation, let us suppose, it has got to go to somebody, on as reasonable grounds as the facts and the law admit. But as a line to deal with a person's fears or expectations about his own future, it seems to have no sense at all. If A's fears can extend to what will happen to the A-body-person in (v), I do not see how they can be rationally diverted from the fate of the exactly similar person in (vi) by his being told that someone would have a reason in the latter situation which he would not have in the former for deciding to call another person A.

Thus, to sum up, it looks as though there are two presen-

tations of the imagined experiment and the choice associated
with it, each of which carries conviction, and which lead to
contrary conclusions. The idea, moreover, that the situation
after the experiment is conceptually undecidable in the relevant
respect seems not to assist, but rather to increase, the puzzlement; while the idea (so often appealed to in these matters)
that it is conventionally decidable is even worse. Following from
all that, I am not in the least clear which option it would be
wise to take if one were presented with them before the experiment. I find that rather disturbing.

Whatever the puzzlement, there is one feature of the arguments which have led to it which is worth picking out, since it
runs counter to something which is, I think, often rather vaguely supposed. It is often recognized that there are "first-personal"
and "third-personal" aspects of questions about persons, and
that there are difficulties about the relations between them. It
is also recognized that "mentalistic" considerations (as we may
vaguely call them) and considerations of bodily continuity are
involved in questions of personal identity (which is not to say
that there are mentalistic and bodily criteria of personal identity). It is tempting to think that the two distinctions run in
parallel: roughly, that a first-personal approach concentrates
attention on mentalistic considerations, while a third-personal
approach emphasizes considerations of bodily continuity. The
present discussion is an illustration of exactly the opposite. The
first argument, which led to the "mentalistic" conclusion that
A and *B* would change bodies and that each person should
identify himself with the destination of his memories and character, was an argument entirely conducted in third-personal
terms. The second argument, which suggested the bodily continuity identification, concerned itself with the first-personal
issue of what *A* could expect. That this is so seems to me
(though I will not discuss it further here) of some significance.

I will end by suggesting one rather shaky way in which
one might approach a resolution of the problem, using only the
limited materials already available.

The apparently decisive arguments of the first presentation,
which suggested that *A* should identify himself with the *B*-body-
person, turned on the extreme neatness of the situation in satis-

fying, if any could, the description of "changing bodies." But this neatness is basically artificial; it is the product of the will of the experimenter to produce a situation which would naturally elicit, with minimum hesitation, that description. By the sorts of methods he employed, he could easily have left off earlier or gone on further. He could have stopped at situation (v), leaving B as he was; or he could have gone on and produced two persons each with A-like character and memories, as well as one or two with B-like characteristics. If he had done either of those, we should have been in yet greater difficulty about what to say; he just chose to make it as easy as possible for us to find something to say. Now if we had some model of ghostly persons in bodies, which were in some sense actually moved around by certain procedures, we could regard the neat experiment just as the *effective* experiment: the one method that really did result in the ghostly persons' changing places without being destroyed, dispersed, or whatever. But we cannot seriously use such a model. The experimenter has not in the sense of that model *induced* a change of bodies; he has rather produced the one situation out of a range of equally possible situations which we should be most disposed to call a change of bodies. As against this, the principle that one's fears can extend to future pain whatever psychological changes precede it seems positively straightforward. Perhaps, indeed, it is not; but we need to be shown what is wrong with it. Until we are shown what is wrong with it, we should perhaps decide that if we were the person A then, if we were to decide selfishly, we should pass the pain to the B-body-person. It would be risky: that there is room for the notion of a *risk* here is itself a major feature of the problem.

NOTES

1. Sydney S. Shoemaker, *Self-Knowledge and Self-Identity* (Ithaca, N. Y., 1963), p. 23 f.
2. This of course does not have to be the crucial question, but it seems one fair way of taking up the present objection.
3. For a more detailed treatment of issues related to this, see Bernard Williams, *Imagination and the Self,* British Academy (London, 1966); reprinted in P. F. Strawson, ed., *Studies in Thought and Action* (Oxford, 1968).

Derek Parfit

14

Personal Identity

We can, I think, describe cases in which, though we know the answer to every other question, we have no idea how to answer a question about personal identity. These cases are not covered by the criteria of personal identity that we actually use.

Do they present a problem?

It might be thought that they do not, because they could never occur. I suspect that some of them could. (Some, for instance, might become scientifically possible.) But I shall claim that even if they did they would present no problem.

My targets are two beliefs: one about the nature of personal identity, the other about its importance.

The first is that in these cases the question about identity must have an answer.

No one thinks this about, say, nations or machines. Our criteria for the identity of these do not cover certain cases. No one thinks that in these cases the questions "Is it the same nation?" or "Is it the same machine?" must have answers.

Some people believe that in this respect they are different. They agree that our criteria of personal identity do not cover certain cases, but they believe that the nature of their own identity through time is, somehow, such as to guarantee that in these cases questions about their identity must have answers. This belief might be expressed as follows: "Whatever happens

This article is reprinted from *The Philosophical Review,* vol. 80, no. 1 (January, 1971), by courtesy of the editor and of D. Parfit.

between now and any future time, either I shall still exist, or I shall not. Any future experience will either be *my* experience, or it will not."

This first belief—in the special nature of personal identity—has, I think, certain effects. It makes people assume that the principle of self-interest is more rationally compelling than any moral principle. And it makes them more depressed by the thought of aging and of death.

I cannot see how to disprove this first belief. I shall describe a problem case. But this can only make it seem implausible.

Another approach might be this. We might suggest that one cause of the belief is the projection of our emotions. When we imagine ourselves in a problem case, we do feel that the question "Would it be me?" must have an answer. But what we take to be a bafflement about a further fact may be only the bafflement of our concern.

I shall not pursue this suggestion here. But one cause of our concern is the belief which is my second target. This is that unless the question about identity has an answer, we cannot answer certain important questions (questions about such matters as survival, memory, and responsibility).

Against this second belief my claim will be this. Certain important questions do presuppose a question about personal identity. But they can be freed of this presupposition. And when they are, the question about identity has no importance.

I

We can start by considering the much discussed case of the man who, like an amoeba, divides.[2]

Wiggins has recently dramatized this case.[3] He first referred to the operation imagined by Shoemaker.[4] We suppose that my brain is transplanted into someone else's (brainless) body, and that the resulting person has my character and apparent memories of my life. Most of us would agree, after thought, that the resulting person is me. I shall here assume such agreement.[5]

Wiggins then imagined his own operation. My brain is divided, and each half is housed in a new body. Both resulting people have my character and apparent memories of my life.

What happens to me? There seem only three possibilities: (1) I do not survive; (2) I survive as one of the two people; (3) I survive as both.

The trouble with (1) is this. We agreed that I could survive if my brain were successfully transplanted. And people have in fact survived with half their brains destroyed. It seems to follow that I could survive if half my brain were successfully transplanted and the other half were destroyed. But if this is so, how could I *not* survive if the other half were also successfully transplanted? How could a double success be a failure?

We can move to the second description. Perhaps one success is the maximum score. Perhaps I shall be one of the resulting people.

The trouble here is that in Wiggins' case each half of my brain is exactly similar, and so, to start with, is each resulting person. So how can I survive as only one of the two people? What can make me one of them rather than the other?

It seems clear that both of these descriptions—that I do not survive, and that I survive as one of the people—are highly implausible. Those who have accepted them must have assumed that they were the only possible descriptions.

What about our third description: that I survive as both people?

It might be said, "If 'survive' implies identity, this description makes no sense—you cannot be two people. If it does not, the description is irrelevant to a problem about identity."

I shall later deny the second of these remarks. But there are ways of denying the first. We might say, "What we have called 'the two resulting people' are not two people. They are one person. I do survive Wiggins' operation. Its effect is to give me two bodies and a divided mind."

It would shorten my argument if this were absurd. But I do not think it is. It is worth showing why.

We can, I suggest, imagine a divided mind. We can imagine a man having two simultaneous experiences, in having each of which he is unaware of having the other.

We may not even need to imagine this. Certain actual cases, to which Wiggins referred, seem to be best described in these terms. These involve the cutting of the bridge between the hemispheres of the brain. The aim was to cure epilepsy. But the result appears to be, in the surgeon's words, the creation of "two separate spheres of consciousness,"[6] each of which controls one half of the patient's body. What is experienced in each is, presumably, experienced by the patient.

There are certain complications in these actual cases. So let us imagine a simpler case.

Suppose that the bridge between my hemispheres is brought under my voluntary control. This would enable me to disconnect my hemispheres as easily as if I were blinking. By doing this I would divide my mind. And we can suppose that when my mind is divided I can, in each half, bring about reunion.

This ability would have obvious uses. To give an example: I am near the end of a maths exam, and see two ways of tackling the last problem. I decide to divide my mind, to work, with each half, at one of two calculations, and then to reunite my mind and write a fair copy of the best result.

What shall I experience?

When I disconnect my hemispheres, my consciousness divides into two streams. But this division is not something that I experience. Each of my two streams of consciousness seems to have been striaghtforwardly continuous with my one stream of consciousness up to the moment of division. The only changes in each stream are the disappearance of half my visual field and the loss of sensation in, and control over, half my body.

Consider my experiences in what we can call my "right-handed" stream. I remember that I assigned my right hand to the longer calculation. This I now begin. In working at this calculation I can see, from the movements of my left hand, that I am also working at the other. But I am not aware of working at the other. So I might, in my right-handed stream, wonder how, in my left-handed stream, I am getting on.

My work is now over. I am about to reunite my mind. What should I, in each stream, expect? Simply that I shall suddenly seem to remember just having thought out two calculations, in thinking out each of which I was not aware of thinking out the other. This, I submit, we can imagine. And if my mind was divided, these memories are correct.

In describing this episode, I assumed that there were two

series of thoughts, and that they were both mine. If my two hands visibly wrote out two calculations, and if I claimed to remember two corresponding series of thoughts, this is surely what we should want to say.

If it is, then a person's mental history need not be like a canal, with only one channel. It could be like a river, with islands, and with separate streams.

To apply this to Wiggins' operation: we mentioned the view that it gives me two bodies and a divided mind. We cannot now call this absurd. But it is, I think, unsatisfactory.

There were two features of the case of the exam that made us want to say that only one person was involved. The mind was soon reunited, and there was only one body. If a mind was permanently divided and its halves developed in different ways, the point of speaking of one person would start to disappear. Wiggins' case, where there are also two bodies, seems to be over the borderline. After I have had his operation, the two "products" each have all the attributes of a person. They could live at opposite ends of the earth. (If they later met, they might even fail to recognize each other.) It would become intolerable to deny that they were different people.

Suppose we admit that they are different people. Could we still claim that I survived as both, using "survive" to imply identity?

We could. For we might suggest that two people could compose a third. We might say, "I do survive Wiggins' operation as two people. They can be different people, and yet be me, in just the way in which the Pope's three crowns are one crown."[7]

This is a possible way of giving sense to the claim that I survive as two different people, using "survive" to imply identity. But it keeps the language of identity only by changing the concept of a person. And there are obvious objections to this change.[8]

The alternative, for which I shall argue, is to give up the language of identity. We can suggest that I survive as two different people without implying that I am these people.

When I first mentioned this alternative, I mentioned this objection: "If your new way of talking does not imply identity, it cannot solve our problem. For that is about identity. The problem is that all the possible answers to the question about identity are highly implausible."

We can now answer this objection.

We can start by reminding ourselves that this is an objection only if we have one or both of the beliefs which I mentioned at the start of this paper.

The first was the belief that to any question about personal identity, in any describable case, there must be a true answer. For those with this belief, Wiggins' case is doubly perplexing. If all the possible answers are implausible, it is hard to decide which of them is true, and hard even to keep the belief that one of them must be true. If we give up this belief, as I think we should, these problems disappear. We shall then regard the case as like many others in which, for quite unpuzzling reasons, there *is* no answer to a question about identity. (Consider "Was England the same nation after 1066?")

Wiggins' case makes the first belief implausible. It also makes it trivial. For it undermines the second belief. This was the belief that important questions turn upon the question about identity. (It is worth pointing out that those who have only this second belief do not think that there must *be* an answer to this question, but rather that we must decide upon an answer.)

Against this second belief my claim is this. Certain questions do presuppose a question about personal identity. And because these questions *are* important, Wiggins' case does present a problem. But we cannot solve this problem by answering the question about identity. We can solve this problem only by taking these important questions and prizing them apart from the question about identity. After we have done this, the question about identity (though we might for the sake of neatness decide it) has no further interest.

Because there are several questions which presuppose identity, this claim will take some time to fill out.

We can first return to the question of survival. This is a special case, for survival does not so much presuppose the retaining of identity as seem equivalent to it. It is thus the general relation which we need to prize apart from identity. We can then consider particular relations, such as those involved in memory and intention.

"Will I survive?" seems, I said, equivalent to "Will there be some person alive who is the same person as me?"

If we treat these questions as equivalent, then the least unsatisfactory description of Wiggins' case is, I think, that I survive with two bodies and a divided mind.

Several writers have chosen to say that I am neither of the resulting people. Given our equivalence, this implies that I do not survive, and hence, presumably, that even if Wiggins' operation is not literally death, I ought, since I will not survive it, to regard it *as* death. But this seemed absurd.

It is worth repeating why. An emotion or attitude can be criticized for resting on a false belief, or for being inconsistent. A man who regarded Wiggins' operation as death must, I suggest, be open to one of these criticisms.

He might believe that his relation to each of the resulting people fails to contain some element which is contained in survival. But how can this be true? We agreed that he *would* survive if he stood in this very same relation to only *one* of the resulting people. So it cannot be the nature of this relation which makes it fail, in Wiggins' case, to be survival. It can only be its duplication.

Suppose that our man accepts this, but still regards division as death. His reaction would now seem wildly inconsistent. He would be like a man who, when told of a drug that could double his years of life, regarded the taking of this drug as death. The only difference in the case of division is that the extra years are to run concurrently. This is an interesting difference. But it cannot mean that there are *no* years to run.

I have argued this for those who think that there must, in Wiggins' case, be a true answer to the question about identity. For them, we might add, "Perhaps the original person does lose his identity. But there may be other ways to do this than to die. One other way might be to multiply. To regard these as the same is to confuse nought with two."

For those who think that the question of identity is up for decision, it would be clearly absurd to regard Wiggins' operation as death. These people would have to think, "We could have chosen to say that I should be one of the resulting people. If we had, I should not have regarded it as death. But since we have chosen to say that I am neither person, I *do.*" This is hard even to understand.[9]

My first conclusion, then, is this. The relation of the original person to each of the resulting people contains all that interests us—all that matters—in any ordinary case of survival. This is why we need a sense in which one person can survive as two.[10]

One of my aims in the rest of this paper will be to suggest such a sense. But we can first make some general remarks.

II

Identity is a one-one relation. Wiggins' case serves to show that what matters in survival need not be one-one.

Wiggins' case is of course unlikely to occur. The relations which matter are, in fact, one-one. It is because they are that we can imply the holding of these relations by using the language of identity.

This use of language is convenient. But it can lead us astray. We may assume that what matters *is* identity and, hence, has the properties of identity.

In the case of the property of being one-one, this mistake is not serious. For what matters is in fact one-one. But in the case of another property, the mistake *is* serious. Identity is all-or-nothing. Most of the relations which matter in survival are, in fact, relations of degree. If we ignore this, we shall be led into quite ill-grounded attitudes and beliefs.

The claim that I have just made—that most of what matters are relations of degree—I have yet to support. Wiggins' case shows only that these relations need not be one-one. The merit of the case is not that it shows this in particular, but that it makes the first break between what matters and identity. The belief that identity *is* what matters is hard to overcome. This is shown in most discussions of the problem cases which actually occur: cases, say, of amnesia or of brain damage. Once Wiggins' case has made one breach in this belief, the rest should be easier to remove.[11]

To turn to a recent debate: most of the relations which matter can be provisionally referred to under the heading "psychological continuity" (which includes causal continuity). My claim is thus that we use the language of personal identity in order to imply such continuity. This is close to the view that psychological continuity provides a criterion of identity.

Williams has attacked this view with the following argument. Identity is a one-one relation. So any criterion of identity must appeal to a relation which is logically one-one. Psychological continuity is not logically one-one. So it cannot provide a criterion.[12]

Some writers have replied that it is enough if the relation appealed to is always in fact one-one.[13]

I suggest a slightly different reply. Psychological continuity is a ground for speaking of identity when it is one-one.

If psychological continuity took a one-many or branching form, we should need, I have argued, to abandon the language of identity. So this possibility would not count against this view.

We can make a stronger claim. This possibility would count in its favor.

The view might be defended as follows. Judgments of personal identity have great importance. What gives them their importance is the fact that they imply psychological continuity. This is why, whenever there is such continuity, we ought, if we can, to imply it by making a judgment of identity.

If psychological continuity took a branching form, no coherent set of judgments of identity could correspond to, and thus be used to imply, the branching form of this relation. But what we ought to do, in such a case, is take the importance which would attach to a judgment of identity and attach this importance directly to each limb of the branching relation. So this case helps to show that judgments of personal identity do derive their importance from the fact that they imply psychological continuity. It helps to show that when we can, usefully, speak of identity, this relation is our ground.

This argument appeals to a principle which Williams put forward.[14] The principle is that an important judgment should be asserted and denied only on importantly different grounds.

Williams applied this principle to a case in which one man is psychologically continuous with the dead Guy Fawkes, and a case in which two men are. His argument was this. If we treat psychological continuity as a sufficient ground for speaking of identity, we shall say that the one man is Guy Fawkes. But we could not say that the two men are, although we should have the same ground. This disobeys the principle. The remedy is to deny that the one man is Guy Fawkes, to insist that sameness of the body is necessary for identity.

Williams' principle can yield a different answer. Suppose we regard psychological continuity as more important than sameness of the body.[15] And suppose that the one man really is psychologically (and causally) continuous with Guy Fawkes. If he is, it would disobey the principle to deny that he is Guy Fawkes, for we have the same important ground as in a normal case of identity. In the case of the two men, we again have the same important ground. So we ought to take the importance from the judgment of identity and attach it directly to this ground. We ought to say, as in Wiggins' case, that each limb of the branching relation is as good as survival. This obeys the principle.

To sum up these remarks: even if psychological continuity is neither logically, nor always in fact, one-one, it can provide a criterion of identity. For this can appeal to the relation of *nonbranching* psychological continuity, which is logically one-one.[16]

The criterion might be sketched as follows. "X and Y are the same person if they are psychologically continuous and there is no person who is contemporary with either and psychologically continuous with the other." We should need to explain what we mean by "psychologically continuous" and say how much continuity the criterion requires. We should then, I think, have described a sufficient condition for speaking of identity.[17]

We need to say something more. If we admit that psychological continuity might not be one-one, we need to say what we ought to do if it were not one-one. Otherwise our account would be open to the objections that it is incomplete and arbitrary.[18]

I have suggested that if psychological continuity took a branching form, we ought to speak in a new way, regarding what we describe as having the same significance as identity. This answers these objections.[19]

We can now return to our discussion. We have three remaining aims. One is to suggest a sense of "survive" which does not imply identity. Another is to show that most of what matters in survival are relations of degree. A third is to show that none of these relations needs to be described in a way that presupposes identity.

We can take these aims in the reverse order.

III

The most important particular relation is that involved in memory. This is because it is so easy to believe that its description must refer to identity.[20] This belief about memory is an important cause of the view that personal identity has a special nature. But it has been well discussed by Shoemaker[21] and by Wiggins.[22] So we can be brief.

It may be a logical truth that we can only remember our own experiences. But we can frame a new concept for which this is not a logical truth. Let us call this "q-memory."

To sketch a definition[23] I am q-remembering an experience if (1) I have a belief about a past experience which seems in itself like a memory belief, (2) someone did have such an experience, and (3) my belief is dependent upon this experience in the same way (whatever that is) in which a memory of an experience is dependent upon it.

According to (1) q-memories seem like memories. So I q-remember *having* experiences.

This may seem to make q-memory presuppose identity. One might say, "My apparent memory of *having* an experience is an apparent memory of *my* having an experience. So how could I q-remember my having other people's experiences?"

This objection rests on a mistake. When I seem to remember an experience, I do indeed seem to remember *having* it.[24] But it cannot be a part of what I seem to remember about this experience that I, the person who now seems to remember it, am the person who had this experience.[25] That I am is something that I automatically assume. (My apparent memories sometimes come to me simply as the belief that *I* had a certain experience.) But it is something that I am justified in assuming only because I do not in fact have q-memories of other people's experiences.

Suppose that I did start to have such q-memories. If I did, I should cease to assume that my apparent memories must be about my own experiences. I should come to assess an apparent memory by asking two questions: (1) Does it tell me about a past experience? (2) If so, whose?

Moreover (and this is a crucial point) my apparent memories would now come to me *as* q-memories. Consider those of my apparent memories which do come to me simply as beliefs about my past: for example, "I did that." If I knew that I could q-remember other people's experiences, these beliefs would come to me in a more guarded form: for example, "Someone— probably I—did that." I might have to work out who it was.

I have suggested that the concept of q-memory is coherent. Wiggins' case provides an illustration. The resulting people, in his case, both have apparent memories of living the life of the original person. If they agree that they are not this person, they will have to regard these as only q-memories. And when they are asked a question like "Have you heard this music before?" they might have to answer "I am sure that I q-remember hearing it. But I am not sure whether I remember hearing it. I am not sure whether it was I who heard it, or the original person."

We can next point out that on our definition every memory is also a q-memory. Memories are, simply, q-memories of one's own experiences. Since this is so, we could afford now to drop the concept of memory and use in its place the wider concept q-memory. If we did, we should describe the relation between an experience and what we now call a "memory" of this experience in a way which does not presuppose that they are had by the same person.[26]

This way of describing this relation has certain merits. It vindicates the "memory criterion" of personal identity against the charge of circularity.[27] And it might, I think, help with the problem of other minds.

But we must move on. We can next take the relation between an intention and a later action. It may be a logical truth that we can intend to perform only our own actions. But intentions can be redescribed as q-intentions. And one person could q-intend to perform another person's actions.

Wiggins' case again provides the illustration. We are supposing that neither of the resulting people is the original person. If so, we shall have to agree that the original person can, before the operation, q-intend to perform their actions. He might, for example, q-intend, as one of them, to continue his present career, and, as the other, to try something new.[28] (I say "q-intend *as* one of them" because the phrase "q-intend that one of them" would not convey the directness of the relation which is involved. If I intend that someone else should do something, I cannot get him to do it simply by forming this intention. But if I am the original person, and he is one of the resulting people, I can.)

The phrase "q-intend *as* one of them" reminds us that we need a sense in which one person can survive as two. But we can first point out that the concepts of q-memory and q-intention give us our model for the others that we need: thus, a man who can q-remember could q-recognize, and be a q-witness of, what he has never seen; and a man who can q-intend could have q-ambitions, make q-promises, and be q-responsible for.

To put this claim in general terms: many different relations are included within, or are a consequence of, psychological continuity. We describe these relations in ways which presuppose the continued existence of one person. But we could describe them in new ways which do not.

This suggests a bolder claim. It might be possible to think of experiences in a wholly "impersonal" way. I shall not develop this claim here. What I shall try to describe is a way of thinking of our own identity through time which is more flexible, and less misleading, than the way in which we now think.

This way of thinking will allow for a sense in which one person can survive as two. A more important feature is that it treats survival as a matter of degree.

IV

We must first show the need for this second feature. I shall use two imaginary examples.

The first is the converse of Wiggins' case: fusion. Just as division serves to show that what matters in survival need not be one-one, so fusion serves to show that it can be a question of degree.

Physically, fusion is easy to describe. Two people come together. While they are unconscious, their two bodies grow into one. One person then wakes up.

The psychology of fusion is more complex. One detail we have already dealt with in the case of the exam. When my mind was reunited, I remembered just having thought out two calculations. The one person who results from a fusion can, similarly, q-remember living the lives of the two original people. None of their q-memories need be lost.

But some things must be lost. For any two people who fuse together will have different characteristics, different desires, and different intentions. How can these be combined?

We might suggest the following. Some of these will be compatible. These can coexist in the one resulting person. Some will be incompatible. These, if of equal strength, can cancel out, and if of different strengths, the stronger can be made weaker. And all these effects might be predictable.

To give examples—first, of compatibility: I like Palladio and intend to visit Venice. I am about to fuse with a person who likes Giotto and intends to visit Padua. I can know that the one person we shall become will have both tastes and both intentions. Second, of incompatibility: I hate red hair, and always vote Labour. The other person loves red hair, and always votes Conservative. I can know that the one person we shall become will be indifferent to red hair, and a floating voter.

If we were about to undergo a fusion of this kind, would we regard it as death?

Some of us might. This is less absurd than regarding division as death. For after my division the two resulting people will be in every way like me, while after my fusion the one resulting person will not be wholly similar. This makes it easier to say, when faced with fusion, "I shall not survive," thus continuing to regard survival as a matter of all-or-nothing.

This reaction is less absurd. But here are two analogies which tell against it.

First, fusion would involve the changing of some of our characteristics and some of our desires. But only the very self-satisfied would think of this as death. Many people welcome treatments with these effects.

Second, someone who is about to fuse can have, before-hand, just as much "intentional control" over the actions of the resulting individual as someone who is about to marry can have, beforehand, over the actions of the resulting couple. And the choice of a partner for fusion can be just as well considered as the choice of a marriage partner. The two original people can make sure (perhaps by "trial fusion") that they do have compatible characters, desires, and intentions.

I have suggested that fusion, while not clearly survival, is not clearly failure to survive, and hence that what matters in survival can have degrees.

To reinforce this claim we can now turn to a second example. This is provided by certain imaginary beings. These beings are just like ourselves except that they reproduce by a process of natural division.

We can illustrate the histories of these imagined beings with the aid of a diagram. The lines on the diagram represent the spatiotemporal paths which would be traced out by the bodies of these beings. We can call each single line (like the double line) a "branch"; and we can call the whole structure a "tree." And let us suppose that each "branch" corresponds to what is thought of as the life of one individual. These individuals are

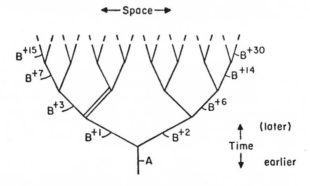

referred to as "A," "B+1," and so forth.

Now, each single division is an instance of Wiggins' case. So A's relation to both B+1 and B+2 is just as good as survival. But what of A's relation to B+30?

I said earlier that what matters in survival could be provisionally referred to as "psychological continuity." I must now distinguish this relation from another, which I shall call "psychochological connectedness."

Let us say that the relation between a q-memory and the experience q-remembered is a "direct" relation. Another "direct" relation is that which holds between a q-intention and the q-intended action. A third is that which holds between different expressions of some lasting q-characteristic.

"Psychological connectedness," as I define it, requires the holding of these direct psychological relations. "Connectedness" is not transitive, since these relations are not transitive. Thus, if X q-remembers most of Y's life, and Y q-remembers most of Z's life, it does not follow that X q-remembers most of Z's life. And if X carries out the q-intentions of Y, and Y carries out the q-intentions of Z, it does not follow that X carries out the q-intentions of Z.

"Psychological continuity," in contrast, only requires overlapping chains of direct psychological relations. So "continuity" is transitive.

To return to our diagram. A is psychologically continuous with B+30. There are between the two continuous chains of overlapping relations. Thus, A has q-intentional control over B+2, B+2 has q-intentional control over B+6, and so on up to B+30. Or B+30 can q-remember the life of B+14, B+14 can q-remember the life of B+6, and so on back to A.[29]

A, however, need *not* be psychologically connected to B+30. Connectedness requires direct relations. And if these beings are like us, A cannot stand in such relations to every individual in his indefinitely long "tree." Q-memories will weaken with the passage of time, and then fade away. Q-ambitions, once fulfilled, will be replaced by others. Q-characteristics will gradually change. In general, A stands in fewer and fewer direct psychological relations to an individual in his "tree" the more remote that individual is. And if the individual is (like B+30) sufficiently remote, there may be between the two *no* direct psychological relations.

Now that we have distinguished the general relations of psychological continuity and psychological connectedness, I suggest that connectedness is a more important element in survival. As a claim about our own survival, this would need more arguments than I have space to give. But it seems clearly true for my imagined beings. A is as close psychologically to B+1 as I today am to myself tomorrow. A is as distant from B+30 as I am from my great-great-grandson.

Even if connectedness is not more important than continuity, the fact that one of these is a relation of degree is enough to show that what matters in survival can have degrees. And in any case the two relations are quite different. So our imagined beings would need a way of thinking in which this difference is recognized.

V

What I propose is this.

First, A can think of any individual, anywhere in his "tree," as "a descendant self." This phrase implies psychological continuity. Similarly, any later individual can think of any earlier individual on the single path[30] which connects him to A as "an ancestral self."

Since psychological continuity is transitive, "being an ancestral self of" and "being a descendant self of" are also transitive.

To imply psychological connectedness I suggest the phrases "one of my future selves" and "one of my past selves."

These are the phrases with which we can describe Wiggins' case. For having past and future selves is, what we needed, a way of continuing to exist which does not imply identity through time. The original person does, in this sense, survive Wiggins' operation: the two resulting people are his later selves. And they can each refer to him as "my past self." (They can share a past self without being the same self as each other.)

Since psychological connectedness is not transitive, and is a matter of degree, the relations "being a past self of" and "being a future self of" should themselves be treated as relations of degree. We allow for this series of descriptions: "my most recent self," "one of my earlier selves," "one of my distant selves," "hardly one of *my* past selves (I can only *q*-remember a few of his experiences)," and, finally, "not in any way one of *my* past selves—just an ancestral self."

This way of thinking would clearly suit our first imagined beings. But let us now turn to a second kind of being. These reproduce by fusion as well as by division.[31] And let us suppose that they fuse every autumn and divide every spring. This yields the following diagram:

If A is the individual whose life is represented by the three-lined "branch," the two-lined "tree" represents those lives which are psychologically continuous with A's life. (It can be seen that each individual has his own "tree," which overlaps with many others.)

For the imagined beings in this second world, the phrases "an ancestral self" and "a descendant self" would cover too much to be of much use. (There may well be pairs of dates such that every individual who ever lived before the first date was an ancestral self of every individual who ever will live after the second date.) Conversely, since the lives of each individual last for only half a year, the word "I" would cover too little to do all of the work which it does for us. So part of this work would have to be done, for these second beings, by talk about past and future selves.

We can now point out a theoretical flaw in our proposed way of thinking. The phrase "a past self of" implies psychological connectedness. Being a past self of is treated as a relation of degree, so that this phrase can be used to imply the varying degrees of psychological connectedness. But this phrase can imply only the degrees of connectedness between different lives. It cannot be used within a single life. And our way of delimiting successive lives does not refer to the degrees of psychological connectedness. Hence there is no guarantee that this phrase, "a past self of," could be used whenever it was needed. There is no guarantee that psychological connectedness will not vary in degree within a single life.

This flaw would not concern our imagined beings. For they divide and unite so frequently, and their lives are in consequence so short, that within a single life psychological connectedness would always stand at a maximum.

But let us look, finally, at a third kind of being.

In this world there is neither division nor union. There are a number of everlasting bodies, which gradually change in appearance. And direct psychological relations, as before, hold only over limited periods of time. This can be illustrated with a third diagram (which is found below). In this diagram the two shadings represent the degrees of psychological connectedness to their two central points.

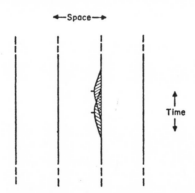

These beings could not use the way of thinking that we have proposed. Since there is no branching of psychological continuity, they would have to regard themselves as immortal. It might be said that this is what they are. But there is, I suggest, a better description.

Our beings would have one reason for thinking of themselves as immortal. The parts of each "line" are all psychologically continuous. But the parts of each "line" are not all psychologically connected. Direct psychological relations hold only between those parts which are close to each other in time. This gives our beings a reason for *not* thinking of each "line" as corresponding to one single life. For if they did, they would have no way of implying these direct relations. When a speaker says, for example, "I spent a period doing such and such," his hearers would not be entitled to assume that the speaker has any memories of this period, that his character then and now are in any way similar, that he is now carrying out any of the plans or intentions which he then had, and so forth. Because the word "I" would carry none of these implications, it would not have for these "immortal" beings the usefulness which it has for us.[32]

To gain a better way of thinking, we must revise the way of thinking that we proposed above. The revision is this. The distinction between successive selves can be made by reference, not to the branching of psychological continuity, but to the degrees of psychological connectedness. Since this connectedness is a matter of degree, the drawing of these distinctions can be left to the choice of the speaker and be allowed to vary from context to context.

On this way of thinking, the word "I" can be used to imply the greatest degree of psychological connectedness. When the connections are reduced, when there has been any marked change of character or style of life, or any marked loss of memory, our imagined beings would say, "It was not I who did that, but an earlier self." They could then describe in what ways, and to what degree, they are related to this earlier self.

This revised way of thinking would suit not only our "immortal" beings. It is also the way in which we ourselves could think about our lives. And it is, I suggest, surprisingly natural.

One of its features, the distinction between successive selves, has already been used by several writers. To give an example, from Proust: "we are incapable, while we are in love, of acting as fit predecessors of the next persons who, when we are in love no longer, we shall presently have become. . . ."[33]

Although Proust distinguished between successive selves, he still thought of one person as being these different selves. This we would not do on the way of thinking that I propose. If I say, "It will not be me, but one of my future selves," I do not imply that I will be that future self. He is one of my later selves, and I am one of his earlier selves. There is no underlying person who we both are.

To point out another feature of this way of thinking. When I say, "There is no person who we both are," I am only giving my decision. Another person could say, "It will be you," thus deciding differently. There is no question of either of these decisions being a mistake. Whether to say "I," or "one of my future selves," or "a descendant self" is entirely a matter of choice. The matter of fact, which must be agreed, is only whether the disjunction applies. (The question "Are X and Y the same person?" thus becomes "Is X *at least* an ancestral [or descendant] self of Y?")

VI

I have tried to show that what matters in the continued existence of a person are, for the most part, relations of degree. And I have proposed a way of thinking in which this would be recognized.

I shall end by suggesting two consequences and asking one question.

It is sometimes thought to be especially rational to act in our own best interests. But I suggest that the principle of self-interest has no force. There are only two genuine competitors in this particular field. One is the principle of biased rationality: do what will best achieve what you actually want. The other is the principle of impartiality: do what is in the best interests of everyone concerned.

The apparent force of the principle of self-interest derives, I think, from these two other principles.

The principle of self-interest is normally supported by the principle of biased rationality. This is because most people care about their own future interests.

Suppose that this prop is lacking. Suppose that a man does not care what happens to him in, say, the more distant future. To such a man, the principle of self-interest can only be propped up by an appeal to the principle of impartiality. We must say,

"Even if you don't care, you ought to take what happens to you then equally into account." But for this, as a special claim, there seem to me no good arguments. It can only be supported as part of the general claim, "You ought to take what happens to everyone equally into account."[34]

The special claim tells a man to grant an *equal* weight to all the parts of his future. The argument for this can only be that all the parts of his future are *equally* parts of *his* future. This is true. But it is a truth too superficial to bear the weight of the argument. (To give an analogy: The unity of a nation is, in its nature, a matter of degree. It is therefore only a superficial truth that all of a man's compatriots are *equally* his compatriots. This truth cannot support a good argument for nationalism.)[35]

I have suggested that the principle of self-interest has no strength of its own. If this is so, there is no special problem in the fact that what we ought to do can be against our interests. There is only the general problem that it may not be what we want to do.

The second consequence which I shall mention is implied in the first. Egoism, the fear not of near but of distant death, the regret that so much of one's *only* life should have gone by—these are not, I think, wholly natural or instinctive. They are all strengthened by the beliefs about personal identity which I have been attacking. If we give up these beliefs, they should be weakened.

My final question is this. These emotions are bad, and if we weaken them we gain. But can we achieve this gain without, say, also weakening loyalty to, or love of, other particular selves? As Hume warned, the "refined reflections which philosophy suggests . . . cannot diminish . . . our vicious passions . . . without diminishing . . . such as are virtuous. They are . . . applicable to all our affections. In vain do we hope to direct their influence only to one side."[36]

That hope *is* vain. But Hume had another: that more of what is bad depends upon false belief. This is also my hope.

NOTES

1. I have been helped in writing this by D. Wiggins, D. F. Pears, P. F. Strawson, A. J. Ayer, M. Woods, N. Newman, and (through his publications) S. Shoemaker.

2. Implicit in John Locke, *Essay Concerning Human Understanding*, ed. by John W. Yolton, vol. 2, chap. 27, sec. 18 (London, 1961) and discussed by (among others) A. N. Prior in "Opposite Number," *Review of Metaphysics*, 11 (1957-1958), and "Time, Existence and Identity," *Proceedings of the Aristotelian Society*, vol. 57 (1965-1966); J. Bennett in "The Simplicity of the Soul," *Journal of Philosophy*, vol. 64 (1967); and R. Chisholm and S. Shoemaker in "The Loose and Popular and the Strict and the Philosophical Senses of Identity," in *Perception and Personal Identity: Proceeding of the 1967 Oberlin Colloquium in Philosophy*, ed. Norman Care and Robert H. Grimm (Cleveland, 1967).

3. David Wiggins, *Identity and Spatio-Temporal Continuity* (Oxford, 1967), p. 50.

4. Sydney S. Shoemaker, *Self-Knowledge and Self-Identity* (Ithaca, N. Y., 1963), p. 22.

5. Those who would disagree are not making a mistake. For them my argument would need a different case. There must be some multiple transplant, faced with which these people would both find it hard to believe that there must be an answer to the question about personal identity, and be able to be shown that nothing of importance turns upon this question.

6. R. W. Sperry, in *Brain and Conscious Experience,* ed. J. C. Eccles (New York, 1966), p. 299.

7. Cf. David Wiggins, *op. cit,* p. 40.

8. Suppose the resulting people fight a duel. Are there three people fighting, one on each side, and one on both? And suppose one of the bullets kills. Are there two acts, one murder and one suicide? How many people are left alive? One? Two? (We could hardly say, "One and a half.") We could talk in this way. But instead of saying that the resulting people are the original person—so that the pair is a trio—it would be far simpler to treat them as a pair, and describe their relation to the original person in some new way. (I owe this suggested way of talking, and the objections to it, to Michael Woods.)

9. Cf. Sydney Shoemaker, in *Perception and Personal Identity,* p. 54.

10. Cf. David Wiggins, *op. cit.*

11. Bernard Williams' "The Self and the Future," *Philosophical Review,* 79 (1970), 161-180, is relevant here. He asks the question "Shall I survive?" in a range of problem cases, and he shows how natural it is to believe (1) that this question must have an answer, (2) that the answer must be all-or-nothing, and (3) that there is a "risk" of our reaching the wrong answer. Because these beliefs are so natural, we should need in undermining them to discuss their causes. These, I think, can be found in the ways in which we misinterpret what it is to remember (cf. Sec.III below) and to anticipate (cf. Williams' "Imagination and the Self," *Proceedings of the British Academy*, 52 [1966], 105-124); and also in the way in which certain features of our egoistic concern—e.g., that it is simple, and applies to all imagin-

able cases—are "projected" onto its object. (For another relevant discussion, see Terence Penelhum's *Survival and Disembodied Existence* [London, 1970], final chapters.)

12. "Personal Identity and Individuation," *Proceedings of the Aristotelian Society*, 57 (1956-1957), 229-253; also *Analysis*, 21 (1960-1961), 43-48.

13. J. M. Shorter, "More about Bodily Continuity and Personal Identity," *Analysis*, 22 (1961-1962), 79-85; and Mrs. J. M. R. Jack (unpublished), who requires that this truth be embedded in a causal theory.

14. *Analysis*, 21 (1960-1961), 44.

15. For the reasons given by A. M. Quinton in "The Soul," *Journal of Philosophy*, 59 (1962), 393-409.

16. Cf. S. Shoemaker, "Persons and Their Pasts," *American Philosophical Quarterly*, 7 (1970), 269; and "Wiggins on Identity," *Philosophical Review*, 79 (1970), 542.

17. But not a necessary condition, for in the absence of psychological continuity bodily identity might be sufficient.

18. Cf. Bernard Williams, "Personal Identity and Individuation," *Proceedings of the Aristotelian Society*, 57 (1956-1957), 240-241, and *Analysis*, 21 (1960-1961), 44; and also Wiggins, *op. cit.*, p. 38: "if coincidence under [the concept] f is to be *genuinely* sufficient we must not withhold identity . . . simply because transitivity is threatened."

19. Williams produced another objection to the "psychological criterion," that it makes it hard to explain the difference between the concepts of identity and exact similarity (*Analysis*, 21 [1960-1961], 48). But if we include the requirement of causal continuity we avoid this objection (and one of those produced by Wiggins in his note 47).

20. Those philosophers who have held this belief, from Butler onward, are too numerous to cite.

21. *Op. cit.*

22. In a paper on Butler's objection to Locke (not yet published).

23. I here follow Shoemaker's "quasi-memory." Cf. also Penelhum's "retrocognition," in his article on "Personal Identity," in the *Encyclopedia of Philosophy*, ed. Paul Edwards.

24. As Shoemaker put it, I seem to remember the experience "from the inside" (*op. cit.*).

25. This is what so many writers have overlooked. Cf. Thomas Reid: "My memory testifies not only that this was done, but that it was done by me who now remember it" ("Of Identity," in *Essays on the Intellectual Powers of Man*, ed. A. D. Woozley [London, 1941], p. 203). This mistake is discussed by A. B. Palma in "Memory and Personal Identity," *Australasian Journal of Philosophy*, 42 (1964), 57.

26. It is not logically necessary that we only q-remember our own experiences. But it might be necessary on other grounds. This possibility is intriguingly explored by Shoemaker in his "Persons and Their Pasts" (*op. cit.*). He shows that q-memories can provide a knowledge of the world only if the observations which are q-remembered trace out fairly continuous spatiotemporal paths. If the observations which are q-remembered traced out a network of frequently interlocking paths, they could not, I think, be usefully ascribed to persisting observers, but would have to be referred to in some more complex way. But in fact the observations which

are q-remembered trace out single and separate paths; so we can ascribe them to ourselves. In other words, it is epistemologically necessary that the observations which are q-remembered should satisfy a certain general condition, one particular form of which allows them to be usefully self-ascribed.

27. Cf. Wiggins' paper on Butler's objection to Locke.

28. There are complications here. He could form *divergent* q-intentions only if he could distinguish, in advance, between the resulting people (e.g., as "the left-hander" and "the right-hander"). And he could be confident that such divergent q-intentions would be carried out only if he had reason to believe that neither of the resulting people would change their (inherited) mind. Suppose he was torn between duty and desire. He could not solve this dilemma by q-intending, as one of the resulting people, to do his duty, and, as the other, to do what he desires. For the one he q-intended to do his duty would face the same dilemma.

29. The chain of continuity must run in one direction of time. B+2 is not, in the sense I intend, psychologically continuous with B+1.

30. Cf. David Wiggins, *op. cit.*

31. Cf. Sydney Shoemaker in "Persons and Their Pasts," *op. cit.*

32. Cf. Austin Duncan Jones, "Man's Mortality," *Analysis,* 28 (1967-1968), 65-70.

33. *Within a Budding Grove* (London, 1949), I, 226 (my own translation).

34. Cf. Thomas Nagel's *The Possibility of Altruism* (Oxford, 1970), in which the special claim is in effect defended as part of the general claim.

35. The unity of a nation we seldom take for more than what it is. This is partly because we often think of nations, not as units, but in a more complex way. If we thought of ourselves in the way that I proposed, we might be less likely to take our own identity for more than what it is. We are, for example, sometimes told, "It is irrational to act against your own interests. After all, it will be you who will regret it." To this we could reply, "No, not me. Not even one of my future selves. Just a descendant self."

36. "The Sceptic," in "Essays Moral, Political and Literary," *Humes's Moral and Political Philosophy* (New York, 1959), p. 349.

PART VI

THE UNITY OF
CONSCIOUSNESS

Thomas Nagel

15

Brain Bisection and
the Unity of Consciousness

I

There has been considerable optimism recently, among philosophers and neuroscientists, concerning the prospect for major
discoveries about the neurophysiological basis of mind. The
support for this optimism has been extremely abstract and general. I wish to present some grounds for pessimism. That type
of self-understanding may encounter limits which have not been
generally foreseen: the personal, mentalist idea of human beings
may resist the sort of coordination with an understanding of
humans as physical systems, that would be necessary to yield
anything describable as an understanding of the physical basis
of mind. I shall not consider what alternatives will be open to
us if we should encounter such limits. I shall try to present
grounds for believing that the limits may exist—grounds derived
from extensive data now available about the interaction between
the two halves of the cerebral cortex, and about what happens
when they are disconnected. The feature of the mentalist conception of persons which may be recalcitrant to integration with
these data is not a trivial or peripheral one, that might easily be
abandoned. It is the idea of a *single* person, a single subject of
experience and action, that is in difficulties. The difficulties
may be surmountable in ways I have not foreseen. On the other

This article is reprinted from *Synthese,* vol. 22 (1971), by courtesy of the
editor and Professor Nagel.

hand, this may be only the first of many dead ends that will emerge as we seek a physiological understanding of the mind.

To seek the physical basis or realization of features of the phenomenal world is in many areas a profitable first line of inquiry, and it is the line encouraged, for the case of mental phenomena, by those who look forward to some variety of empirical reduction of mind to brain, through an identity theory, a functionalist theory, or some other device. When physical reductionism is attempted for a phenomenal feature of the external world, the results are sometimes very successful, and can be pushed to deeper and deeper levels. If, on the other hand, they are not entirely successful, and certain features of the phenomenal picture remain unexplained by a physical reduction, then we can set those features aside as *purely* phenomenal, and postpone our understanding of them to the time when our knowledge of the physical basis of mind and perception will have advanced sufficiently to supply it. (An example of this might be the moon illusion, or other sensory illusions which have no discoverable basis in the objects perceived.)

However, if we encounter the same kind of difficulty in exploring the physical basis of the phenomena of the mind itself, we cannot adopt the same line of retreat. That is, if a phenomenal feature of mind is left unaccounted for by the physical theory, we cannot postpone the understanding of it to the time when we study the mind itself—for that is exactly what we are supposed to be doing. To defer to an understanding of the basis of mind which lies beyond the study of the physical realization of certain aspects of it is to admit the irreducibility of the mental to the physical. A clearcut version of this admission would be some kind of dualism. But if one is reluctant to take such a route, then it is not clear what one should do about central features of the mentalistic idea of persons which resist assimilation to an understanding of human beings as physical system. It may be true of some of these features that we can neither find an objective basis for them, nor give them up. It may be impossible for us to abandon certain ways of conceiving and representing ourselves, no matter how little support they get from scientific research. This, I suspect, is true of the idea of the unity of a person: an idea whose validity may be called into question with the help of recent discoveries about the functional duality of the cerebral cortex. It will be useful to present those results here in outline.

II

The higher connections between the two cerebral hemispheres have been severed in men, monkeys, and cats, and the results have led some investigators to speak of the creation of two separate centers of consciousness in a single body. The facts are as follows.[1]

By and large, the left cerebral hemisphere is associated with the right side of the body and the right hemisphere with the left side. Tactual stimuli from one side are transmitted to the opposite hemisphere—with the exception of the head and neck, which are connected to both sides. In addition, the left

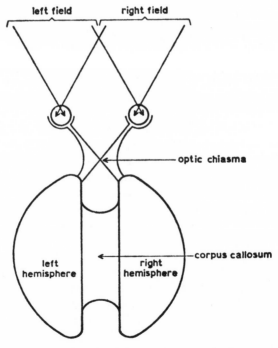

Fig. 1. A very schematic top view of the eyes and cerebral cortex.

half of each retina, i.e., that which scans the right half of the visual field, sends impulses to the left hemisphere, and impulses from the left half of the visual field are transmitted by the right half of each retina to the right hemisphere. Auditory impulses from each ear are to some degree transmitted to both hemispheres. Smells, on the other hand, are transmitted ipsilaterally: the left nostril transmits to the left hemisphere and the right nostril to the right. Finally, the left hemisphere usually controls the production of speech.

Both hemispheres are linked to the spinal column and peripheral nerves through a common brain stem, but they also communicate directly with one another, by a large transverse band of nerve fibres called the corpus callosum, plus some smaller pathways. These direct cerebral commissures play an essential role in the ordinary integration of function between the hemispheres of normal persons. It is one of the striking features of the subject that this fact remained unknown, at least in the English-speaking world, until the late 1950's, even though a number of patients had had their cerebral commissures surgically severed in operations for the treatment of epilepsy a decade earlier. No significant behavioral or mental effects on these patients could be observed, and it was conjectured that the corpus callosum had no function whatever, except perhaps to keep the hemispheres from sagging.

Then R. E. Myers and R. W. Sperry introduced a technique for dealing with the two hemispheres separately.[2] They sectioned the optic chiasma of cats, so that each eye sent direct information (information about the opposite half of the visual field) only to one side of the brain. It was then possible to train the cats in simple tasks using one eye, and to see what happened when one made them use the other eye instead. In cats whose callosum was intact, there was very good transfer of learning. But in some cats, they severed the corpus callosum as well as the optic chiasma; and in these cases nothing was transmitted from one side to the other. In fact the two severed sides could be taught conflicting discriminations simultaneously, by giving the two eyes opposite stimuli during a single course of reinforcement. Nevertheless this capacity for independent function did not result in serious deficits of behavior. Unless inputs to the two hemispheres were artificially segregated, the animal seemed normal (though if a split-brain monkey gets hold of a peanut with both hands, the result is sometimes a tug of war).

Instead of summarizing all the data, I shall concentrate on the human cases, a reconsideration of which was prompted by the findings with cats and monkeys.[3] In the brain-splitting operation for epilepsy, the optic chiasma is left intact, so one cannot get at the two hemispheres separately just through the two eyes. The solution to the problem of controlling visual input is to flash signals on a screen, on one or other side of the midpoint of the patient's gaze, long enough to be perceived but not long enough to permit an eye movement which would bring the signal to the opposite half visual field and hence to the opposite side of the brain. This is known as tachistoscopic stimulation. Tactile inputs through the hands are for the most part very efficiently segregated, and so are smells through the two nostrils. Some success has even been achieved recently in segregating auditory input, since each ear seems to signal more powerfully to the contralateral than to the ipsilateral hemisphere. As for output, the clearest distinction is provided by speech, which is exclusively the product of the left hemisphere.[4] Writing is a less clear case: it can occasionally be produced in rudimentary form by the right hemisphere, using the left hand. In general, motor control is contralateral, i.e., by the opposite hemisphere, but a certain amount of ipsilateral control sometimes occurs, particularly on the part of the left hemisphere.

The results are as follows. What is flashed to the right half of the visual field, or felt unseen by the right hand, can be reported verbally. What is flashed to the left half field or felt by the left hand cannot be reported, though if the word "hat" is flashed on the left, the left hand will retrieve a hat from a group of concealed objects if the person is told to pick out what he has seen. At the same time he will insist verbally that he saw nothing. Or, if two different words are flashed to the two half fields (e.g., "pencil" and "toothbrush") and the individual is told to retrieve the corresponding object from beneath a screen, with both hands, then the hands will search the collection of objects independently, the right hand picking up the pencil and discarding it while the left hand searches for it, and the left hand similarly rejecting the toothbrush which the right hand lights upon with satisfaction.

If a concealed object is placed in the left hand and the person is asked to guess what it is, wrong guesses will elicit an annoyed frown, since the right hemisphere, which receives the tactile information, also hears the answers. If the speaking hemisphere should guess correctly, the result is a smile. A smell fed to the right nostril (which stimulates the right hemisphere) will elicit a verbal denial that the subject smells anything, but if asked to point with the left hand at a corresponding object he will succeed in picking out, e.g., a clove of garlic, protesting all the while that he smells absolutely nothing, so how can he possibly point to what he smells. If the smell is an unpleasant one like that of rotten eggs, these denials will be accompanied by wrinklings of the nose and mouth, and guttural exclamations of disgust.[5]

One particularly poignant example of conflict between the hemispheres is as follows. A pipe is placed out of sight in the patient's left hand, and he is then asked to write with his left hand what he was holding. Very laboriously and heavily, the left hand writes the letters P and I. Then suddenly the writing speeds up and becomes lighter, the I is converted to an E, and the word is completed as PENCIL. Evidently the left hemisphere has made a guess based on the appearance of the first two letters, and has interfered, with ipsilateral control. But then the right hemisphere takes over control of the hand again, heavily crosses out the letters ENCIL, and draws a crude picture of a pipe.[6]

There are many more data. The split brain patient cannot tell whether shapes flashed to the two half visual fields or held out of sight in the two hands are the same or different—even if he is asked to indicate the answer by nodding or shaking his head (responses available to both hemispheres). The subject cannot distinguish a continuous from a discontinuous line flashed across both halves of the visual field, if the break comes in the middle. Nor can he tell whether two lines meet at an angle, if the joint is in the middle. Nor can he tell whether two spots in opposite half-fields are the same or different in color—though he can do all these things if the images to be compared fall within a single half field. On the whole the right hemisphere does better at spatial relations tests, but is almost incapable of calculation. It appears susceptible to emotion, however. For example, if a photograph of a naked woman is flashed to the left half field of a male patient, he will grin broadly and perhaps blush, without being able to say what has pleased him, though he may say "Wow, that's quite a machine you've got there."

All this is combined with what appears to be complete normalcy in ordinary activities, when no segregation of input to the two hemispheres has been artificially created. Both sides fall asleep and wake up at the same time. The patients can play the piano, button their shirts, swim, and perform well in other activities requiring bilateral coordination. Moreover they do not report any sensation of division or reduction of the visual field. The most notable deviation in ordinary behavior was in a patient whose left hand appeared to be somewhat hostile to the patient's wife. But by and large the hemispheres cooperate admirably, and it requires subtle experimental techniques to get them to operate separately. If one is not careful, they will give each other peripheral cues, transmitting information by audible, visible, or otherwise sensorily perceptible signals which compensate for the lack of a direct commissural link. (One form of communication is particularly difficult to prevent, because it is so direct: both hemispheres can move the neck and facial muscles, and both can feel them move; so a response produced in the face or head by the right hemisphere can be detected by the left, and there is some evidence that they send signals to one another via this medium.)[7]

III

What one naturally wants to know about these patients is how many minds they have. This immediately raises questions about the sense in which an ordinary person can be said to have one mind, and what the conditions are under which diverse experiences and activities can be ascribed to the same mind. We must have some idea what an ordinary person is one of in order to understand what we want to know whether there is *one or two* of, when we try to describe these extraordinary patients.

However, instead of beginning with an analysis of the unity of the mind, I am going to proceed by attempting to apply the ordinary, unanalyzed conception directly in the interpretation of these data, asking whether the patients have one mind, or two, or some more exotic configuration. My conclusion will be that the ordinary conception of a single, countable mind cannot be applied to them at all, and that there is no number of such minds that they possess, though they certainly engage in mental activity. A clearer understanding of the idea of an individual mind should emerge in the course of this discussion but the difficulties which stand in the way of its application to the split-brain cases will provide ground for more general doubts. The concept may not be applicable to ordinary human beings either, for it embodies too simple a conception of the way in which human beings function.

Nevertheless I shall employ the notion of an individual mind in discussing the cases initially, for I wish to consider systematically how they might be understood in terms of countable minds, and to argue that they cannot be. After having done this, I shall turn to ordinary people like you and me.

There appear to be five interpretations of the experimental data which utilize the concept of an individual mind.

(1) The patients have one fairly normal mind associated with the left hemisphere, and the responses emanating from the nonverbal right hemisphere are the responses of an automaton, and are not produced by conscious mental processes.

(2) The patients have only one mind, associated with the left hemisphere, but there also occur (associated with the right hemisphere) isolated conscious mental phenomena, not integrated into a mind at all, though they can perhaps be ascribed to the organism.

(3) The patients have two minds, one which can talk and one which can't.

(4) They have one mind, whose contents derive from both hemispheres and are rather peculiar and dissociated.

(5) They have one normal mind most of the time, while the hemispheres are functioning in parallel, but two minds are elicited by the experimental situations which yield the interesting results. (Perhaps the single mind splits in two and reconvenes after the experiment is over.)

I shall argue that each of these interpretations is unacceptable for one reason or another.

IV

Let me first discuss hypotheses (1) and (2), which have in common the refusal to ascribe the activities of the right hemisphere to a mind, and then go on to treat hypotheses (3), (4), and (5), all of which associate a mind with the activities of the right hemisphere, though they differ on what mind it is.

The only support for hypothesis (1), which refuses to ascribe consciousness to the activities of the right hemisphere at all, is the fact that the subject consistently denies awareness of the activities of that hemisphere. But to take this as proof that the activities of the right hemisphere are unconscious is to beg the question, since the capacity to give testimony is the exclusive ability of the left hemisphere, and of course the left hemisphere is not conscious of what is going on in the right. If on the other hand we consider the manifestations of the right hemisphere itself, there seems no reason in principle to regard verbalizability as a *necessary* condition of consciousness. There may be other grounds for the ascription of conscious mental states that are sufficient even without verbalization. And in fact, what the right hemisphere can do on its own is too elaborate, too intentionally directed and too psychologically intelligible to be regarded merely as a collection of unconscious automatic responses.

The right hemisphere is not very intelligent and it cannot talk; but it is able to respond to complex visual and auditory stimuli, including language, and it can control the performance of discriminatory and manipulative tasks requiring close attention—such as the spelling out of simple words with plastic letters. It can integrate auditory, visual, and tactile stimuli in order to follow the experimenter's instructions, and it can take certain aptitude tests. There is no doubt that if a person were deprived of his left hemisphere entirely, so that the only capacities remaining to him were those of the right, we should not on that account say that he had been converted into an automaton.

Though speechless, he would remain conscious and active, with a diminished visual field and partial paralysis on the right side from which he would eventually recover to some extent. In view of this, it would seem arbitrary to deny that the activities of the right hemisphere are conscious, just because they occur side by side with those of the left hemisphere, about whose consciousness there is no question.

I do not wish to claim that the line between conscious and unconscious mental activity is a sharp one. It is even possible that the distinction is partly relative, in the sense that a given item of mental activity may be assignable to consciousness or not, depending on what other mental activities of the same person are going on at the same time, and whether it is connected with them in a suitable way. Even if this is true, however, the activities of the right hemisphere in split-brain patients do not fall into the category of events whose inclusion in consciousness depends on what else is going on in the patient's mind. Their determinants include a full range of psychological factors, and they demand alertness. It is clear that attention, even concentration is demanded for the tasks of the concealed left hand and tachistoscopically stimulated left visual field. The subjects do not take their experimental tests in a dreamy fashion: they are obviously in contact with reality. The left hemisphere occasionally complains about being asked to perform tasks which the right hemisphere can perform, because it does not know what is going on when the right hemisphere controls the response. But the right hemisphere displays enough awareness of what it is doing to justify the attribution of conscious control in the absence of verbal testimony. If the patients did not deny any awareness of those activities, no doubts about their consciousness would arise at all.

The considerations that make the first hypothesis untenable also serve to refute hypothesis (2), which suggests that the activities of the right hemisphere are conscious without belonging to a mind at all. There may be problems about the intelligibility of this proposal, but we need not consider them here, because it is rendered implausible by the high degree of organization and intermodal coherence of the right hemisphere's mental activities. They are not free-floating, and they are not organized in a fragmentary way. The right hemisphere follows instructions, integrates tactile, auditory and visual stimuli, and does most of the things a good mind should do. The data present us not merely with slivers of purposive behavior, but with a system capable of learning, reacting emotionally, following instructions, and carrying out tasks which require the integration of diverse psychological determinants. It seems clear that the right hemisphere's activities are not unconscious, and that they belong to something having a characteristically mental structure: a subject of experience and action.

V

Let me now turn to the three hypotheses according to which the conscious mental activities of the right hemisphere are ascribed to a mind. They have to be considered together, because the fundamental difficulty about each of them lies in the impossibility of deciding among them. The question, then, is whether the patients have two minds, one mind, or a mind that occasionally splits in two.

There is much to recommend the view that they have two minds, i.e. that the activities of the right hemisphere belong to a mind of their own.[8] Each side of the brain seems to produce its own perceptions, beliefs, and actions, which are connected with one another in the usual way, but not to those of the opposite side. The two halves of the cortex share a common body, which they control through a common midbrain and spinal cord. But their higher functions are independent not only physically but psychologically. Functions of the right hemisphere are inaccessible not only to speech but to any direct combination with corresponding functions of the left hemisphere—i.e., with functions of a type that the right hemisphere finds easy on its home ground, like shape or color discrimination.

One piece of testimony by the patients' left hemispheres may appear to argue against two minds. They report no diminution of the visual field, and little absence of sensation on the left side. Sperry dismisses this evidence on the ground that it is comparable to the testimony of victims of scotoma (partial destruction of the retina), that they notice no gaps in their visual field—although these gaps can be discovered by others observing their perceptual deficiences. But we need not assume that an elaborate confabulatory mechanism is at work in the left hemisphere to account for such testimony. It is perfectly possible that although there are two minds, the mind associated with each hemisphere receives, through the common brain stem, a certain amount of crude ipsilateral stimulation, so that the speaking mind has a rudimentary and undifferentiated appendage to the left side of its visual field, and vice versa for the right hemisphere.[9]

The real difficulties for the two-minds hypothesis coincide with the reasons for thinking we are dealing with one mind— namely the highly integrated character of the patients' relations to the world in ordinary circumstances. When they are not in the experimental situation, their startling behavioral dissociation disappears, and they function normally. There is little doubt that information from the two sides of their brains can be pooled to yield integrated behavioral control. And although this is not accomplished by the usual methods, it is not clear that this settles the question against assigning the integrative functions to a single mind. After all, if the patient is permitted to touch things with both hands and smell them with both nostrils, he arrives at a unified idea of what is going on around him and what he is doing, without revealing any left-right inconsistencies in his behavior or attitudes. It seems strange to suggest that we are not in a position to ascribe all those experiences to the same person, just because of some peculiarities about how the integration is achieved. The people who *know* these patients find it natural to relate to them as single individuals.

Nevertheless, if we ascribe the integration to a single mind, we must also ascribe the experimentally evoked dissociation to that mind, and that is not easy. The experimental situation reveals a variety of dissociation or conflict that is unusual not only because of the simplicity of its anatomical basis, but because such a wide *range* of functions is split into two noncommunicating branches. It is not as though two conflicting volitional centers shared a common perceptual and reasoning apparatus. The split is much deeper than that. The one-mind hypothesis must therefore assert that the contents of the individual's single consciousness are produced by two independent control systems in the two hemispheres, each having a fairly complete mental structure. If this dual control were accomplished during experimental situations by temporal alternation, it would be intelligible, though mysterious. But that is not the hypothesis, and the hypothesis as it stands does not supply us with understanding. For in these patients there appear to be things happening *simultaneously* which cannot fit into a single mind: simultaneous attention to two incompatible tasks, for example, without interaction between the purposes of the left and right hands.

This makes it difficult to conceive what it is like to *be* one of these people. Lack of interaction at the level of a preconscious control system would be comprehensible. But lack of interaction in the domain of visual experience and conscious intention threatens assumptions about the unity of consciousness which are basic to our understanding of another individual as a person. These assumptions are associated with our conception of ourselves, which to a considerable extent constrains our understanding of others. And it is just these assumptions, I believe, that make it impossible to arrive at an interpretation of the cases under discussion in terms of a countable number of minds.

Roughly, we assume that a single mind has sufficiently immediate access to its conscious states so that, for elements of experience or other mental events occurring simultaneously or in close temporal proximity, the mind which is their subject can also experience the simpler *relations* between them if it attends to the matter. Thus, we assume that when a single person has two visual impressions, he can usually also experience the sameness or difference of their coloration, shape, size, the relation of their position and movement within his visual field, and so forth. The same can be said of cross-modal connections. The experiences of a single person are thought to take place in an *experientially* connected domain, so that the relations among experiences can be substantially captured in experiences of those relations.[10]

Split-brain patients fail dramatically to conform to these assumptions in experimental situations, and they fail over the simplest matters. Moreover the dissociation holds between two classes of conscious states each characterized by significant *internal* coherence: normal assumptions about the unity of consciousness hold intrahemispherically, although the requisite comparisons cannot be made across the interhemispheric gap.

These considerations lead us back to the hypothesis that the patients have two minds each. It at least has the advantage of enabling us to understand what it is like to *be* these individuals, so long as we do not try to imagine what it is like to be both of them at the same time. Yet the way to a comfortable acceptance of this conclusion is blocked by the compelling behavioral integration which the patients display in ordinary life, in comparison to which the dissociated symptoms evoked by the experimental situation seem peripheral and atypical. We are faced with diametrically conflicting bodies of evidence, in a case which does not admit of arbitrary decision. There is a powerful inclination to feel that there must be *some* whole number of minds in those heads, but the data prevent us from deciding how many.

This dilemma makes hypothesis (5) initially attractive, especially since the data which yield the conflict are to some extent gathered at different times. But the suggestion that a second mind is brought into existence only during experimental situations loses plausibility on reflection. First, it is entirely ad hoc: it proposes to explain one change in terms of another without suggesting any explanation of the second. There is nothing about the experimental situation that might be expected to produce a fundamental internal change in the patient. In fact it produces no anatomical changes and merely elicits a noteworthy set of symptoms. So unusual an event as a mind's popping in and out of existence would have to be explained by something more than its explanatory convenience.

But secondly, the behavioral evidence would not even be explained by this hypothesis, simply because the patients' integrated responses and their dissociated responses are not clearly separated in time. During the time of the experiments the patient is functioning largely as if he were a single individual: in his posture, in following instructions about where to focus his eyes, in the whole range of trivial behavioral control involved in situating himself in relation to the experimenter and the experimental apparatus. The two halves of his brain cooperate completely except in regard to those very special inputs that reach them separately and differently. For these reasons hypothesis (5) does not seem to be a real option; if two minds are operating in the experimental situation, they must be operating largely in harmony although partly at odds. And if there are two minds then, why can there not be two minds operating essentially in parallel the rest of the time?

Nevertheless the psychological integration displayed by the patients in ordinary life is so complete that I do not believe it is possible to accept that conclusion, nor any conclusion involving the ascription to them of a whole number of minds. These cases fall midway between ordinary persons with intact brains (between whose cerebral hemispheres there is also cooperation, though it works largely via the corpus callosum), and pairs of individuals engaged in a performance requiring exact behavioral coordination, like using a two-handed saw, or playing a duet. In the latter type of case we have two minds which communicate by subtoe peripheral cues; in the former we have a single mind. Nothing taken from either of those cases can compel us to assimilate the split-brain patient to one or the other of them. If we decided that they definitely had two minds, then it would be problematical why we didn't conclude on anatomical grounds that everyone has two minds, but that we don't notice it except in these odd cases because most pairs of minds in a single body run in perfect parallel due to the direct communication between the hemispheres which provide their anatomical bases. The two minds each of us has running in harness would be much the same except that one could talk and the other couldn't. But it is clear that this line of argument will get us nowhere. For if the idea of a single mind applies to anyone it applies to ordinary individuals with intact brains, and if it does not apply to them it ought to be scrapped, in which case there is no point in asking whether those with split brains have one mind or two.[11]

VI

If I am right, and there is no whole number of individual minds that these patients can be said to have, then the attribution of conscious, significant mental activity does not require

the existence of a single mental subject. This is extremely puzzling in itself, for it runs counter to our need to construe the
mental states we ascribe to others on the model of our own.
Something in the ordinary conception of a person, or in the
ordinary conception of experience, leads to the demand for an
account of these cases which the same conception makes it
impossible to provide. This may seem a problem not worth
worrying about very much. It is not so surprising that, having
begun with a phenomenon which is radically different from anything else previously known, we should come to the conclusion
that it cannot be adequately described in ordinary terms. However, I believe that consideration of these very unusual cases
should cause us to be skeptical about the concept of a single
subject of consciousness as it applies to ourselves.

The fundamental problem in trying to understand these
cases in mentalistic terms is that we take ourselves as paradigms
of psychological unity, and are then unable to project ourselves
into their mental lives, either once or twice. But in thus using
ourselves as the touchstone of whether another organism can be
said to house an individual subject of experience or not, we are
subtly ignoring the possibility that our own unity may be
nothing absolute, but merely another case of integration, more
or less effective, in the control system of a complex organism.
This system speaks in the first person singular through our
mouths, and that makes it understandable that we should think
of its unity as in some sense numerically absolute, rather than
relative and a function of the integration of its contents.

But this is quite genuinely an illusion. The illusion consists
in projecting inward to the center of the mind the very subject
whose unity we are trying to explain: the individual person
with all his complexities. The ultimate account of the unity of
what we call a single mind consists of an enumeration of the
types of functional integration that typify it. We know that
these can be eroded in different ways, and to different degrees.
The belief that even in their complete version they can be explained by the presence of a numerically single subject is an
illusion. Either this subject contains the mental life, in which
case it is complex and its unity must be accounted for in terms
of the unified operation of its components and functions, or

else it is an extensionless point, in which case it explains nothing.

An intact brain contains two cerebral hemispheres each of which possesses perceptual, memory, and control systems adequate to run the body without the assistance of the other. They cooperate in directing it with the aid of a constant two-way internal communication system. Memories, perceptions, desires and so forth therefore have duplicate physical bases on both sides of the brain, not just on account of similarities of initial input, but because of subsequent exchange. The cooperation of the undetached hemispheres in controlling the body is more efficient and direct than the cooperation of a pair of detached hemisphere, but it is cooperation nonetheless. Even if we analyze the idea of unity in terms of functional integration, therefore, the unity of our own consciousness may be less clear than we had supposed. The natural conception of a single person controlled by a mind possessing a single visual field, individual faculties for each of the other senses, unitary systems of memory, desire, belief, and so forth, may come into conflict with the physiological facts when it is applied to ourselves.

The concept of a person might possibly survive an application to cases which require us to speak of two or more persons in one body, but it seems strongly committed to some form of whole number countability. Since even this seems open to doubt, it is possible that the ordinary, simple idea of a single person will come to seem quaint some day, when the complexities of the human control system become clearer and we become less certain that there is anything very important that we are *one* of. But it is also possible that we shall be unable to abandon the idea no matter what we discover.[12]

NOTES

1. The literature on split brains is sizeable. An excellent recent survey is Michael S. Gazzaniga, *The Bisected Brain* (New York: Appleton-Century-Crofts, 1970). Its nine-page list of references is not intended to be a complete bibliography of the subject, however. Gazzaniga has also written a brief popular exposition: "The Split Brain in Man," *Scientific American* 217 (1967), 24. The best general treatment for philosophical purposes is

to be found in several papers by R. W. Sperry, the leading investigator in the field: "The Great Cerebral Commissure," *Scientific American* 210 (1964), 42; "Brain Bisection and Mechanisms of Consciousness" in *Brain and Conscious Experience,* ed. Eccles, J. C. (Berlin: Springer-Verlag, 1966); "Mental Unity Following Surgical Disconnections of the Cerebral Hemispheres," *The Harvey Lectures,* Series 62 (New York, Academic Press, 1968), p. 293; "Hemisphere Deconnection and Unity in Conscious Awareness," *American Psychologist* 23 (1968), 723. Several interesting papers are to be found in *Functions of the Corpus Callosum: Ciba Foundation Study Group No. 20,* ed. G. Ettlinger (London: J. and A. Churchill, 1965).

2. Myers and Sperry, "Interocular Transfer of a Visual Form Discrimination Habit in Cats after Section of the Optic Chiasm and Corpus Callosum," *Anatomical Record* 115 (1953), 351; Myers, "Interocular Transfer of Pattern Discrimination in Cats Following Section of Crossed Optic Fibers," *Journal of Comparative and Physiological Psychology* 48 (1955), 470.

3. The first publication of these results was M. S. Gazzaniga, J. E. Bogen, and R. W. Sperry, "Some Functional Effects of Sectioning the Cerebral Commissures in Man," *Proceedings of the National Academy of Sciences* 48 (1962), pt 2, p. 1765. Interestingly, the same year saw publication of a paper proposing the interpretation of a case of human brain *damage* along similar lines, suggested by the earlier findings with animals. Cf. N. Geschwind and E. Kaplan, "A Human Cerebral Deconnection Syndrome," *Neurology* 12 (1962), 675. Also of interest is Geschwind's long two-part survey of the field, which takes up some philosophical questions explicitly: "Disconnexion Syndromes in Animals and Man," *Brain* 88 (1965), 247-294, 585-644. Parts of it are reprinted, with other material, in *Boston Studies in the Philosophy of Science,* Vol. IV (1969). See also his paper "The Organization of Language and the Brain," *Science* 170 (1970), 940.

4. There are individual exceptions to this, as there are to most generalizations about cerebral function: left-handed people tend to have bilateral linguistic control, and it is common in early childhood. All the subjects of these experiments, however, were right-handed, and displayed left cerebral dominance.

5. H. W. Gordon and R. W. Sperry, "Lateralization of Olfactory Perception in the Surgically Separated Hemispheres of Man," *Neuropsychologia* 7 (1969), 111. One patient, however, was able to say in these circumstances that he smelled something unpleasant, without being able to describe it further.

6. Reported in Jerre Levy, *Information Processing and Higher Psychological Functions in the Disconnected Hemispheres of Human Commissurotomy Patients* (Ph.D. diss., California Institute of Technology, 1969).

7. Moreover, the condition of radical disconnection may not be stable: there may be a tendency toward the formation of new interhemispheric pathways through the brain stem, with the lapse of time. This is supported partly by observation of commissurotomy patients, but more importantly by cases of agenesis of the callosum. People who have grown up without one have learned to manage without it; their performance on the tests is much closer to normal than that of recently operated patients. (Cf. Saul and Sperry, "Absence of Commissurotomy Symptoms with

Agenesis of the Corpus Callosum," *Neurology* 18 [1968].) This fact is very important, but for the present I shall put it aside to concentrate on the immediate results of disconnection.

8. It is Sperry's view. He puts it as follows: "Instead of the normally unified single stream of consciousness, these patients behave in many ways as if they have two independent streams of conscious awareness, one in each hemisphere, each of which is cut off from and out of contact with the mental experiences of the other. In other words, each hemisphere seems to have its own separate and private sensations; its own perceptions; its own concepts; and its own impulses to act, with related volitional, cognitive, and learning experiences. Following the surgery, each hemisphere also has thereafter its own separate chain of memories that are rendered inaccessible to the recall process of the other." (*American Psychologist* 23, 724.)

9. There is some direct evidence for such primitive ipsilateral inputs, both visual and tactile; cf. Gazzaniga, *The Bisected Brain,* chap. 3.

10. The two can of course diverge, and this fact underlies the classic philosophical problem of inverted spectra, which is only distantly related to the subject of this paper. A type of relation can hold between elements in the experience of a single person that cannot hold between elements of the experience of distinct persons: looking similar in color, for example. Insofar as our concept of similarity of experience in the case of a single person is dependent on his experience of similarity, the concept is not applicable between persons.

11. In case anyone is inclined to embrace the conclusion that we all have two minds, let me suggest that the trouble will not end there. For the mental operations of a single hemisphere, such as vision, hearing, speech, writing, verbal comprehension, etc., can to a great extent be separated from one another by suitable cortical deconnections; why then should we not regard *each* hemisphere as inhabited by several cooperating minds with specialized capacities? Where is one to stop? If the decision on the number of minds associated with a brain is largely arbitrary, the original point of the question has disappeared.

12. My research was supported in part by the National Science Foundation.

PART VII

SELECTIONS FOR THE SECOND EDITION

Sydney Shoemaker

16

Persons and Their Pasts

Persons have, in memory, a special access to facts about their own past histories and their own identities, a kind of access they do not have to the histories and identities of other persons and other things. John Locke thought this special access important enough to warrant a special mention in his definition of "person," viz., "a thinking, intelligent being, that has reason and reflection, *and can consider itself as itself, the same thinking thing, in different times and places. . . .*"[1] In this paper I shall attempt to explain the nature and status of this special access and to defend Locke's view of its conceptual importance. I shall also attempt to correct what now seem to me to be errors and oversights in my own previous writings on this topic.

I

As a first approximation, the claim that persons have in memory a special access to their own past histories can be expressed in two related claims, both of which will be considerably qualified in the course of this paper. The first is that it is a necessary condition of its being true that a person remembers a given past event that he, that same person, should have observed or experienced the event, or known if it in some other direct way, at the time of its occurrence. I shall refer to this as the "previous awareness condition" for remembering.[2]

This article is reprinted from *The American Philosophical Quarterly*, Vol. 7, No. 4 (October 1970), pp. 269–285, by courtesy of the editor and of Professor Shoemaker.

The second claim is that an important class of first person memory claims are in a certain respect immune to what I shall call "error through misidentification." Consider a case in which I say, on the basis of my memory of a past incident, "I shouted that Johnson should be impeached," and compare this with a case in which I say, again on the basis of my memory of a past incident, "John shouted that Johnson should be impeached." In the latter case it could turn out that I do remember someone who looked and sounded just like John shouting that Johnson should be impeached, but that the man who shouted this was nevertheless not John—it may be that I misidentified the person as John at the time I observed the incident, and that I have preserved this misidentification in memory, or it may be that I subsequently misidentified him as John on the basis of what I (correctly) remembered about him. Here my statement would be false, but its falsity would not be due to a mistake or fault of my memory; my memory could be as accurate and complete as any memory could be without precluding this sort of error. But this sort of misidentification is not possible in the former case. My memory report could of course be mistaken, for one can misremember such incidents, but it could not be the case that I have a full and accurate memory of the past incident but am mistaken in thinking that the person I remember shouting was myself. I shall speak of such memory judgments as being immune to error through misidentification with respect to the first person pronouns, or other "self-referring" expressions, contained in them.[3]

I do not contend that all memory claims are immune to error through misidentification with respect to the first person pronouns contained in them. If I say "I blushed when Jones made that remark" because I remember seeing in a mirror someone, whom I took (or now take) to be myself, blushing, it could turn out that my statement is false, not because my memory is in any way incomplete or inaccurate, but because the person I saw in the mirror was my identical twin or double.[4] In general, if at some past time I could have known of someone that he was φ, and could at the same time have been mistaken in taking that person to be myself, then the subsequent memory claims I make about that past occasion will be subject to error through misidentification with respect to the first person pronouns. But if, as is frequently the

case, I could not have been mistaken in this way in the past in
asserting what I then knew by saying "I *am* ɸ," then my subsequent memory claim "I *was* ɸ" will be immune to error through
misidentification relative to 'I'; that is, it is impossible in such
cases that I should accurately remember someone being ɸ but
mistakenly take that person to be myself. We might express this
by saying that where the present tense version of a judgment is
immune to error through misidentification relative to the first person pronouns contained in it, this immunity is *preserved* in memory.[5] Thus if I claim on the strength of memory that I saw John
yesterday, and have a full and accurate memory of the incident, it
cannot be the case that I remember someone seeing John but have
misidentified that person as myself; my memory claim "I saw
John" is subject to error through misidentification with respect to
the term "John" (for it could have been John's twin or double
that I saw), but not with respect to 'I'.

II

In his early paper, "Personal Identity," H. P. Grice held that the
proposition "One can only remember one's own past experiences"
is analytic, but pointed out that this would be analytic in only a
trivial way "if 'memory' were to be defined in terms of 'having
knowledge of one's own past experiences'." He says that "even if
we were to define 'memory' in this sort of way, we should still
be left with a question about the proposition, 'one can only have
knowledge of one's own past experiences,' which seems to me a
necessary proposition."[6] Now I doubt very much if Grice, or any
other philosopher, would now want to hold that is necessarily
true, or that it is true at all, that one's own past experiences are
the only past experiences of which one can have knowledge. But
one does not have to hold this to hold, with Grice, that it is not
just a trivial analytic truth that one's own experiences are the
only ones that one can remember, i.e., that it is not the case that
the necessity of this truth derives merely from the fact that we
refuse to *call* someone's having knowledge of a past experience a
case of his remembering it unless the past experience belonged to
the rememberer himself.

Grice's remarks are explicitly about memory of past experiences, but they raise an important question about all sorts of "event memory." Supposing it to be a necessary truth that the previous witnessing condition must be satisfied in any genuine case of remembering, is this necessarily true because we would refuse to *count* knowing about a past event as remembering it if the previous awareness condition were not satisfied, or is it necessary for some deeper reason? I think that many philosophers would hold that if this is a necessary truth at all, it is so only in the former way, i.e., in such a way as to make its necessity trivial and uninteresting. Thus G. C. Nerlich, in a footnote to his paper "On Evidence for Identity," sa–ys that it is true only of *our* world, not of all possible worlds, that only by being identical with a witness to past events can one have the sort of knowledge of them one has in memory.[7] On this view it is logically possible that we should have knowledge of past events which we did not ourselves witness, of experiences we did not ourselves have, and of actions we did not ourselves perform, that is in all important respects like the knowledge we have of past events, experiences, and actions in remembering them. If one takes this view it will seem a matter of small importance, if indeed it is true, that the having of such knowledge could not be called "remembering."

It is of course not absolutely clear just what it means to speak of knowledge as being "in all important respects like" memory knowledge, if this is not intended to imply that the knowledge *is* memory knowledge. Presumably, knowledge of past events that is "just like" memory knowledge must not be inferred from present data (diaries, photographs, rock strata, etc.) on the basis of empirical laws and generalizations. But while this is necessary, it is not sufficient. When a person remembers a past event there is a correspondence between his present cognitive state and some past cognitive and sensory state of his that existed at the time of the remembered event and consisted in his experiencing the event or otherwise being aware of its occurrence.[8] I shall say that remembering a past event involves there being a correspondence between the rememberer's present cognitive state and a past cognitive and sensory state that was "of" the event.[9] In actual memory this past cognitive and sensory state is always a past state of the rememberer himself. What we need to consider is whether there could be a kind of knowledge of past events such that someone's having this sort of knowledge of an event does involve there being a correspondence between his present cognitive state and a past cognitive and sensory state that was of the event, but such that this correspondence, although otherwise just like that which exists in memory, does not necessarily involve that past state's having been a state of the very same person who subsequently has the knowledge. Let us speak of such knowledge, supposing for the moment that it is possible, as "quasi-memory knowledge," and let us say that a person who has this sort of knowledge of a past event "quasi-remembers" that past event. Quasi-remembering, as I shall use the term, includes remembering as a special case. One way of characterizing the difference between quasi-remembering and remembering is by saying that the former is subject to a weaker previous awareness condition than the latter. Whereas someone's claim to remember a past event implies that he himself was aware of the event at the time of its occurrence, the claim to quasi-remember a past event implies only that someone or other was aware of it. Except when I indicate otherwise, I shall use the expression "previous awareness condition" to refer to the stronger of these conditions.

Our faculty of memory constitutes our most direct access to the past, and this means, given the previous awareness condition, that our most direct access to the past is in the first instance an access to *our own* past histories. One of the main questions I shall be considering in this paper is whether it is conceivable that our most direct access to the past should be a faculty of quasi-remembering which is not a faculty of remembering. Is it conceivable that we should have, as a matter of course, knowledge that is related to past experiences and actions other than our own in just the way in which, as things are, our memory knowledge is related to our own past experiences and actions? In our world all quasi-remembering is remembering; what we must consider is whether the world could be such that most quasi-remembering is not remembering.

Before going on to consider this question I should mention two reasons why I think it important. The first is its obvious bearing on the question of the relationship between the concepts of memory and personal identity. If there can be quasi-remembering that is not remembering, and if remembering can be defined as quasi-remembering that is of events the quasi-rememberer was aware of at the time of their occurrence (thus making it a trivial analytic truth that one can remember an event only if one was previously aware of it), then it would seem that any attempt to define or analyze the notion of personal identity in terms of the notion of remembering will be viciously circular. I shall have more to say about this in Sect. V. But this question also has an important bearing on the question of how a person's memory claims concerning his own past are grounded. In previous writings I have claimed, and made a great deal of the claim, that our memory knowledge of our own past histories, unlike our knowledge of the past histories of other things, is not grounded on criteria of identity.[10] Strawson makes a similar claim in *The Bounds of Sense,* saying that "When a man (a subject of experience) ascribes a current or directly remembered state of consciousness to himself, no use whatever of any criteria of personal identity is required to justify his use of the pronoun 'I' to refer to the subject of that experience." He remarks that "it is because Kant recognized this truth that his treatment of the subject is so greatly superior to Hume's."[11] Now it can easily seem that this claim follows immediately from the fact that remembering necessarily involves the satisfaction of the previous awareness condition. If one remembers a past experience then it has to have been one's own, and from this it may seem to follow that it makes no sense to inquire concerning a remembered experience whether it was one's own and then to try to answer this question on the basis of empirical criteria of identity. But suppose that it were only a trivial analytic truth that remembering involves the satisfaction of the previous awareness condition, and suppose that it were possible to quasi-remember experiences other than one's own. If this were so one might remember a past experience but not know whether one was remembering it or only quasi-remembering it. Here, it seems, it would be perfectly appropriate to employ a criterion of identity to determine whether the quasi-remembered experience was one's own, i.e., whether one remembered it as opposed to merely quasi-remembering it. Thus the question of whether the knowledge of our own identities provided us by memory is essentially non-critical turns on the question of whether it is possible to quasi-remember past actions and experiences without remembering them.

III

There is an important respect in which my characterization of quasi-remembering leaves that notion inadequately specified. Until now I have been ignoring the fact that a claim to remember a past event implies, not merely that the rememberer experienced such an event, but that his present memory is in some way *due to,* that it came about *because of,* a cognitive and sensory state the rememberer had at the time he experienced the event. I am going to assume, although this is controversial, that it is part of the previous awareness condition for memory that a veridical memory must not only correspond to, but must also stand in an appropriate *causal* relationship to, a past cognitive and sensory state of the rememberer.[12] It may seem that if quasi-memory is to be as much like memory as possible, we should yield a similar requirement into the previous awareness condition for quasi-memory, i.e., that we should require that a veridical quasi-memory must not only correspond to, but must also stand in an appropriate causal relationship to, a past cognitive and sensory state of someone or other. On the other hand, it is not immediately obvious that building such a requirement into the previous awareness condition for quasi-memory would not make it equivalent to the previous awareness condition for memory, and thus destroy the intended difference between memory and quasi-memory. But there is no need for us to choose between a previous awareness condition that includes the causal requirement and one that does not, for it is possible and useful to consider both. In the present section I shall assume that the previous awareness condition for quasi-memory does not include the causal requirement, and that it includes nothing more than the requirement that a quasi-memory must, to be a veridical quasi-memory of a given event, correspond in content to a past cognitive and sensory state that was of that event. In the sections that follow I shall consider the consequences of strengthening this condition to include a causal requirement.

The first thing we must consider is what becomes of the immunity of first person memory claims to error through misidentification if we imagine the faculty of memory replaced by a faculty of quasi-memory. As things are now, there is a difference between, on the one hand, remembering an action of someone else's—this might consist, for example, in having a memory of seeing someone do the action—and, on the other hand, remembering *doing* an action, which can be equated with remembering *oneself* doing the action. In the case of quasi-remembering the distinction corresponding to this is that between, on the one hand, the sort of quasi-memory of a past action whose corresponding past cognitive and sensory state belonged to someone who was watching someone else do the action, and, on the other hand, the sort of quasi-memory of a past action whose corresponding past cognitive and sensory state belonged to the very person who did the action. Let us call these, respectively, quasi-memories of an action "from the outside" and quasi-memories of an action "from the inside." Now whereas I can remember an action from the inside only if it was my action, a world in which there is quasi-remembering that is not remembering will be one in which it is not true that any action one quasi-remembers from the inside is thereby an action he himself did. So—assuming that ours may be such a world—if I quasi-remember an action from the inside, and say on this basis that I did the action, my statement will be subject to error through misidentification; it may be that my quasi-memory of the action is as accurate and complete as it could be, but that I am mistaken in thinking that I am the person who did it. There is another way in which a first person quasi-memory claim could be mistaken through misidentification. If there can be quasi-remembering that is not remembering, it will be possible for a person to quasi-remember an action of his own from the outside. That is, one might quasi-remember an action of one's own as it appeared to someone else who observed it; one might, as it were, quasi-remember it through the eyes of another person. But of course, if I were to quasi-remember someone who looks like me doing a certain action, and were to say on that basis that I did the action, I might be mistaken through no fault of my quasi-memory; it might be that the person who did the action was my identical twin or someone disguised to look like me.

What I have just said about the quasi-remembering of past actions also applies to the quasi-remembering of past experiences and of other mental phenomena. If I remember a past pain from the inside—i.e., remember the pain itself, or remember having the pain, as opposed to remembering seeing someone manifest pain behavior—then the pain must have been mine. But the fact that I *quasi*-remember a pain from the inside will be no guarantee that the pain was mine. Any quasi-memory claim to have been in pain on some past occasion, or to have had a certain thought, or to have made a certain decision, will be subject to error through misidentification.

What is shown by the foregoing is that the immunity of first person memory claims to error through misidentification exists only because remembering requires the satisfaction of the previous awareness condition, and that this feature disappears once we imagine this requirement dropped. Quasi-memory, unlike memory, does not preserve immunity to error through misidentification relative to the first person pronouns. To consider the further consequences of replacing memory with quasi-memory, I must first say something more about memory.

To refer to an event of a certain sort as one that one remembers does not always uniquely identify it, since one may remember more than one event of a given sort, but it does go some way toward identifying it. In referring to an event in this way one to a certain extent locates it in space and time, even if the description of the event contains no place-names, no names of objects by reference to which places can be identified, and no dates or other temporal indicators. For in saying that one remembers the event one locates it within a spatio-temporal region which is defined by one's own personal history. The spatiotemporal region which is "rememberable" by a given person can be charted by specifying the intervals of past time during which the person was conscious and by specifying the person's spatial location, and indicating what portions of his environment he was in a position to witness, at each moment during these intervals. If someone reports that he remembers an event of a certain kind, we know that unless his memory is mistaken an event of that kind occurred within the spatiotemporal region rememberable by him, and in principle we can chart this region by tracing his history back to its beginning.

Ordinarily, of course, we have far more knowledge than this of the spatiotemporal location of a remembered event, for usually a memory report will fix this position by means of dates, place-names, and other spatial and temporal indicators. But it must be noted that memory claims are subject to error through misidentification with respect to spatial indicators. If a man says "I remember an explosion occurring right in front of that building," it is possible for this to be false even if the memory it expresses is accurate and detailed; the remembered explosion may have occurred, not in front of the building indicated, but in front of another building exactly like it. This remains true no matter how elaborate and detailed we imagine the memory claim to be. For any set of objects that has actually existed in the world, even if this be as extensive as the set of buildings, streets, parks, bridges, etc., that presently make up New York City, it is logically possible that there should somewhere exist, or that there should somewhere and at some time have existed, a numerically different but exactly similar set of objects arranged in exactly the same way. So memory claims are, in principle, subject to error through misidentification even with respect to such place names as "New York City." Here I am appealing to what Strawson has referred to as the possibility of "massive reduplication."[13]

When a memory report attempts to fix the location of a remembered event by reference to some landmark, we are ordinarily justified in not regarding it as a real possibility that the claim involves error through misidentification owing to the reduplication of that landmark. Certainly we are so justified if the landmark is New York City. But it is important to see why this is so. It is not that we have established that nowhere and at no time has there existed another city exactly like New York; as a self-consistent, unrestricted, negative existential claim, this is something that it would be impossible in principle for us to establish.[14] What we can do and do know is that New York is not reduplicated within any spatiotemporal region of which anyone with whom we converse can have had experience. Whether or not New York is reduplicated in some remote galaxy or at some remote time in the past, we know that the man who claims to remember doing or experiencing something in a New York-like city cannot have been in any such duplicate. And from this we can conclude that if he does remember doing or experiencing something in a New York-like city, then it was indeed in New York, and not in any duplicate of it, that the remembered action or event occurred. But we can conclude this only because remembering involves the satisfaction of the previous awareness condition.

Even when a landmark referred to in someone's memory claim is reduplicated within the spatio-temporal region rememberable by that person, we can often be confident that the claim does not involve error through misidentification. Suppose that someone locates a remembered event, say an explosion, by saying that it occurred in front of his house, and we know that there are many houses, some of which he has seen, that are exactly like his. If he reported that he had simply found himself in front of his house, with no recollection of how he had gotten there, and that after seeing the explosion he had passed out and awakened later in a hospital, we would think it quite possible that he had misidentified the place at which the remembered explosion occurred. But suppose instead that he reports that he remembers walking home from work, seeing the explosion in front of his house, and then going inside and being greeted by his family. Here a misidentification of the place of the explosion would require the reduplication, not merely of his house, but also of his family, his place of work, and the route he follows in walking home from work. We could know that no such reduplication exists within the spatiotemporal region of which he has had experience, and could conclude that his report did not involve an error through misidentification. But again, what would enable us to conclude this is the fact that remembering involves the satisfaction of the previous awareness condition.

Presumably, what justifies any of us in using such expressions as "New York" and "my house" in his own memory reports are considerations of the same kind as those that justify others in ruling out the possibility that claims containing such expressions involve error through misidentification. What justifies one is the knowledge that certain sorts of reduplication do not in fact occur within the spatio-temporal regions of which any of us have had experience. Normally no such justification is needed for the use of 'I' in memory reports; this is what is involved in saying that memory claims are normally immune to error through misidentification relative to the first person pronouns. But what makes such a justification possible in the case of "New York" is the same as what makes it unnecessary in the case of 'I', namely the fact that remembering involves the satisfaction of the previous awareness condition. So it is because of this fact that remembering can provide us, not merely with the information that an event of a certain sort has occurred somewhere or other in the vicinity of persons and things satisfying certain general descriptions, but with the information that such an event occurred in a certain specified place, in a certain specifiable spatial relationship to events presently observed, and in the vicinity of certain specified persons or things. But this is also to say that it is this fact about remembering that makes it possible for us to know that an object or person to which one remembers something happening is, or is not, identical with an object or person presently observed. And it will emerge later that it is also this fact about remembering that makes it possible to know that different memories are, or are not, of events in the history of a single object or person.

But now let us consider the consequences of replacing the faculty of memory by a faculty of quasi-memory. Quasi-remembering does not necessarily involve the satisfaction of the previous awareness condition, and first person quasi-memory claims are, as we have seen, subject to error through misidentification. It is a consequence of this that even if we are given that someone's faculty of quasi-memory is highly reliable, in the sense that when he seems to quasi-remember an event of a certain sort he almost always does quasi-remember such an event, nevertheless his quasi-memory will provide neither him nor us with any positive information concerning the spatial location of the events he quasi-remembers, or with any information concerning the identity, or concerning the history, of any object or person to which he quasi-remembers something happening. The fact that he quasi-remembers an event of a certain sort will not provide us with the information that such an event has occurred within the spatiotemporal region of which he has had experience. But in consequence of this, if he attempts to locate the quasi-remembered event by reference to some object or place known to us, e.g., New York or Mt. Everest, it is impossible for us to rule out on empirical grounds the possibility that his claim involves error through misidentification owing to the reduplication of that object or place. To rule this out we would have to have adequate grounds for asserting, not merely that there is no duplicate of New York (say) in the spatiotemporal region of which he has had experience, but that at no place and time has there been a duplicate of New York. And this we could not have.[15] But this means that in expressing his quasi-memories he could not be justified in using such expressions as "New York" and "Mt. Everest," or such expressions as 'I', "this," and "here," to refer to the places, persons, and things in or to which he quasi-remembers certain things happening. The most he could be entitled to assert on the basis of his quasi-memories would be a set of general propositions of the form "An event of type ϕ at some time occurred in the history of an object of type A while it stood in relations $R_1, R_2, R_3 \ldots$ to objects of types $B, C, D \ldots$" And given only a set of propositions of this sort, no matter how extensive, one could not even begin to reconstruct any part of the history of the world; one could not even have grounds for asserting that an object mentioned in one proposition in the set was one and the same as an object mentioned in another proposition of the set.

So far I have been ignoring the fact that the events and actions we remember generally have temporal duration, and the fact that we sometimes remember connected sequences of events and actions lasting considerable lengths of time. What will correspond to this if remembering is replaced with quasi-remembering? If someone says "I remember doing X and then doing Y," it would make no sense to say to him, "Granted that your memory is accurate, and that such a sequence of actions did occur, are you sure that it was one and the same person who did both X and Y?" But now suppose that someone says "I quasi-remember doing X and then doing Y," and that the world is such that there is quasi-remembering that is not remembering. Here it is compatible with the accuracy of the man's quasi-memory that he should be mistaken in thinking that he himself did X and Y. And as I shall now try to show, it must also be compatible with the accuracy of this man's quasi-memories that he should be mistaken in thinking even that one and the same person did both X and Y.

Suppose that at time t_1 a person, call him A, does action Y and has while doing it a quasi-memory from the inside of the immediately previous occurrence of the doing of action X. A's having this quasi-memory of the doing of X is of course compatible with X's having been done by someone other than himself. At t_1 A's cognitive state includes this quasi-memory from the inside of the doing of X together with knowledge from the inside of the doing of Y; we might say that it includes knowledge from the inside of the action sequence X-followed-by-Y. But now suppose that at a later time t_2 someone, call him B, has a quasi-memory corresponding to the cognitive state of A at t_1. It would seem that B's quasi-memory will be a quasi-memory from the inside of the action sequence X-followed-by-Y. This quasi-memory will be veridical in the sense that it corresponds to a past cognitive state that was itself a state of knowledge, yet its being veridical in this way is compatible with X and Y having been done by different persons. If A were mistakenly to assert at t_1 that X and Y were done by the same person, his mistake would not be due to a faulty quasi-memory. And if B's cognitive state at t_2 corresponds to A's cognitive state at t_1, then if B were mistaken at t_2 in thinking that X and Y were done by the same person, this mistake would not be due to a faulty-quasi-memory.

If, as I have been arguing, someone's quasi-remembering from the inside the *action* sequence X-followed-by-Y provides no guarantee that X and Y were done by the same person, then by the same reasoning someone's quasi-remembering the *event* sequence X-followed-by-Y provides no guarantee that X and Y were witnessed by the same person, and therefore no guarantee that they occurred in spatial proximity to one another. But any temporally extended event can be thought of as a succession of temporally and spatially contiguous events; e.g., a stone's rolling down a hill can be thought of as consisting in its rolling half of the way down followed by its rolling the other half of the way. Suppose, then, that someone has a quasi-memory of the following event sequence: stone rolling from top of hill to middle followed by stone rolling from middle of hill to bottom. If we knew this to be a memory, and not just a quasi-memory, we would know that if it is veridical then one and the same person observed both of these events, one immediately after the other, and this together with the contents of the memory could guarantee that one and the same hill and one and the same stone were involved in both, and that a single stone had indeed rolled all the way down a hill. But the veridicality of this quasi-memory *qua* quasi-memory would be compatible with these events having been observed by different persons, and with their involving different stones and different hills; it would be compatible with no stone's having rolled all of the way down any hill. And since any temporally extended event can be thought of as a succession of temporally and spatially contiguous events, it follows that someone's quasi-remembering what is ostensibly a temporally extended event of a certain kind is always compatible with there actually being no such event that he quasi-remembers, for it is compatible with his quasi-memory being, as it were, compounded out of quasi-memories of a number of different events that were causally unrelated and spatio-temporally remote from one another. The knowledge of the past provided by such a faculty of quasi-memory would be minimal indeed.[16]

IV

But now we must consider the consequences of strengthening the previous awareness condition for quasi-remembering to include the requirement that a veridical quasi-memory must not only correspond to, but must also stand in an appropriate causal relationship to, a past cognitive and sensory state of someone or other. Clearly, much of what I have said about quasi-remembering ceases to hold once its previous awareness condition is strengthened in this way. If, as is commonly supposed, causal chains must be spatiotemporally continuous, then if quasi-memory claims implied the satisfaction of this strengthened previous awareness condition they would, when true, provide some information concerning the location of the quasi-remembered events and actions. We would know at a minimum that the spatiotemporal relationship between the quasi-remembered event and the making of the quasi-memory claim is such that it is possible for them to be linked by a spatiotemporally continuous causal chain, and if we could trace the causal ancestry of the quasi-memory we could determine precisely when and where the quasi-remembered event occurred. Thus if we construe the previous awareness condition of quasi-memory as including this causal requirement, it seems that a faculty of quasi-remembering could enable us to identify past events and to reidentify persons and things, and it seems at first glance (though not, I think, on closer examination) that it would enable us to do this without giving us a special access to our own past histories.

It must be stressed that this strengthened previous awareness condition is an improvement on the weaker one *only* on the assumption that causal chains (or at any rate the causal chains that link cognitive and sensory states with subsequent quasi-memories) must be spatiotemporally continuous, or at least must satisfy a condition similar to spatiotemporal continuity. If the sort of causality operating here allowed for action at a spatial or temporal distance, and if there were no limit on the size of the spatial or temporal gaps that could exist in a causal chain linking a cognitive and sensory state with a subsequent quasi-memory, then the claim that a quasi-memory originated in a corresponding cognitive and sensory state would be as unfalsifiable, and as uninformative, as the claim that it corresponds to a past cognitive and sensory state of someone or other.

To consider the consequences of strengthening the previous awareness condition for quasi-memory in the way just suggested I shall have to introduce a few technical expressions. First, I shall use the expressions "quasi$_c$-remember" and "quasi$_c$-memory" when speaking of the sort of quasi-remembering whose previous awareness condition includes the causal requirement. Second, I shall use the term "M-type causal chain" to refer to the sort of causal chain that must link a quasi$_c$-memory with a corresponding past cognitive and sensory state if they are to be "of" the same event, or if the former is to be "of" the latter. Since quasi$_c$-remembering is to be as much like remembering as is compatible with the failure of the strong previous awareness condition, M-type causal chains should resemble as much as possible the causal chains that are responsible for actual remembering, i.e., should resemble them as much as is compatible with their sometimes linking mental states belonging to different persons. At any given time a person can be said to have a total mental state which includes his memories or quasi$_c$-memories and whatever other mental states the person has at that time. Let us say that two total mental states, existing at different times, are directly M-connected if the later of them contains a quasi$_c$-memory which is linked by an M-type causal chain to a corresponding cognitive and sensory state contained in the earlier. And let us say, by way of giving a recursive definition, that two total mental states are M-connected if either (1) they are directly M-connected, or (2) there is some third total mental state to which each of them is M-connected.[17]

Now there are two cases we must consider. Either the world will be such, or it will not, that a total mental state existing at a particular time can be M-connected with at most one total mental state existing at each other moment in time. Or, what comes to the same thing, either the world will be such, or it will not, that no two total mental states existing at the same time can be M-connected. Let us begin by considering the case in which the former of these alternatives holds. This is the case that will exist if there is no "branching" of M-type causal chains, i.e., if it never happens that an M-type causal chain branches into two such chains which then produce quasi$_c$-memories belonging to different and simultaneously existing total mental states, and if it never happens that different M-type causal chains coalesce and produce in a single total mental state quasi$_c$-memories whose corresponding past cognitive and sensory states belonged to different and simultaneously existing total mental states. This is presumably the situation that exists in the actual world. And I think that in any world in which this situation exists M-connected total mental states will be, to use a term of Bertrand Russell's, "copersonal," i.e., states of one and the same person, and quasi$_c$-remembering will reduce to remembering. There seems to me to be at least this much truth in the claim that memory is constitutive of personal identity.[18] (But more about this in Sect. V.)

Now let us consider the case in which M-type causal chains do sometimes branch, and in which, as a result, it can happen that two or more simultaneously existing total mental states are M-connected. Here we cannot claim that if two total mental states are M-connected they are thereby copersonal without committing ourselves to the unattractive conclusion that a person can be in two different places, and can have two different total mental states, at one and the same time. But it is still open to us to say that if a total mental state existing at time t_1 and a total mental state existing at time t_2 are M-connected then they are copersonal *unless* the M-type chain connecting them branched at some time during the interval t_1–t_2. If we can say this, as I think we can, then even in a world in which there is branching of M-type causal chains the fact that a person quasi$_c$-remembers a past event or action would create a presumption that he, that same person, experienced the event or did the action, and therefore a presumption that the quasi$_c$-memory was actually a memory. This presumption would stand as long as there was no evidence that the M-type causal chain linking the past action or experience with the subsequent quasi$_c$-memory had branched during the interval between them.

Worlds of the sort we are now considering, i.e., worlds in which M-type causal chains sometimes branch, could be of several kinds. Consider first a world in which people occasionally undergo fission or fusion; i.e., people sometimes split, like amoebas, both offshoots having quasi$_c$-memories of the actions done prior to the fission by the person who underwent it, and two people sometimes coalesce into a single person who then has quasi$_c$-memories of both of their past histories. Here we cannot say that a person did whatever actions he quasi$_c$-remembers from the inside without running afoul of Leibniz' Law and the principle of the transitivity of identity. But we can say something close to this. Suppose that someone, call him Jones, splits into two persons, one of whom is I and the other is someone I shall call Jones II. Both Jones I and II have quasi$_c$-memories from the inside of Jones's past actions, and no one else does. If anyone now alive is identical with Jones it is either myself or Jones II, and any objection to saying that I am Jones is equally an objection to saying that Jones II is Jones. I think that we can say here that I am identical with Jones if anyone now alive is identical with him. Or suppose that two people, call them Brown and Smith, coalesce, resulting in me. I have quasi$_c$-memories from the inside of Brown's actions and also of Smith's actions. There are serious objections to identifying me with either Brown or Smith, but it seems clear here that if anyone now alive is identical with either Brown or Smith, I am. So in such a world the following principle holds: if at time t a person A quasi$_c$-remembers a past action X from the inside then A is identical with the person who did X if anyone alive at t is identical with him.[19]

But I think that we can imagine a world in which this principle would not hold. In the case in which two persons coalesce the M-type causal chains involved might be represented by a river having two "forks" of equal width. Suppose that instead of this we have an M-type causal chain, or a connected set of such causal chains, that could be represented by a river having several small tributaries. For example, suppose, very fancifully, that memories were stored, by some sort of chemical coding, in the blood rather than in brain cells, and that as a result of being given a blood transfusion one sometimes acquired quasi$_c$-memories "from the inside" of a few of the actions of the blood donor. Here the blood transfusion would be a "tributary" into what apart from its tributaries would be the sort of M-type causal chain that occurs in the history of a single person. Now I do not think that we would deny that A, existing at time t_2 was the same person as B, who existed at an earlier time t_1, merely because A quasi$_c$-remembers from the inside, as the result of a blood transfusion, an action at t_1 that was not done by B. Nor would we deny that another person C, the blood donor, is the person who did that past action merely because there is someone other than himself, namely A, who quasi$_c$-remembers it from the inside. So here it would not be true that if at time t a person quasi-remembers a past action from the inside then he is identical with the person who did it if anyone existing at t is identical with the person who did it.

Yet even in such a world it seems essential that in any total mental state the memories, i.e., the quasi$_c$-memories produced by the past history of the person whose total mental state it is, should outnumber the quasi$_c$-memories produced by any given tributary. If the quasi$_c$-memories produced by a given tributary outnumbered the memories then surely the tributary would not be a tributary at all, but would instead be the main stream. But this implies that if a person quasi$_c$-remembers an action from the inside then, in the absence of evidence to the contrary, he is entitled to regard it as more likely that the action was done by him than that it was done by any other given person. And this, taken together with my earlier point that if someone quasi$_c$-remembers an action from the inside there is a presumption that he is the person who did it, gives us a sense in which quasi$_c$-memory can be said to provide the quasi$_c$-rememberer with "special access" to his own past history. This is of course a much weaker sense of "special access" than that explained in Sect. I—but in this sense it will be true in *any* possible world, and not merely in ours, that people have a special access to their own past histories.

V

In the preceding sections it was assumed that remembering, as opposed to (mere) quasi$_c$-remembering, necessarily involves the satisfaction of the strong previous awareness condition; that is, it was assumed that in any genuine case of event memory the memory must correspond to a past cognitive and sensory state of the rememberer himself. And this is commonly supposed in discussions of memory and personal identity. But it is not really clear that this assumption is correct. For consider again the hypothetical case in which a man's body "splits" like an amoeba into two physiologically identical bodies, and in which both offshoots produce memory claims corresponding to the past life of the original person. Or, to take a case that lies closer to the realm of real possibility, consider the hypothetical case in which a human brain is split, its two hemispheres are transplanted into the newly vacated skulls of different bodies, and both transplant recipients survive, regain consciousness, and begin to make memory claims that correspond to the past history of the brain "donor."[20] In neither case can we identify both of the physiological offshoots of a person with the original person, unless we are willing to take the drastic step of giving up Leibniz' Law and the transitivity of identity. But is it clear that it would be wrong to say that each of the offshoots remembers the actions, experiences, etc., of the original person? There is, to be sure, an awkwardness about saying that each offshoot remembers *doing* an action done by the original person, for this seems to imply that an action done by one and only one person was done by each of the two non-identical offshoots. But perhaps we can say that each of the offshoots does remember the action "from the inside." In our world, where such bizarre cases do not occur, the only actions anyone remembers from the inside are those that he himself performed, so it is not surprising that the only idiomatic way of reporting that one

remembers an action from the inside is by saying that one
remembers doing the action. But this need not prevent us from
describing my hypothetical cases by saying that both offshoots do
remember the actions of the original person, and it does not seem
to me unnatural to describe them in this way. If this is a correct
way of describing them, then perhaps my second sort of quasi-
remembering, i.e., quasi$_c$-remembering, turns out to be just
remembering, and the previous awareness condition for remembering turns out to be the causal requirement discussed in the
preceding section rather than the stronger condition I have been
assuming it to be.

If the suggestion just made about the conditions for remembering is correct, the logical connection between remembering
and personal identity is looser than I have been supposing it to
be. Yet adopting this suggestion does not prevent one from defending the claim that remembering is constitutive of and criterial
for personal identity; on the contrary, this makes it possible to
defend the letter of this claim, and not just its spirit, against the
very common objection that any attempt to analyze personal identity in terms of memory will turn out to be circular.

Bishop Butler objected against Locke's account of personal
identity that "one should really think it self-evident, that consciousness of personal identity presupposes, and therefore cannot
constitute, personal identity, any more than knowledge, in any
other case, can constitute truth, which it presupposes."[21] More recently several writers have argued that while "*S* remembers doing
A" entails "*S* did *A*" (and so entails "*S* is identical with the person who did *A*"), this is only because "*S* remembers doing *A*"
is elliptical for "*S* remembers himself doing *A*."[22] To offer as a
partial analysis of the notion of personal identity, and as a criterion of personal identity, the formula "If *S* remembers (himself)
doing action *A, S* is the same as the person who did *A*" would be
like offering as a partial definition of the word "red," and as a
criterion of redness, the formula "If *S* knows that *X* is red, then *X*
is red." In both cases the concept allegedly being defined is illic-
itly employed in the formulation of the defining condition. Likewise, it has been argued that while someone's remembering a
past event is a sufficient condition of his being identical with a
witness to the event, we cannot use the former as a criterion for

the latter, since in order to establish that a person really does remember a given past event we have to establish that he, that very person, was a witness to the event. And if this is so, the formula "If S remembers E, S is identical with someone who witnessed E" will be circular if offered as a partial analysis of the concept of personal identity.[23]

Such objections assume that remembering involves the satisfaction of the strong previous awareness condition, and they can be avoided on the assumption that the previous awareness condition is weaker than this, e.g., is that given for quasi$_c$-remembering in Sect. IV. Or, better, they can be avoided if we explicitly use "remember" in a "weak" sense ("remember$_w$") rather than in a "strong" sense ("remember$_s$"), the strength of the sense depending on the strength of the associated previous awareness condition. Although there are perhaps other possibilities, let us take "remember$_w$" to be synonymous with "quasi$_c$-remember." Clearly, to establish that S remembers$_w$ event E (or remembers$_w$ action A from the inside) it is not necessary to establish that S himself witnessed E (or did A), for it will be enough if S is the offshoot of someone who witnessed E (did A). And while we cannot claim that statements about what events or actions a man remembers$_w$ logically entail statements about his identity and past history, this does not prevent the truth of the former from being criterial evidence for, and from being partially constitutive of, the truth of the latter. For we can still assert as a logical truth that if S remembers$_w$ event E (or remembers$_w$ action A from the inside), *and* if there has been no branching of M-type causal chains during the relevant stretch of S's history, then S is one of the witnesses of E (is the person who did A). Here we avoid the circularity that Butler and others have thought to be involved in any attempt to give an account of personal identity, and of the criteria of personal identity, in terms of memory.

In the actual world, people remember$_s$ whatever they remember$_w$, and this makes it difficult to settle the question of whether it is the weak or the strong sense of "remember" that is employed in ordinary discourse. It is possible that this question has no answer; since branching of M-type causal chains does not in fact occur, and is seldom envisaged, people have had no practical motive for distinguishing between the strong and the weak senses of "remember." But I do not think that this question is especially important. We can defend the spirit of the claim that memory is a criterion of personal identity without settling this question, although in order to defend the letter of that claim we must maintain that in its ordinary use "remember" means "remember$_w$."

At this point I should say something about why it is important to insist on the claim that there is a causal element in the notion of memory. For this claim has recently come under attack.[24] It has been argued that the notion of memory should be analyzed in terms of the *retention,* rather than the causation, of knowledge, and that the notion of retention is not itself a causal notion. Now I have no objection to saying that remembering$_s$ consists in the retention of knowledge. But I believe that unless we understand the notion of retention, as well as that of memory, as involving a causal component, we cannot account for the role played by the notion of memory, or even the concept of similarity, in judgments of personal identity.

Here it will be useful to consider a hypothetical case I have discussed at some length elsewhere.[25] Let us suppose that the brain from the body of one man, Brown, is transplanted into the body of another man, Robinson, and that the resulting creature—I call him "Brownson"—survives and upon regaining consciousness begins making memory claims corresponding to the past history of Brown rather than that of Robinson. We can also suppose that Brownson manifests personality traits strikingly like those previously manifested by Brown and quite unlike those manifested by Robinson. Although Brownson has Robinson's (former) body, I doubt if anyone would want to say that Brownson is Robinson, and I think that most people would want to say that Brownson is (is the same person as) Brown.

But what can we offer as evidence that Brownson is Brown? Clearly the mere correspondence of Brownson's ostensible memories to Brown's past history, and the similarity of Brownson's personality to Brown's, is far from being sufficient evidence. And it is equally clear that the notion of the *retention* of knowledge and traits is of no use here. To be sure, once we take ourselves to have established that Brownson is Brown we can say that Brownson retains knowledge, and also personality traits, acquired by Brownson in the past. But the latter assertion presupposes the identity of Brownson and Brown, and cannot without circularity be offered as evidence for it. Indeed, the circularity is the same as what would be involved in offering as evidence of this identity the fact that Brownson remembers$_s$ Brown's past experiences and actions.

We do not, however, beg the question about identity if we take Brownson's possession of what used to be Brown's brain, together with the empirical facts about the role played by the brain in memory, as establishing that Brown's ostensible memories are directly M-connected with Brown's past actions and experiences, i.e., are causally related to them in essentially the same ways as people's memories are generally connected with their own past experiences and actions. This in turn establishes that Brownson quasi$_c$-remembers, and so remembers$_w$, Brown's past experiences and actions. And from this in turn, and from the fact that we have good reason to suppose that no other person's memories are M-connected with Brown's past history in this way, i.e., that there has been no "branching" of M-type causal chains, we can conclude that Brownson is Brown.[26]

We can reason in this way only if we can assert that there is a causal connection between Brownson's past history and Brownson's ostensible memories. And this, it seems to me, we are clearly entitled to do. Given that Brownson has Brown's former brain, there is every reason to think that had Brown's history been different in certain ways, there would (*ceteris paribus*) be corresponding differences in what Brownson ostensibly remembers. I can see no reason for doubting that such counterfactuals assert causal connections. Similar remarks can be made about the similarity between Brownson's and Brown's personality traits. Given that Brownson has Brown's former brain, we have reason to think that had Brown developed a different set of personality traits, Brownson would (*ceteris paribus*) have those personality traits rather than the ones he has. And while we cannot naturally speak of Brown's having a certain trait at one time as causing Brownson to have the same trait at a subsequent time, we can speak of the former as being an important part of a causally sufficient condition for the latter. It is only where we suppose that the traits of things at different times are causally related in this way that we are entitled to take the similarity of something at one time and something at another time as evidence of identity.

VI

We are now in a position to reassess the view, mentioned in Sec. II, that the knowledge of our own pasts and our own identities provided us by memory is essentially "noncriterial." If I remember$_s$ an action or experience from the inside, and know that I do, it makes no sense for me to inquire whether that action or experience was my own. But it seems logically possible that one should remember$_w$ an action or experience from the inside (i.e., quasi$_c$-remember it) without remembering$_s$ it. So if one remembers$_w$ an action or experience from the inside it can make sense to inquire whether it was one's own (whether one remembers$_s$ it), and it would seem offhand that there is no reason why one should not attempt to answer this question on the basis of criteria of personal identity.

But while an action I remember$_w$ from the inside can fail to be mine, there is only one way in which this can happen, namely through there having been branching in the M-type causal chain linking it with my present memory. So in asking whether the action was mine, the only question I can significantly be asking is whether there was such branching. If I go on to verify that there was no branching, I thereby establish that a sufficient criterion of personal identity is satisfied. If instead I conclude on inductive grounds that there was no branching, relying on my general knowledge that M-type causal chains seldom or never branch (or that it is physiologically impossible for them to do so), I thereby conclude that a sufficient criterion of personal identity is satisfied. But an important part of what the satisfaction of this criterion consists in, namely my remembering$_w$ the past action from the inside, is not something I establish, and not something I conclude on inductive grounds, but is something I necessarily presuppose in inquiring concerning my relation to the remembered$_w$ action. In cases where one remembers$_w$ a past action from the inside, and knows of it only on that basis, one cannot significantly inquire concerning it whether one does remember$_w$ it—for as I tried to bring out in my discussion of quasi-remembering, there is no way of knowing the past that stands to remembering$_w$ as remembering$_w$ stands to remembering$_s$, i.e., is such that one can know of a past event in this way and regard it as an open question whether in so knowing of it one is remembering$_w$ it. So in such cases the satisfaction of this part of the memory criterion for personal identity is a precondition of one's being able to raise the question of identity, and cannot be something one establishes in attempting to answer that question.

That one remembers$_w$ a past action is not (and could not be) one of the things one remembers$_w$ about it, and neither is the fact that there is no branching in the M-type causal chain linking it with one's memory of it. And normally there is no set of remembered$_w$ features of an action one remembers$_w$ from the inside, or of the person who did the action, by which one identifies the action as one's own and the agent as oneself. If one has not identified a remembered person as oneself on the basis of his remembered$_w$ features, then of course it cannot be the case that one has *mis*identified him on this basis. This is not to say that there is no basis on which one might misidentify a remembered$_w$ person as oneself. If there can, logically, be remembering$_w$ that is not remembering$_s$, then where one remembers$_w$ an action from the inside one's judgment that one did the action will not be logically immune to error through misidentification in the sense defined in Sec. II—though given the contingent fact that all remembering$_w$ is remembering$_s$, such judgments can be said to have a *de facto* immunity to error through misidentification. But the sort of error through misidentification to which a statement like "I saw a canary" is liable, if based on a memory$_w$ from the inside, is utterly different from that to which a statement like "John saw a canary" is liable when based on a memory$_w$ of the incident reported. If the making of the latter statement involves an error through misidentification, this will be because either (1) the speaker misidentified someone as John at the time the reported incident occurred, and retained this misidentification in memory, or (2) at some subsequent time, perhaps at the time of speaking, the speaker misidentified a remembered$_w$ person as John on the basis of his remembered$_w$ features. But if I remember$_w$ from the inside someone seeing a canary, and am mistaken in thinking that person to have been myself, it is absurd to suppose that this mistake originated at the time at which the remembered$_w$ seeing occurred. Nor, as I have said, will this be a misidentification based on the remembered$_w$ features of the person who saw the canary. What could be the basis for a misidentification in this case is the mistaken belief that there is no branching in the M-type causal chain linking one's memory with the past incident. But a misidentification on this basis, while logically possible, would be radically unlike the misidentifications that actually occur in the making of third person reports.

VII

Because I have taken seriously the possibility of worlds in which M-type causal chains sometimes branch, and thus the possibility of quasi$_c$-remembering (remembering$_w$) that is not remembering$_s$, I have had to qualify and weaken my initial claims about the "special access" people have to their own past histories. But if our concern is with the elucidation of our present concept of personal identity, and with personal identity as something that has a special sort of importance for us, then it is not clear that the possibility of such worlds, and the qualifications this requires, should be taken as seriously as I have taken them. For there is reason to think (1) that some of our concepts, perhaps including the concept of a person, would necessarily undergo significant modification in their application to such worlds, and (2) that in such worlds personal identity would not *matter* to people in quite the way it does in the actual world.

There are important connections between the concept of personal identity and the concepts of various "backward looking" and "forward looking" mental states. Thus the appropriate objects of remorse, and of a central sort of pride, are past actions done by the very person who is remorseful or proud, and the appropriate objects of fear and dread, and of delighted anticipation, are events which the subject of these emotions envisages as happening to himself. And intentions have as their "intentional objects" actions to be done by the very person who has the intention. It is difficult to see how the notion of a person could be applied, *with these conceptual connections remaining intact,* to a world in which M-type causal chains frequently branch, e.g., one in which persons frequently undergo fission. If I remember$_w$ from the inside a cruel or deceitful action, am I to be relieved of all tendency to feel remorse if I discover that because of fission someone else remembers$_w$ it too? May I not feel proud of an action I remember$_w$ from the inside even though I know that I am only one of several offshoots of the person who did it, and so cannot claim to be identical with him? Am I not to be afraid of horrible things I expect to happen to my future offshoots, and not to view with pleasant anticipation the delights that are in prospect for them? And is it to be impossible, or logically inappropriate, for me knowingly to form intentions, and make decisions and plans, which because of the prospect of immanent fission will have to be carried out by my offshoots rather than by me? To the extent that I can imagine such a world, I find it incredible to suppose that these questions must be answered in the affirmative. The prospect of immanent fission might not be appealing, but it seems highly implausible to suppose that the only rational attitude toward it would be that appropriate to the prospect of immanent death (for fission, unlike death, would be something "lived through"). It seems equally implausible to suppose that a person's concern for the well-being of his offshoots should be construed as altruism; surely this concern would, or at any rate could, be just like the self-interested concern each of us has for his own future well-being. Yet a negative answer to my rhetorical questions would suggest that either the concept of a person or such concepts as those of pride, remorse, fear, etc., would undergo significant modification in being applied to such a world.[27]

A person's past history is the most important source of his knowledge of the world, but it is also an important source of his knowledge, and his conception, of himself; a person's "self-image," his conception of his own character, values, and potentialities, is determined in a considerable degree by the way in which he views his own past actions. And a person's future history is the primary focus of his desires, hopes, and fears.[28] If these remarks do not express truths about the concept of personal identity, they at least express truths about the *importance* of this concept in our conceptual scheme, or in our "form of life." It seems plausible to suppose that in a world in which fission was common personal identity would not have this sort of importance. Roughly speaking, the portion of past history that would matter to a person in this special way would be that which it is possible for him to remember$_w$, and not merely that which it is possible for him to remember$_s$. And the focus of people's "self-interested" attitudes and emotions would be the future histories of their offshoots, and of their offshoots' offshoots, and so on, as well as their own future histories. In the actual world it is true both that (1) remembering$_w$ is always remembering$_s$ (and thus that there is special access in the strong sense characterized in Sect. I), and that (2) the primary focus of a person's "self-interested" attitudes and emotions is his own past and future history. It is surely no accident that (1) and (2) go together.[29]

NOTES

1. Locke, *Essay Concerning Human Understanding,* Bk. II, Chap. 27, sec. 9 (London, 1912). Italics added.

2. In their paper "Remembering" (*The Philosophical Review,* vol. 75 [April, 1966]) C. B. Martin and Max Deutscher express what I call the previous awareness condition by saying that "a person can be said to remember something happening or, in general, remember something directly, only if he has observed or experienced it." Their notion of direct remembering seems to be much the same as Norman Malcolm's notion of "personal memory" (see his "Three Lectures on Memory" in *Knowledge and Certainty* [Englewood Cliffs, N.J., 1963], pp. 203–221). To remember that Caesar invaded Britain I need not have had any experience of the invasion, but no one who lacked such experience could directly or personally remember that Caesar invaded Britain. In this paper I am primarily concerned with memories that are of events, i.e., of something happening, and do not explicitly consider what Malcolm calls "factual memory," i.e., memories *that* such and such was (or is, or will be) the case, but what I say can be extended to cover all cases of direct or personal memory. Martin and Deutscher hold, and I agree, that remembering something happening is always direct remembering.

There are apparent counterexamples to the previous witnessing condition as I have formulated it. I can be said to remember Kennedy's assassination, which is presumably an event, yet I did not witness or observe it, and the knowledge I had of it at the time was indirect. But while I can be said to remember the assassination, I could hardly be said to remember Kennedy being shot (what I do remember is hearing about it, and the impact this made on me and those around me). Perhaps I can be said to remember the assassination because we sometimes mean by "the assassination" not only the events in Dallas but their immediate effects throughout the nation and world. In any case, when I speak of memories of events in this paper I mean what Martin and Deutscher speak of as memories of something happening.

3. Although self-reference is typically done with first person pronouns, it can be done with names, and even with definite descriptions—as when De Gaulle says "De Gaulle intends . . . ," and the chairman of a meeting says "The Chair recognizes. . . ." In such cases these expressions are "self-referring," not merely because their reference is in fact to the speaker, but also because the speaker intends in using them to refer to himself.

4. There is a subtle distinction between this sort of case and cases like the following, which I would not count as a case of error through misidentification. Suppose that Jones says "You are a fool," and I mistakenly think that he is speaking to me. Subsequently I say "I remember Jones calling me a fool," and my statement is false through no fault of my memory. While this is a case of knowing *that* Jones called someone (someone or other) a fool and mistakenly thinking that he was calling me a fool, it is not a case of knowing *of* some particular person that Jones called him a fool but mistakenly identifying that person as oneself. Whereas in the other case we can say, not merely that I know that someone or other blushed, mistakenly think that it was I, but I know *of* some particular person (namely the man I saw in the mirror) that he blushed and have mistakenly identified him as myself.

5. I have discussed the immunity to error through misidentification of first person present tense statements in my paper "Self-Reference and Self-Awareness," *The Journal of Philosophy,* vol. 65, 19 (1968). In that paper I made the mistake of associating this feature with the peculiarities of the first-person pronouns. But in fact present tense statements having the appropriate sorts of predicates are immune to error to misidentification with respect to any expressions that are "self-referring" in the sense of footnote 3, including names and definite descriptions. If someone says "De Gaulle intends to remove France from NATO," and is using "De Gaulle" to refer to himself, his statement is in the relevant sense immune to error through misidentification, regardless of whether he is right in thinking his name is "De Gaulle" and that he is the President of France.

6. H. P. Grice, "Personal Identity," *Mind,* vol. 50 (1941), p. 344.

7. G. C. Nerlich, "On Evidence for Identity," *Australian Journal of Philosophy,* vol. 37 (1959), p. 208.

8. I am not here endorsing the view, which I in fact reject, that remembering consists in the having of an image, or some other sort of mental "representation," in which the memory content is in some way encoded. It is sufficient for the existence at *t* of the "cognitive state" of remembering such and such that it be true of the person at *t* that he remembers such and such; I am not here committing myself to any account of what, if anything, someone's remembering such and such "consists in."

9. I should make it clear that I am not saying that what we remember is always, or even normally, a past cognitive and sensory state. I am not propounding the view, which is sometimes held but which is clearly false, that "strictly speaking" one can remember only one's own past experiences. I am saying only that if a person remembers an event that occurred at time *t* then at *t* there must have been a corresponding cognitive and sensory state—which the person may or may not remember—that was of that event. It would not be easy to specify just what sort of correspondence is required here, and I shall

not attempt to do so. But I take it as obvious that the claim to remember firing a gun requires, for its truth, a different sort of past cognitive and sensory state than the claim to remember hearing someone else fire a gun, and that the latter, in turn, requires a different sort of past cognitive and sensory state than the claim to remember seeing someone fire a gun. Sometimes one remembers a past event but no longer remembers just how one knew of it at the time of its occurrence; in such a case one's memory, because of vagueness and incompleteness, corresponds to a wider range of possible cognitive and sensory states than (say) a memory of seeing the event or a memory of being told about it.

10. See my book *Self-Knowledge and Self-Identity* (Ithaca, N.Y., 1963), especially Chap. Four, and my paper "Personal Identity and Memory," *Journal of Philosophy,* vol. 56 (1959), pp. 868–882.

11. P. F. Strawson, *The Bounds of Sense* (London, 1966), p. 165.

12. I owe to Normal Malcolm the point that to be memory knowledge one's knowledge must be in some way due to, must exist because of, a past cognitive and sensory state of oneself—see his "Three Lectures on Memory" (*op. cit.*). Malcolm holds that "due to" does not here express a causal relationship, but I have been persuaded otherwise by Martin's and Deutscher's "Remembering" (*op. cit.*). See also my paper "On Knowing Who One Is" (*Common Factor,* No. 4, 1966), and David Wiggins' *Identity and Spatio-Temporal Continuity* (Oxford, 1967), especially p. 50 ff. The view that there is a causal element in the concept of memory is attacked by Roger Squires in his recent paper "Memory Unchained" (*The Philosophical Review,* vol. 78 [1969] pp. 178–196); I make a very limited reply to this in Sect. V of this paper.

13. P. F. Strawson, *Individuals* (London 1959), p. 20.

14. It will perhaps be objected that the dictum that unrestricted negative existential claims are unfalsifiable in principle is brought into question by the possibility that we might discover—what some cosmologists would there is good reason for believing—that space and past time are finite. If we discovered this, why shouldn't we be able, at least in principle, to establish that at no place does there exist, and at no time in the past has there existed, a duplicate of New York?

One way of countering this objection would be to introduce the possibility, which has been argued by Anthony Quinton in his paper "Spaces and Times" (*Philosophy,* vol. 57 [1962] pp. 130–141), of there being a multiplicity of different and spatially unrelated spaces. Establishing that there is no duplicate of New York in our space would not establish that there is no space in which there is such a duplicate, and if it is possible for there to be multiplicity of spaces there would seem to be no way in which the latter could be established.

But we needn't have recourse to such recondite possibilities in order to counter the objection, if it is viewed as an objection to my claim that it is the fact that remembering involves the satisfaction of the previous awareness condition that makes it possible for us to rule out the possibility that memory claims are false through misidentification owing to the reduplication of landmarks. For to discover that space or past time is finite, and that massive reduplication does not occur, one would have to have a vast amount of empirical information about the world, including information about the histories of particular things. But, as I think the remainder of my discussion should make clear, one could not be provided with such information by memory (or by quasi-memory) unless one were *already* entitled in a large number of cases to refer to particular places and things in one's memory reports without having to regard it as possible that one's references were mistaken owing to massive reduplication. So this entitlement would have to precede the discovery that space and past time are finite, and could not depend on it.

15. The point made in the preceding footnote can now be expressed by saying that even if we, who have the faculty of memory, could establish that at no place and time has there been a duplicate of New York, this could not be established by someone whose faculty of knowing the past was a faculty of quasi-memory.

16. It may be objected that I have overlooked one way in which a quasi-rememberer might begin to reconstruct his own past history, and the histories of other things, from the information provided him by his quasi-memories. The quasi-rememberer's difficulties would be solved if he had a way of sorting out those of his quasi-memories that are his own past, i.e., are memories, from those that are not. But it may seem that the quasi-rememberer could easily tell which of his quasi-memories of the very *recent* past are of his own past, namely by noting which of them have contents very similar to the contents of his *present* experiences; e.g., if he quasi-remembers from the inside the very recent seeing of a scene that resembles very closely the scene he presently sees, it may seem that he can justifiably conclude that the quasi-remembered seeing was his own. And it may seem that by starting in this way he could trace back his own history by finding among his quasi-memories a subset of situations that form a spatiotemporally continuous series of situations, that series terminating in the situation he presently perceives.

This objection assumes that the quasi-rememberer can know the degree of recentness of the situations of which he has quasi-memories, but I shall not here question this assumption. What I shall question is the assumption that if the quasi-rememberer knows that a quasi-remembered scene occurred only a moment or so ago, and that it closely resembles the scene he presently sees, he is entitled to believe that it is numerically the same scene as the one he presently sees and that in all probability it was he who saw it. For of course it could be the case that there is somewhere else a duplicate of the scene he sees, and that his quasi-memory is of that duplicate. It will perhaps be objected that while this is logically possible (given the possibility of quasi-remembering that is not remembering), it is highly improbable. But while it may be intrinsically improbable that a highly complicated situation should be reduplicated within some limited spatiotemporal area, it does not seem intrinsically improbable that such a situation should be reduplicated somewhere or other in the universe—unless the universe is finite, which is something the quasi-rememberer could have no reason for believing (see footnotes 14 and 15). Moreover, one could not be in a position to know how rare or frequent such reduplication is in fact, and therefore how likely or unlikely it is that a given situation is reduplicated, unless one already had a way of reidentifying places and things. So the quasi-rememberer could not be in a position to know this, for he could have a way of reidentifying places and things only if he were already in a position to rule out reduplication as improbable.

17. It is worth mentioning that if quasi$_c$-remembering is to be as much like remembering as possible then not just any causal chain linking a past cognitive and sensory state with a subsequent quasi$_c$-memory can be allowed to count as an M-type causal chain. For as Martin and Deutscher (*op. cit.*) point

out, there are various sorts of cases in which a man's knowledge of a past event is causally due to his previous experience of it but in which the causal connection is obviously not of the right kind to permit us to say that he remembers the event. E.g., I have completely forgotten the event, but know of it now because you told me about it, and you came to know about it through my telling you about it prior to my forgetting it. It is easier to decide in particular cases whether the causal connection is "of the right kind" than it is to give a general account of what it is for the causal connection to be of the right kind, i.e., what it is for there to be an M-type causal chain. I shall not attempt to do the latter here. The notion of an M-type causal chain would of course be completely useless if it were impossible to determine in any particular case whether the causal connection is "of the right kind" without already having determined that the case is one of remembering—but I shall argue in Sect. V that this is not impossible.

18. In his paper "Bodily Continuity and Personal Identity: A Reply" (*Analysis,* vol. 21 [1960] pp. 42–48), B. A. O. Williams says that "identity is a one-one relation, and . . . no principle can be a criterion of identity for things of type T if it relies on what is logically a one-many or many-many relation between things of type T," and remarks that the relation "being disposed to make sincere memory claims which exactly fit the life of" is a many-one relation and "hence cannot possibly be adequate in logic to constitute a criterion of identity" (pp. 44–45). Now it may seem that my version of the view that memory is a criterion of personal identity is open to the same objection, for if M-type causal chains can branch and coalesce then the relation "has a quasi-memory which is linked by an M-type causal chain with a cognitive and sensory state of" is not logically a one-one relation. But while this relationship is not logically one-one, the relationship "has a quasi-memory which is linked by a *nonbranching* M-type causal chain with a cognitive and sensory state of" is logically one-one, and it is the holding of the latter relationship that I would hold to be a criterion, in the sense of being a sufficient condition, for personal identity.

19. A. N. Prior has defended the view that in cases of fission *both* offshoots can be identified with the original person, although not with each other. This of course involves modifying the usual account of the logical features of identity. See his " 'Opposite Number' " (*Review of Metaphysics,* vol. 11 [1957] pp. 196–201), and his "Time, Existence and Identity" (*Proceedings of the Aristotelian Society,* 1965–1966). Roderick Chisholm takes a very different view. Considering the supposition that "you knew that your body, like that of an amoeba, would one day undergo fission and that you would go off, so to speak, in two different directions," he says "it seems to me, first, that there is no possibility whatever that *you* would be *both* the person on the right and the person on the left. It seems to me, secondly, that there *is* a possibility that you would be one or the other of those two persons" ("The Loose and Popular and the Strict and Philosophical Senses of Identity," in *Perception and Personal Identity,* ed. by Norman S. Care and Robert H. Grimm [Cleveland, 1969], p. 106). It is not clear to me whether Chisholm would hold that one (but not both) of the offshoots might be me if the memories of each stood in the same causal relationships to my actions and experiences as the memories of the other, and if each resembled me, in personality, appearance, etc., as much as the other. If so, I would disagree.

20. See Wiggins, *op. cit.,* p. 53, where such a case is discussed.

21. Joseph Butler, "Of Personal Identity," First Dissertation to the *Analogy of Religion.* Reprinted in Flew, ed., *Body, Mind and Death,* (New York, 1964), pp. 166–172.

22. See A. J. Ayer, *The Problem of Knowledge,* (Harmondsworth, Middlesex, 1956), p. 196, and B. A. O. Williams, "Personal Identity and Individuation," in Gustavsen (ed.) *Essays in Philosophical Psychology* (New York, 1964), pp. 327–b 28 (originally published in the *Proceedings of the Aristotelian Society,* vol. 57, 1956–57).

23. See Williams, *op. cit.,* p. 329, and my *Personal Identity and Memory,* pp. 869–870 and p. 877. In the latter, and in *Self-Knowledge and Self-Identity,* I attempt to reduce the force of this objection by arguing that it is a "conceptual truth" that memory claims are generally true, and that we can therefore be entitled to say that a person remembers a past event without already having established, or having inductive evidence, that some other criterion of personal identity (one not involving memory) is satisfied. This way of handling the objection no longer seems to me satisfactory.

24. See Squires' "Memory Unchained," *op. cit.*

25. *Self-Knowledge and Self-Identity,* pp. 23–25 and 245–47.

26. In *Self-Knowledge and Self-Identity* I held that saying that Brownson is Brown would involve making a "decision" about the relative weights to be assigned to different criteria of personal identity, and that in the absence of such a decision there is no right answer to the question whether Brownson is Brown. I have come to believe that there is a right answer to this question, namely that Brownson is Brown, and that my former view overlooked the importance of the causal component in the notion of memory—see my treatment of this example in "On Knowing Who One Is," *op. cit.*

27. On this and related questions, see my exchange with Chisholm in *Perception and Personal Identity, op. cit.*

28. This is not to deny the possibility or occurrence of unselfish attitudes and emotions. Even the most unselfish man, who is willing to suffer that others may prosper, does not and cannot regard the pleasures and pains that are in prospect for him in the same light as he regards those that are in prospect for others. He may submit to torture, but he would hardly be human if he could regularly view his own future sufferings with the same detachment (which is not indifference) as he views the future sufferings of others.

29. This is a considerably revised version of a paper which was read at a conference on "The Concept of a Person" at the University of Michigan in November 1967, and at the University of British Columbia and the University of Saskatchewan at Saskatoon in the Spring of 1969. I am grateful to Harry Frankfurt, Robert Nozick, and Michael Slote for criticisms of the earlier versions of the paper.

William Uzgalis

17

Selections from the
Clarke-Collins Correspondence

*The correspondence between Samuel Clarke (1675–1729) and
Anthony Collins (1676–1729) took its inspiration from a book
published in 1706 by Henry Dodwell that put forward the view
that the soul was not naturally, but only supernaturally, immortal.
The work was the subject of a public refutation by Clarke, who
found the possibility of naturally thinking matter implausible.
Collins wrote a defense of Dodwell in a public "Letter to Mr.
Dodwell," to which Clarke responded. Over the next two years
Clarke wrote three more defenses of his original letter to Henry
Dodwell, and Collins wrote three replies. Each of these was longer than its predecessor. Clarke, who became increasingly irri-
tated as the debate continued, had the final word in "The Fourth
Defense of an Argument." While the central issue of the correspondence is whether it is possible for consciousness to inhere in
a material system and thus for matter to think, the discussion toward the end turned to other issues, such as free will and deter-
minism and the adequacy of Collins' account of personal identity.
Collins was a protégé and an admirer of Locke; his theory of
personal identity was based on Locke's, relying on links of memory rather than identity of immaterial substance. And Locke's*

These selections are taken from Samuel Clarke, *The Works of Samuel Clarke,* vols.
1–4 (1738; reprinted, New York: Garland Press, 1978). The editor is grateful to Trip
McCrossin, who prepared a transcription of the 1738 edition into modern typescript,
modernizing punctuation and correcting a few grammatical errors.

speculations that matter might think were behind Collins' defense of Dodwell on this topic.

The following selections focus on Clarke and Collins' discussion of personal identity as it develops from the issue of thinking matter.

COLLINS: IT'S CONCEIVABLE THAT MATTER THINKS

In "A Reply to Mr. Clarke's Defense" Collins makes the claim that it is the brain that is conscious and thinks (Clarke, Works, *p. 768).*

. . . for the different in the single and separate parts of a system of matter, by uniting in one operation or power to operate, are the causes of the existence of that power which did not exist in the particles singly. And thus it may be conceived that there is a power in all those particles that compose the brain to contribute to the act of thinking before they are united under that form, though while they are disunited they have no more of consciousness than any being which produces sweetness in us (that is made up of parts wherein different powers inhere) when under a particular form has a power to produce sweetness in us when its parts are disunited and separated.

CLARKE: THINKING MATTER IS A CONTRADICTION

In "A Second Defense of an Argument" Clarke claims that consciousness arising from the brain is a contradiction (Clarke, Works, *p. 787).*

And here I cannot but take notice that, besides the contradictions before-mentioned, you have, by choosing to annex consciousness to so flux a substance as the brain or the spirits in it, fallen into another very great absurdity. For if the brain or spirits be the subject of consciousness, and the parts of the brain or spirits be (as they certainly are, whatever question may be made concerning any original *solid stamina* of the body) in perpetual flux and change, it will follow that that consciousness by which I *not only remember* that certain things were done many years since, but also *am conscious that they were done by me, by the very same individual conscious being* who now remembers them—it will follow, I say, that that consciousness is transferred from one subject to another. That is to say, that it is a real quality which subsists without inhering in any subject at all.

At the end of "A Second Defense of an Argument" Clarke sets forth his whole argument in fifteen propositions (Clarke, Works, *pp. 795–99).*

Having thus at large endeavored to give you particular satisfaction in every one of the difficulties you proposed, I shall conclude with briefly repeating the strength of the argument in a few plain and easy *propositions,* and so leave it to the judgment of the inquisitive and impartial reader.

(Note: by consciousness *in the following propositions, the reader may understand indifferently either the* reflex act—by which a man knows his thoughts to be his own thoughts *(which is the strict and* most proper sense of the word)—or the direct act of thinking, *or* the power or capacity of thinking, *or (which is of the same import)* simple sensation, *or the* power of self-motion or beginning motion by the will *the argument holding equally in all or any of these senses, as has been before said.)*

I. Every *System of Matter* consists of a *Multitude of* distinct *Parts.*

> This, I think, is granted by all.

II. Every *real Quality* inheres in some *Subject.*

> This also, I think, is granted by all. For whatever is called a *quality,* and yet inheres not in any *subject,* must either subsist of itself—and then it is a *substance,* not a *quality*—or else it is nothing but a *mere name.*

III. No *individual* or *single quality* of one particle of matter can be the *individual* or *single quality* of another particle.

> The *heat* of one particle is not the *heat* of another. The *gravity,* the *color,* the *figure,* of one particle is not the same individual *gravity, color,* or *figure* of another particle. The *consciousness* or *sensation* of one particle (supposing it to be a quality of matter) is not the *consciousness* or *sensation* of another. If it was, it would follow that the same thing could be *two,* in the same sense and at the same time that it is *one.*
>
> *Note,* from hence may be drawn an evident confutation of that absurd notion which Mr. *Hobbes* suggests in his *Physics* (ch. 25, sect. 5) that *all matter* is essentially *endued with an obscure actual*

sense and perception, but that there is required a number and apt ‚composition of parts to make up *a clear and distinct sensation of consciousness.* For from this notion it would follow that the resulting *sensation* or *consciousness* at last, being but one distinct *sensation* or *consciousness* (as is that of a man) the *sensation* or *consciousness* of every one of the constituent particles, would be the individual *sensation* or *consciousness* of all and each of the rest.

IV. Every *real simple quality* that resides *in* any *whole material system* resides *in* all the *parts* of that system.

The *magnitude* of every *body* is the sum of the *magnitude* of its several *parts.* The *motion* of every *body* is the sum of the *motions* of its several *parts.* The *heat* of every *body* is the sum of the *heat* of its several *parts.* The *color* of every *body* is the sum of the *color* of its several *parts.** And the same is universally true of *every simple quality* residing *in* any *system.* For residing in the *whole* and not residing in the *parts* is *residing* in a thing and not *residing* in it at the same time.

V. Every *real compound quality* that resides *in* any whole material *system* is a number of simple qualities residing *in* all the *parts* of that system—some in one part, some in another.

Thus in the instance of *mixed colors—when* the simples *blue,* suppose, *and yellow* make the *whole* appear *green*—in this case, that *portion* of the system in which any one of the particular simple qualities resides is a *whole* system with respect to that quality, and the quality residing in it resides in the several *particles* of which that *portion of the system* is constituted. And so of the rest.

VI. Every *real quality, simple* or *compound,* that *results from* any whole material *system,* but does not *reside in it, that* is, neither in all its distinct parts, nor in all the parts of some portion of it, according to the explication of the two foregoing propositions, is the mode or quality of some *other substance,* and not of *that.*

All sensible secondary qualities—heat, *color, smell, taste, sound,* and the like—are of this kind, being in reality not *qualities* of the *bodies* they are ascribed to, but *modes* of the *mind* that perceives them.

*Note, by Heat here is meant that Motion which causes in us the Sensation of Heat. By Color, that Magnitude and Figure which causes particular rays to be transmitted to us, etc.

VII. Every *power, simple* or *compound,* that *results from* any whole material *system,* but does not *reside in it—that* is, in all its parts, in the manner before explained—nor yet resides in any *other substance* as its subject, is no *real quality* at all, but must either be itself a real substance (which seems unintelligible), or else it is nothing but merely an *abstract name* or *notion,* as all *universals* are. Thus the power resulting from the texture of the *rose* to excite in us the sensation of sweetness is nothing but an *abstract name,* signifying a particular motion and figure of certain parts emitted. The power of a *clock* to show the hour of the day is nothing but one *new complex name,* to express at once the several motions of the parts, and particularly the *determinate velocity* of the last wheel to turn round once in twelve hours. Upon the stopping of which *motion* by the touch of a finger or any other impediment, without making any alteration at all in the number, figure, or disposition of the parts of the clock, the *power* wholly ceases. And upon removing the impediment, by which nothing is restored but *mere motion,* the *power* returns again which is therefore no new real quality of the *whole,* but only the *mere motion* of the *parts.* The power of a *pin* to prick is nothing distinct from its mere figure permitting it to enter the skin. The power of a *weight in one scale of a balance* to ascend or descend, upon increasing or diminishing the counterpoint in the other scale, is not a *new real quality* distinct from its *absolute gravity,* though it occasions a new *effect,* there being no alteration at all made in *the weight itself.*

The *power of the eye to see* is not a real quality of the *whole eye,* but merely an *abstract name* signifying a transmitting and refracting of the rays of light in a certain manner through its several parts which effect, by the interpretation or removal of an opaque body, is destroyed or renewed without any alteration at all in the eye itself. A *key,* by having many new locks made fit to it, acquires a *new power* of producing effects which it could not before, and yet no new real quality is produced, nor any alteration at all made in the *key* itself. And so, universally, of all powers of this kind. If these powers were anything else but *mere abstract names,* they would signify qualities subsisting without any subject at all—that is, such as must themselves be distinct substances—which is unintelligible.

VIII. *Consciousness* is neither a *mere abstract name* (such as are the *powers* mentioned in prop. VII), *nor a power of exciting or occasioning modes in a foreign substance* (such as are all the *sensible qualities* of bodies, prop. VI), but *a real quality truly and properly inherent in the subject itself, the thinking Substance.*

If it was *a mere abstract name,* it would be nothing at all in the person that thinks, or in the thinking substance itself, but only a notion framed by the imagination of some other being. For all those powers which are only *abstract names* are not at all in the *things whose powers they are called,* but are only *notions* framed in imagination by the mind that observes, compares, and reasons about different *objects without itself.*

If it was a *power of exciting or occasioning different modes in a foreign substance,* then the *power of thinking* must be before in that foreign substance, and that foreign substance alone would in reality be conscious, and not *this* which excites the different modes in *that foreign substance.* For the power that is in one substance of exciting different modes in another substance presupposes necessarily, in that other substance, the *foundation* of those modes. Thus in the case of all the *sensible qualities* of bodies, the *power of thinking* is beforehand in that being, wherein those qualities excite or occasion *different modes* of thinking.

It remains therefore that it must of necessity be a *real quality truly and properly inhering in the subject itself, the thinking substance,* there being no other *species* of *powers* or *qualities* left to which it can possibly be referred. And this indeed is of itself as evident by every man's experience as it can be rendered by any explication or proof whatsoever.

IX. No *real quality* can result from the *composition* of *different qualities,* so as to be a new quality in the same subject of a *different kind* or *species* from all and every one of the *component qualities.*

If it could, it would be a creation of something out of nothing. From compound motions can arise nothing but motion; from magnitudes nothing but magnitude; from figure nothing but figure; from compositions of magnitude, figure, and motion together nothing but magnitude, figure, and motion; from mechanical powers nothing but mechanical powers; from composition of colors nothing but color, which itself (as appears by microscopes) is still the simple colors of which it was compounded; from mixtures of chemical liquors nothing but ferments which are only mere motions of the particles in mixing, such motions as arise from the placing of iron and a loadstone near each other. Gravity is not a quality of matter arising from its texture or any other power in it, but merely an endeavor to motion, excited by some foreign force or power. Magnetism and electricity are not new qualities resulting from different and unknown powers, but merely emissions of certain streams of matter which produce certain determinate motions. Compositions of colors can never contribute to produce a sound, nor compositions of magnitude and figure to produce a motion; nor necessary and determinate motions to produce a free and indeterminate power of self motion; nor any mechanical powers whatsoever to produce a power not mechanical. And the same must of necessity hold universally true of all qualities and powers whatsoever, whether known or unknown. Because otherwise, as has been before said, there would in the compound be something created out of nothing.

X. *Consciousness* therefore being a real quality (prop. VIII), and of a kind *specifically different* from all other qualities, whether known or unknown, which are themselves acknowledged to be *void of consciousness,* can never possibly result from any composition of such qualities.

This is as evident from the foregoing propositions, as that a *sound* cannot be the result of a mixture of *colors* and *smells,* nor *extension* the result of a composition of parts *unextended,* nor *solidity* the result of parts *unextended,* nor *solidity* the result of parts *not solid—whatever* other different qualities, known or unknown, those constituent parts may be supposed to be endued with.

XI. No individual *quality* can be *transferred* from one *subject* to another.

This is granted by all.

XII. The *spirits* and *particles* of the *brain,* being *loose* and in perpetual *flux,* cannot therefore be the seat of that *consciousness* by which a man not only remembers things done many years since, but also is conscious that *he himself,* the same *individual conscious being,* was the doer of them.

This follows evidently from the foregoing.

XIII. The *consciousness* that a man has at one and the same time is *one consciousness,* and not a *multitude of consciousnesses,* as the *solidity, motion,* or *color* of any piece of matter is a multitude of distinct *solidities, motions,* or *colors.*

This is granted by all who deny that the particles of the brain, which they suppose to constitute a conscious substance, are themselves each of them conscious.

XIV. *Consciousness* therefore cannot at all reside in the substance of the *brain,* or *spirits,* or in any other *material system* as its *subject,* but must be a quality of some *immaterial substance.*

This follows necessarily from the foregoing propositions compared together. For since every possible power of matter, whether known or unknown, must needs be either, first, a *real quality* of matter to which it is ascribed, and then it must inhere in the several distinct parts; or, secondly, a power of exciting or occasioning certain *modes* in some *other Subject;* or, thirdly, a *mere abstract name* or *notion* of what is, properly speaking, no real quality at all, and inheres in no real subject at all. And *consciousness* is acknowledged to be none of these. It follows unavoidably that it must of necessity be a quality of some *immaterial substance.*

XV. Difficulties that arise afterwards concerning *other qualities* of that *immaterial substance,* as whether it be *extended* or *unextended,* do not at all affect the present argument.

For thus even abstract mathematical demonstrations as those concerning the *infinite divisibility of quality,* the *eternity of God,* and his *immensity,* have almost insuperable difficulties on the other side. And yet no man who understands those matters thinks that those difficulties do at all weaken the force, or diminish the certainty, of the demonstrations.

COLLINS: CLARKE HASN'T SHOWN THAT THINKING MATTER IS NOT A CONTRADICTION, OR THAT HIS VIEWS ARE HELPFUL TO RELIGION

In his "Reflections on Mr. Clarke's Second Defense" Anthony Collins takes up Clarke's claim that to annex consciousness to so flux a subject as the brain leads to contradictions (Clarke, Works, *pp. 808–9).*

It is urged by Mr. *Clarke* to *annex consciousness* to so *flux a substance as the brain or the spirits in* it, is *a very great absurdity. For if the parts of the brain or spirits be (as they certainly are) in perpetual flux and change, it will follow that consciousness by which I not only remember that certain things were done many years since, but also am conscious that they were done by the very same individual conscious being who now remembers them—it will follow,* he says, *that the consciousness is transferred from one subject to another. That* is to *say, that it* is *a real quality which subsists without inhering in any subject at all.* In the examination of this argument I think something will appear quite contrary to what Mr. *Clarke* imagines—that it is so far from being absurd to annex human consciousness to so flux a substance as the brain, that it will rather be absurd to annex it to any other substance but so flux a one as the brain. For if we utterly forget, or cease to be conscious of, having done many things in the former parts of our lives which we certainly did, as much as any of those things which we are conscious that we have done; and if in fact we do by degrees forget everything which we do not revive by frequent recollection, and by again and again imprinting our decaying Ideas; and if there be in a determinate time a partial or total flux of particles on our brains; what can better account for our total forgetfulness of some things, our partial forgetfulness of others, than to suppose the substance of our brain in a constant flux? And what can better show that consciousness is not transferred from one subject to another, than our forgetting totally or partially according to the brain's being more or less in a flux? But [if] I will suppose that I am conscious to have done some things, without having one particle of the brain the same that I had when I did those things, how then can I be conscious that I did them, without allowing consciousness to be transferred from one subject to another? This I think contains the strength of Mr. *Clarke's* objection. In answer to which, I will suppose myself conscious at forty of having been carried to a market or fair at five years old, without any particles of matter about me the same which I had at that age. Now in order to retain the consciousness of that action, it is necessary to revive the idea of it before any considerable flux of particles (otherwise I must totally lose the memory of it, as I do several things done in my childhood), and by reviving the idea of that action I imprint afresh the consciousness of having done that action by which the brain has as lively an impression of consciousness (though it be not entirely composed of the same particles) as it had the day after I did the action, or as it has of a triangle or any other new idea not before imprinted on it. Consciousness of having done that action is an idea imprinted on the brain by recollecting or bringing into view our ideas before they are quite worn out— which idea continues in me not only the memory of the action itself, but that I did it. And if there is every now and then a recollection of a past action, Mr. *Clarke* may, by what I have said, conceive a man may be conscious of things done by him, though he has not one particle of matter the same that he had at the doing of those things, without *consciousness being transferred from one subject to another* in any absurd sense of those words.

At the end of his "Reflections on Mr. Clarke's Second Defense" Collins claims that Clarke's arguments are of no use for the ends and purposes of religion. He also comments on Clarke's fifteen propositions (Clarke, Works, *pp. 817–21).*

From these and some other consequences flowing from the foregoing argument, we have so strange a view of the state of man that I conceive there can be no greater service to religion than to show the uselessness of that argument to the ends and purposes of religion. Especially since there are such solid arguments for a future state from topics that can neither be answered by infidels, nor loaded with any absurd consequences.

Mr. *Clarke,* in the conclusion of his *Defense,* has summed up his argument in fifteen propositions which I now propose to consider, that my answer to him may be complete, though all that he advances in them is overthrown in the foregoing reflections.

His propositions are:

1. Every system of matter consists of a multitude of distinct parts.

> This proposition, which he *thinks is granted by all,* is, I am sure, denied by a great many. However, I shall not at present enter into any debate with him concerning it, but continue to suppose it as I have hitherto done.

2. Every real quality inheres in some subject.

3. No individual or *single quality of one particle of matter can be the individual* or *single quality of another particle of matter.*

> These two I grant.

4. Every real simple quality that resides in any whole material system resides in all the parts of that system.

5. Every real compound quality that resides in any whole material system is a number of simple qualities residing in all the parts of that system, some in one part, some in another.

> These two propositions I shall not contend with him about, though he seems to me to confound *simple and compound qualities together.* For in his explication subjoined to his fourth proposition, as an example of what he means by a *simple quality* he instances in the *motion of a body which,* says he, *consists in the sum of the motions of its several parts.* And in his explication subjoined to his fifth proposition, as an example of what he means by *compound qualities* he says, *the simples blue and yellow make the compound color called green.* Now the motion of a clock is to me as much a *compound quality* as the color *green* is a *compound quality.* For the various motions of a clock—its circular, perpendicular, and other

motions—are as specifically different from one another as blue and yellow are from one another. And therefore I confess that I have no clear ideas from Mr. *Clarke's* explications to the terms *simple and compound.*

6. *Every real quality, simple or compound, that results from any whole material system, but does not reside in it—that is, neither in all its distinct parts, nor in all the parts of some portion of it—according to the explication of the two foregoing propositions,* is *the mode of some other substance, and not of that.*

This proposition I grant, on condition that instead of *other substance* be substituted the words *other subject.* For I grant sweetness does not reside in a sugar-loaf—that is, *neither in all the distinct parts, nor in all the parts of some portion of a sugar-loaf, but* is *produced in another* subject (and not in another *substance)* as all other sensations or modes of thinking are. Which subject I contend is material.

7. *Every power, simple or compound, that results from any whole material system, but does not reside in it—that is, in all* its *parts, in the manner before explained—nor yet resides in any other substance as* its *subject,* is *no real quality at all, but must be either itself a real substance (which seems unintelligible), or else* it *is nothing else but merely an abstract name, as all universals are.*

8. *Consciousness is neither a mere abstract name (such as the powers mentioned in prop.* 7), *nor a power of exciting or occasioning different modes in a foreign substance (such as are the sensible qualities of bodies, prop.* 6), *but a real quality truly and properly inhering in the subject itself, the thinking substance.*

Before I answer to this proposition, it is necessary to be very precise in unraveling what seems to be very much perplexed in it. Mr. *Clarke* confounds two things that ought to be separated—viz. *the power of exciting modes in a foreign subject,* and the modes that are excited when he says *sensible qualities in bodies* are *powers of exciting modes in another subject.* Whereas sweetness, sounds, etc., which are vulgarly termed *sensible qualities in bodies,* are only ideas, sensations, or modes of thinking in us, and exist not at all in those bodies of which they are said to be sensible qualities—and therefore the powers in bodies must be something very different from those qualities, as different as a Cause is from an Effect, and (that I may proceed with the greater clearness)—I will suppose those powers to excite modes in another subject to be peculiar modes of motion in certain systems of matter.

Having thus distinguished, I shall answer to this proposition in each of the foregoing senses.

1. I do agree that consciousness is neither a mere abstract name (such as are the powers mentioned in prop. 7), nor does it exist in the brain—as sweetness is vulgarly supposed to do in a rose, and as all sensible qualities in bodies are supposed to do—but is a real quality truly and properly inhering in the subject itself, the brain—as modes of motion do in some bodies, and roundness does in others.

2. I do agree, again, that consciousness is not a mere abstract name, but is a power of the brain answering to the powers in matter that produce sensations in us. For as those powers or modes of motion are peculiar to certain systems of matter, and are not the sums of powers of the same numerical kind, so neither is consciousness the sum of powers of the same numerical kind. And as those systems of matter do by peculiar modes of motion produce ideas in us, so we by the power of thinking can enlarge or abstract ideas—that is, modify them, or cause changes in them, as well as external sensible things can cause modes or changes in us. And therefore consciousness answers, or may be likened to, those powers in some systems of matter that are occasions of modes in another subject, and is at the same time a quality as much inhering in matter as the motion of a clock does in the parts of a clock, or as roundness or any other particular or individual figure in a body.

9. No *real quality can result from the composition of different qualities,* so *as to be a new quality in the same subject of a different kind* or *species from all and every one of the compound qualities.*

According to Mr. *Clarke's* explication of this proposition, I allow this likewise to be true. For *from motion nothing but motion can arise, and from figure nothing but figure.* But this reaches not the case of numerical powers, and particularly reaches not the case of consciousness. A real numerical power, as I suppose consciousness to be, and such as roundness is, may result from the composition of different qualities, as roundness does from different species of figures, and is consequently a new quality in the same subject of a different kind or species from all the component qualities considered together. But motion, being a generical power, does, I agree, consist of the motions of the parts, as figure does of the figures of the parts. And did consciousness answer to figure and motion that would likewise consist of the consciousness of the parts.

10. Consciousness therefore being a real quality (prop. 8), *and of a kind specifically different from all other qualities, whether known or unknown, which are themselves acknowledged to be void of consciousness, can never possibly result from any composition of such qualities.*

Though consciousness be a real quality, and different from all other qualities, whether known or unknown, which are themselves acknowledged to be void of consciousness, it can or may result from such qualities as, singly considered, are void of consciousness. Roundness is a real quality specifically different from other qualities void of roundness, and yet may be the result of composition of such qualities. But in Mr. *Clarke's* sense of real qualities, I allow this proposition to be true. But then it reaches not the case of consciousness, which I deny to be a generical power, but affirm to be only a mode of a generical power.

11. No individual quality can be transferred from one subject to another.

This proposition I allow to be true. The quality of a subject can only be the quality of that subject wherein it exists, and not of another subject. The motion of a system of matter can only be the motion of that system. The consciousness of any being can only be the consciousness of that particular being. And I further observe that the motion of a system of matter one day can never be the motion of the same numerical system the next day, nor the consciousness of yesterday be the same numerical consciousness that I have today, let the being that is conscious in me be divisible or indivisible. The same individual quality can no more be transferred to the same *individual subject* that was formerly the subject of it, than it can be transferred to another subject.

12. The spirits and particles of the brain, being loose and in a perpetual flux, cannot therefore be the seat of that consciousness by which a man not only remembers things done many years since, but also is conscious that he himself, the same individual being, was the doer of them.

Though the spirits of particles of the brain cannot, by being in a perpetual flux, be the seat of that consciousness by which I know myself today to be the same individual conscious being that I was a year ago (for I deny that we have any consciousness at all that we continue the same individual being at different times), yet if it be not absurd for matter to think, matter must at the same time know that it thinks, or be conscious of its thinking. And if it can know at this instant that it thinks, I can see no reason why it may not remember tomorrow what it thinks of today, though some particles will be then wanting which it has at present. And if it can remember at all, then the memory of things may be continued even after we have lost all the particles of matter that we had at the time of the doing them, by continual intermediate repeating, or imprinting afresh our ideas before they are quite lost or worn out. And it is thus as intelligible to me that the memory of things should be preserved by a being in flux, as by a being that is not so. For the individual consciousness today can neither in an individual or divisible being be the individual consciousness tomorrow—that consciousness is a perfectly distinct action in both beings from the preceding consciousness the day before. And whenever Mr. *Clarke* accounts for an indivisible being's remembrance of an action or thought, I promise to account for memory in a divisible being.

13. The consciousness that a man has at one and the same time is one consciousness and not a multitude of distinct consciousnesses, as [the] solidity, motion, or color of any piece of matter is a multitude of distinct solidities, motions, or colors.

14. Consciousness therefore cannot at all reside in the substance of the *brain,* or *spirits* or in any other *material system* as its *subject,* but must be a quality of some *immaterial substance.*

Taking consciousness for a numerical power, either as answering to roundness in a body, or to a motion peculiar to a system of matter, and this proposition by no means follows from those foregoing. For if consciousness be a numerical power, then it answers to never a one of the heads under which he ranks the powers of matter. For it neither answers to an effect residing in no subject at all (if there is any such thing in nature, which I utterly deny there is), nor does it answer to sweetness, or any other sensible qualities exciting in bodies external to us (for they are only modes of thinking or perception in us, and exist not at all in those external bodies). Nor, lastly, is it a power which answers to figure and motion, which I agree consist only in the figures and motions of the parts, but agrees or answers to modes of figure and motion. From all which it is plain that all Mr. *Clarke's* propositions are founded on his considering consciousness to be something else than what I contend it is. And so, though he may demonstrate the impossibility of matter's being conscious in his sense of the term consciousness, yet I deny that he has said one word to prove the impossibility of matter's thinking in the sense for which the term consciousness stands with me—and I suppose with all those that contend for the possibility of matter's thinking or being conscious. So that his demonstration may be granted by me without affecting the question between us, since it relates to a chimera or idea of his own framing. And thus endless demonstrations may be made without understanding things as they really exist, or any truth besides the relations of chimerical ideas. For I grant his demonstration to be good, if consciousness be considered either as a generical power like motion and figure, or as answering to the sweetness of a rose (which is a sensation or mode of thinking in us), or as an effect residing in no substance at all—then consciousness cannot inhere in a system of matter, and his demonstration reaches no farther. But consciousness answering to never a one of these powers, in demonstrating that consciousness in his sense cannot inhere in a system of matter, he has no more reached the question than if he had talked of anything else in the world. For his usage of the term consciousness does not make him one jot nearer the question, than if he had used a different term, or a term that no one would suspect stood for the thing really signified by the term *consciousness.*

15. Difficulties that arise afterwards concerning other qualities of that immaterial substance, as whether it be extended or unextended, do not at all affect the present argument.

. . . [A]s for the difficulty of making immaterial being *unextended,* I will speak to that whenever Mr. *Clarke* defines the terms *unextended* and *being,* that I may see what they stand for when joined together. And then I will show how far considering immaterial being to be an unextended being affects his argument, as I have shown how far considering immaterial being to be an extended being affects it.

Thus I have gone through Mr. *Clarke's* propositions, and shown wherein they fail to clear the point that he ought to have aimed at. And I conclude with this further observation, that he has not drawn up one proposition to show that his argument is of any use to the ends and purposes of religion, allowing it to be ever so true and just.

CLARKE: DIFFICULTIES ABOUT
PERSONAL IDENTITY PRESSED

In his "Third Defense of an Argument" Clarke turns again to the argument about annexing consciousness to so flux a substance as the brain (Clarke, Works, *pp. 843–45).*

I alleged that it is *absurd to annex consciousness to so flux a substance as the brain or spirits because, if such a subject could be the seat of consciousness by which a man not only remembers things many years since, but is also conscious that he himself, the same individual being, was the doer of them, it would follow that consciousness could be transferred from one subject to another—that is, that a quality could subsist without inhering in any subject at all—which all rational men allow to be impossible.* To this you reply that *in order to retain the consciousness of an action, it is necessary to revise the idea of it before any considerable flux of particles, and by reviving the idea of that action I imprint afresh the consciousness of having done that action—by which the brain has as lively an impression of consciousness (though it be not entirely composed of the same particles) as it did the day after it did the same action, or as it has of a triangle or any new idea not before imprinted on it. Consciousness of having done that action is an idea imprinted on the brain by recollecting or bringing into view our ideas before they are quite worn out—which idea continues in me not only the memory of the action itself, but that I did it. And if there is every now and then a recollection of a past action,* it may hereby be *conceived that a man may be conscious of things done by him, though he has not one particle of matter the same that he had at the doing of those things, without consciousness being transferred from one subject to another in any absurd sense of those words.* And again, *if* matter *can know at this instant that it thinks,* you can *see no reason why it may not remember tomorrow what it thinks of today, though some particles will then be wanting which it has at present. And if it can remember at all, the memories of things may be continued even after we have lost all the particles of matter that we had at the doing of them, by continued intermediate repeating or imprinting afresh our ideas before they are quite lost or worn out.* But the fallacy of this reply is very evident. For to affirm that *new matter* perpetually added to a fleeting system may, by repeated impressions add recollections of ideas, participate [in] and have communicated to it *a memory* of what was formerly done by the *whole system,* is not explaining or proving, but begging the question by assuming an impossible hypothesis. But supposing it were *possible* that the *memory* in general of such or such an action's having been done might be preserved in the manner you suppose, yet it is a manifest contradiction that the *consciousness* of its being done by *me,* by *my own individual self* in particular, should continue in me after my whole substance is changed unless *consciousness* could be transferred from one subject to another in the absurdist sense of those words. For to suppose that one should be *conscious* of an action's having been done by itself, which really was not done by it but by another substance, is as plainly supposing an individual quality to be transferred from one subject to another, in the most absurd sense, as it is plain that *consciousness* is a *real individual quality,* and different from bare *general memory.*

If therefore you will answer (which is the only possible seeming evasion in this case) that that which we call *consciousness* is not a *fixed individual numerical quality* like the numerical figure or motion of a solid body, but a *fleeting transferable mode or power* like the roundness or the mode of motion of circles upon the face of a running stream, and that the *person* may still be the same by a continual superaddition of the *like consciousness,* notwithstanding the whole *substance* be changed. Then I say you make *individual personality* to be a mere *external imaginary denomination* and nothing at all in reality just as a *ship* is called the *same ship* after the whole substance is changed by frequent repairs, or a *river* is called the *same river* though the water of it be every day new. The *name* of the ship is the same, but the *ship itself* is not at all the same, and the continued *name* of the river signifies water running in the same channel, but not at all the *same water.* So, if a man at forty years of age has nothing of the same substance in him, neither material nor immaterial, that he had at twenty, he may be called the *same person* by a mere *external imaginary denomination,* in such a sense as a *statue* may be called the *same statue* after its whole substance has been changed by piecemeal. But he cannot be *really and truly* the *same person* unless the *same individual numerical consciousness* can be transferred from one subject to another. For the continued addition or exciting of a *like consciousness* in the new acquired parts, after the manner you suppose, is nothing but a deception and delusion under the form of memory—a making the man to seem to himself to be conscious of having done that which really was not done by him, but by another. And such a consciousness in a man whose substance is wholly changed can no more make it just and equitable for such a man to be punished for an action done by another substance, than the addition of the like consciousness (by the power of God) to two or more new created men, or to any number of men now living, by giving a like modification to the motion of the spirits in the brain of each of them respectively, could make them all to be one and the same individual person, at the same time that they remain several and distinct persons, or make it just and reasonable for all and every one of them to be punished for one and the same individual action done by one only, or perhaps by none of them at all.

Mr. *Locke* himself, in the very place where he contends that consciousness makes the *same individual person,* notwithstanding that the *whole substance* be supposed to be changed, acknowledges expressly

(Book II, ch. 27, sect. 13) that such a continuation of the *same consciousness* in a fleeting substance would be *a representing that to the mind to have been, which really never was, a representing to one intellectual substance as done by itself what I never did, and was perhaps done by some other agent—a representation without reality of matter of fact, as several representations in dreams are—a transferring by a fatal error from one to another, that consciousness which draws reward or punishment with it; a making two* [or two hundred] *thinking substances to be but one* [individual] *person;* and *leaves it to be considered how far this may be an argument against those who would place thinking in a system of fleeting animal spirits.*

To say here that God's *justice and goodness* will not permit him to put any such inevitable deceit upon men, is nothing to the purpose. For, if it be but *naturally possible* for him to do that which, upon supposition of the truth of your notion, will be a *plain contradiction,* this is a certain demonstration that your notion is false. And I think it is a *contradiction plain enough* to say that God's impressing permanently upon a thousand men's minds, after the manner of the representation of a dream, the like consciousness with that which I find in my own mind, would make every one of them to be not persons like me, but the *same individual person* with myself. According to such reasoning as this, accidents need not have any necessary dependence on their substance, and the same individual substance may as well be conceived to exist in a thousand places at once under like accidents, as the same *individuating* accidents or qualities can inhere in a thousand different substances at once. By which same subtlety (as believing *too much* and *too little* have commonly the luck to meet together, like things moving two contrary ways in the same circle), all the absurdities in the doctrine of *transubstantiation* may easily be reconciled.

You *deny that we have any consciousness at all that we continue the same individual being at different times.* If so, it can be to no great purpose for us to dispute about anything. For, before you receive my reply, you may happen possibly to be entirely changed into another substance, and the next time you write may deny that you have any consciousness at all that you continue the same individual being who wrote this remarkable sentence. But to the assertion, I answer either consciousness proves a man to be the same individual being at different times, or else it is a mere deceit and delusion, and by being added in like manner to other substances, might (as I said) make a hundred other men with equal justice liable to the same punishment with himself for any one individual action done by him. But of this, more when I come to speak

of the usefulness and importance of the present argument to the ends
and purposes of religion.

In his "Third Defense of an Argument" Clarke takes up Collins'
challenge to show that his argument is useful for the ends and
purposes of religion (Clarke, Works, *pp. 851–53).*

In the last place, you challenge me to show that my argument is *of any*
use to the ends and purpose of religion. That it is of the *greatest use*
will I suppose easily be granted, if it be evident that the notion I am arguing against is utterly destructive of religion. And in what respects it is
so, I shall give you an instance or two to consider of, and so conclude.

 . . . [I]f the *soul* be nothing but a *system of matter,* and *thinking*
nothing but a *mode of motion,* or *of some other power of matter,* the
doctrine of the *resurrection* (as I before observed) will be inconceivable
and incredible, and the justice of future rewards and punishments impossible to be made out. The notion of the soul's *immateriality* evidently
facilitates the belief of a *resurrection* and of a future retribution by securing a principle of *personal individuality,* upon which the justice of all
reward or punishment is entirely grounded. But if *thinking* be in reality
nothing but a *power* or *mode* which, inhering in a loose and fleeting system of matter, perishes utterly at the dissolution of the body, then the
restoring the power of *thinking* to the same body *at the resurrection* will
not be a raising again of the *same individual person,* but it will be as
truly a *creation* of a *new person* as the addition of the like power of
thinking to a new body *now* would be the *creation* of a *new man.* For as
God's superadding *now* to a new parcel of matter the like *consciousness*
with what I at this time find in myself would not make that new parcel
of matter to be the *same individual person with me,* but only *another*
person like me, so his superadding that *consciousness* at the *resurrection*
to the same particles of dust of which my body was formerly composed
will not be a *restoration* of the *same person,* but a creation of a *new one*
like me. For the sameness of the senseless particles of dust, it is evident
from the flux nature of the substance of our bodies, is not that which
now makes me to be the same person, and therefore cannot be that
which will *then* make me to be so. If my present *consciousness* be
nothing but a *mode of motion* in the fleeting particles of my brain or
spirits, this *consciousness* will be as utterly destroyed at the dissolution
of my body as if the very substance of my body was annihilated. And it
would be just as possible for the *same individual person* to be *created*
again after an *absolute annihilation,* as to be *restored again* after such a

dissolution. But now, if the *same person* after *annihilation* could, by re-storing of the same *consciousness,* be created again, he might as possi-bly be created again by addition of the same *consciousness* to new matter, even before annihilation of the first. From whence it would fol-low that two, or two hundred, several persons might all, by a superaddi-tion of the like *consciousness,* be *one and the same individual person,* at the same time that they remain *several and distinct persons—it* being as easy for God to add *my consciousness* to the new formed matter of one or of one hundred bodies at this *present time,* as to the dust of my pres-ent body at the *time of the* resurrection. And no reason can be given why it would not be as just at any time to punish for my faults a new created man, to whom *my consciousness* is by the power of God superadded, as to punish that person who at the *resurrection* shall by the same power be new made out of the dust of my body with the same *consciousness* su-peradded—it being allowed that *then,* as well as *now,* it is not the same-ness of the particles of dust that makes the *same person.* But if it was, yet that would make no difference in this matter. For the particles of dust which, in the course of twenty years, have successively been part of the substance of my body are enough in quantity to form several bodies, and if the addition of a like consciousness with what I now find in my-self to one of those bodies at the resurrection will make *it* to be the same *individual person* with *me,* the addition of the like consciousness to twenty of them would consequently make every one of them to be (not persons *like* me, but) the same *individual person* with *me,* and with *each other likewise.* Which is the greatest absurdity in the world—an absurdity equal (as I before said) to that of *transubstantiation.* This in-explicable confusion, wherewith your doctrine perplexes the notion of *personal identity* upon which identity the justice of all reward or punish-ment manifestly depends, makes the *resurrection,* in your way of argu-ing, to be inconceivable and impossible. And consequently your doctrine (which supposes the body to be the whole man) is destructive of reli-gion, leaving no room for reward or punishment but in the present life only, and consequently giving men liberty to do everything for their present pleasure or advantage that can be done with a good color, and without being obnoxious to human laws—which is the greatest mischief that can possibly befall mankind. But if the soul be, as we believe, a *permanent indivisible immaterial substance,* then all these difficulties vanish of themselves.

It is here to be observed that all the absurd consequences which I have now (in considering of what use my argument is to *religion*) shown to follow from your doctrine with respect to the *resurrection,* do equally follow from it (as has been before proved) even *without respect to the resurrection.* For as it is absurd to suppose (which you must do in your scheme) that at the resurrection the *same individual person* can be restored merely by the addition of a *like* consciousness with that which utterly perishes at the dissolution of the body to the dust of the same body when recollected again—as this, I say, is plainly absurd—because in the same manner twenty other men formed out of the same dust (of which there is quantity enough belonging to every person that has lived any number of years) may also by an addition of the like consciousness become every one of them *that one same individual person,* at the same time that they remain so many several and distinct persons—so, without regard to any future resurrection, there is the very same absurdity in supposing (as you do) that a man *at this present time,* though he has none of the same substance belonging to him, may yet, merely by a like modification of the motion of his spirits, continue to be *the same individual person he was* twenty years since. There is, I say, the very same absurdity in this supposition as in the former, because there is no difference between supposing that any number of new bodies at the resurrection *coexistently,* or any number of different men now living *contemporarily,* or any number of different bodies *succeeding* one another in one continued form by a perpetual uninterrupted flux of particles (which is the thing you contend for) can be *one and the same individual person* merely by a *like* modification of the figures and motions of the parts respectively, without having anything at all *the same* in them.

To the *propositions* I laid down at the conclusion of my former reply, you have objected nothing but what (I think) is already clearly answered in the foregoing pages.

COLLINS: DEFENSE OF THE MEMORY
THEORY OF PERSONAL IDENTITY

In "An Answer to Mr. Clarke's Third Defense" Collins takes up the arguments Clarke had raised about personal identity (Clarke, Works, pp. 875–79).

His next argument to prove *my notion destructive of religion* is *that the doctrine of the resurrection will be inconceivable and incredible, and justice of rewards and punishments impossible to be made out.* What he says to make out this point, being founded on the question of identity, it will not be amiss to state briefly my opinion before I consider his exception.

1. A particular substance I call the same substance that it was formerly, from its perfect agreement to that idea which I then supposed it

correspondent to. As for instance, the identity of a material substance, at different times, lies in consisting of exactly the same numerical particles, to which no addition or subtraction has been made.

2. A particular mode (as, suppose, any particular mode of motion) not being capable of a continuation of existence—like *being* and *substance—but* perishing the moment it begins, its identity cannot consist in being the same numerical mode of motion at different times, but only in being that mode of motion that it was when it existed, and not another mode of motion. In like manner, any particular act of consciousness is incapable of the continuation of its existence, wherefore its identity can only consist in being that very numerical act of consciousness that it is.

3. The identity of an *oak, animal,* or *man,* consists in a participation of a continued life, under a particular organization of parts. An oak that contains several loads of timber is called the same oak with an oak that was an inch long an hundred years ago, by partaking thence-forward of a continued vegetable life, in a like continued organization of parts. And an animal or man is called the same animal or man at twenty years old that it was a quarter old, by partaking of a continued animal life, under a like continued organization of parts—let this vegetable and animal life in the oak, animal, or man, be united at different times, to ever so different particles of matter.

4. Besides these sorts of identity, there is a fourth, very different from these, which we signify by the word *self,* and sometimes call *personal identity.* Now to understand what it is that constitutes *self* or personal identity, let us consider to what ideas we apply the term *self.* If a man charges me with a murder done by somebody last night, of which I am not conscious, I deny that I did the action, and cannot possibly attribute it to my *self* because I am not conscious that I did it. Again, suppose me to be seized with a short frenzy of an hour, and during that time to kill a man, and then to return to my *self* without the least consciousness of what I have done. I can no more attribute that action to my *self,* than I could the former which I supposed done by another. The mad man and the sober man are really two as distinct persons as any two other men in the world, and will be so considered in a court of judicature, where want of consciousness can be proved. And it will be thought as unjust to punish the sober man for what the mad man did, as to punish one man for another's fault, though the man both sober and mad is the same man. And lastly, should there be so strong a representation to my understanding of a murder done by me (which was really never done at all) so that I could not distinguish it in my mind from something *really* done by me, I can no more help attributing this to my

self, than I can any other action which I really did, and was conscious of. So that it is evident that *self* or personal identity consist solely in consciousness, since when I distinguish my *self* from others, and when I attribute any past actions to my *self,* it is only by extending my consciousness to them. And further, to give the reader an idea of the nature of personal identity, let him consider that our limbs or flesh, while vitally united to *thinking conscious self,* are part of ourselves, but when separated from us are no part of *self,* but that flesh which succeeds in the room of the flesh separated becomes as much a part of *self* as the separated piece of flesh was before. The question then between Mr. *Clarke* and me is whether, upon supposition that personal identity consists in consciousness, and that consciousness is only a mode in a fleeting system of matter, the doctrine of the *resurrection will be incredible,* and *the justice of future rewards and punishments impossible to be made out.* Mr. *Clarke* says *if thinking be in reality nothing but a mode, which inhering in a loose and fleeting system of matter, perishes utterly at the dissolution of the body, then the restoring the power of thinking to the same body at the resurrection, will not be a raising again of the same individual person, but it will be as truly a creation of a new person as the addition of the like power of thinking to a new body now would be the creation of a new man.*

To which I answer that if *personal identity* consists in consciousness, as before explained, and if consciousness be a mode in a fleeting system of matter, consciousness can perish no more at the dissolution of the body than it does every moment we cease to think, or be conscious. Suppose we were taken to pieces every night after we are asleep, and our parts put into the same form and order which they would have been in in the morning had we continued sleeping. I think it is not to be doubted but we should have the same consciousness or memory that we should have had in our natural state. Consciousness is no more created anew in one case than in the other. There is only a suspension of the operation of thinking. Therefore the restoring the power of thinking to the same (or, if you please, a different) body at the resurrection, with a memory or consciousness extending to past actions, will be a raising the same person, and not a creation of a new person *as adding the like power of thinking to a new body now would be the creation of a new man.* Because the identity of man, consisting in a participation of a continued *life* under a particular organization of parts, must be new created whenever such a *life* begins. Whereas, if personal identity consists in consciousness, or a memory extending to past actions, *that* will make anyone as much the same person that he was in his world as anyone is the same person here two days together. *That memory* or *consciousness* preserves him from being a *new person* (the essence whereof, *ex hypothesi,* consists in having a power of thinking that cannot be extended backwards.)

2. But if Mr. *Clarke* means by the *same individual person,* in the paragraph I cited, the *same numerical being* with the *same individual numerical consciousness* at different times, as I suppose he does, since therein consists his notion of personal identity (as the reader may see, if he will read the places referred to in the margin), I do allow that such an individual person cannot be raised at the resurrection. Nay, I think it is demonstrable that there can be no resurrection at all of the *same* person on that supposition. And thus I demonstrate it.

    1. Being as being cannot be rewarded or suffer.

    2. Being only as conscious or thinking can be rewarded or suffer.

    3. Human thinking or consciousness consists of a number of particular acts of thinking or consciousness which, whether they reside in a fleeting or indivisible substance, can each of them have but one existence, and cannot possibly exist at different times as substances do, but perish the moment they begin.

    4. Since it is not possible for those individual numerical acts of thinking or consciousness that are past to exist again, the same numerical being, with the same numerical individual consciousness, cannot exist at two different times, and consequently cannot possibly be rewarded or punished for an action done.

    5. Therefore if personal identity consists in the same numerical being, with the same individual numerical consciousness, there can be no resurrection of the *same person—nay,* there can be no such thing as the *same person* at two different times.

So that, upon the whole, my notion of personal identity is so far from contradicting the doctrine of the resurrection, or making it *impossible or incredible,* that there can only be a resurrection of the *same person* on these principles—that present *consciousness* or memory *is nothing but a present representation of a past action,* and that *personal identity* consists only in having such a *consciousness* or memory. For on these suppositions, a particular consciousness or memory of past actions can begin at the resurrection as well as after a night's sleep. Whereas, if the *same numerical individual consciousness* that existed in this world is to exist at the resurrection, as Mr. *Clarke* maintains, he requires a condition in order to [have] a resurrection that implies a contradiction. There seems to me but one objection more to my notion of *personal identity* that requires a solution, and that is as follows: *that if the addi-*

tion of a like consciousness with what Mr. Clarke *now finds in himself to any system of those particles of dust which, in the course of twenty years, have successively been part of the substance of his body, and are enough to form several bodies at the resurrection, will* constitute *the same person with himself—the addition of the like consciousness to all those systems would consequently make every one of them to be, not persons like* him, *but the same individual person with* him, *and with each other likewise. Which is the greatest absurdity in the world—an absurdity equal to transubstantiation.* It is making *them all to be one and the same individual person at the same time that they remain several and distinct persons.*

    1. To which objection I answer by asking him if these thinking beings can know themselves to be the same or different persons any other way but purely by consciousness? And I ask him whether each of them must not unavoidably think himself the *same person* with Mr. *Clarke?* If each conscious being cannot help thinking himself to be the same person with Mr. *Clarke,* it is past doubt that nothing can be meant by the term *self* but purely a present representation of past actions, or a consciousness extending itself to past actions, without regard to sameness or change of substance. Wherefore I do allow that each of those beings would be the *same person* with Mr. *Clarke—that* is, each of them would have a present representation of the past actions of Mr. *Clarke* (for that is what I understand, and what I think every man must unavoidably signify, by the term *self,* or by *sameness* of person). And if each thinking being is in that sense the *same person* with Mr. *Clarke,* and if sameness of person *or self* consists in having a present representation of a past action, and applying that action to a man's self, let there be ever so many thinking beings that have a present representation of a past action, they can all constitute but one and the same person. Because they all agree in, or have a present representation of, the same past action wherein *self* or personal identity consists—as my consisting of ever so great a bulk of matter, or ever so many distinct beings, does not constitute different persons, but constitutes what we call *self,* by the sympathy and concern I have for each part united to me, though I have a distinct act of sensation for each part that is at any time affected. I suppose Mr. *Clarke,* when he expects *any deference should be given* to an authority he cites against me, will pay the same deference to the same authority that he expects I should. And therefore on this occasion I shall give him Mr. *Locke's* own words, who says *it must be allowed that if the same consciousness can be transferred from one thinking substance to another* (as in a certain sense he evidently shows that it may), *it will be possible that two thinking substances may make but one person.*

2. It is an article of Christian faith that the same numerical particles that are laid in the grave shall be raised at their resurrection. And since God almighty has made that necessary by the declaration of his will, the *same person* will at the resurrection only exist in those very numerical particles that were laid in the grave, by virtue of which personal identity or *self* will begin in the same manner at the resurrection as it does in morning when we awake from sleep. Besides, if God should cause to exist twenty present representations of the same past sinful actions in so many distinct beings, the consequent punishment would be twenty times as much as the final action deserved, and his justice required. Wherefore if God will not punish for punishment's sake—as to be sure he will not—there cannot be two distinct thinking beings with, each of them, a consciousness extended to the same past actions, and attributing them to themselves.

3. But supposing that each of these twenty distinct beings is the *same person* with Mr. *Clarke* (which, *ex hypothesi* is true), and supposing further that they can be considered as distinct *persons* from one another (which yet is not the case, as the reader may see by what I have said before), yet I humbly conceive Mr. *Clarke* will not upon recollection say this is an absurdity equal to *transubstantiation,* but will rather choose to call it *a difficulty that cannot be perfectly cleared,* when he considers that it is one of the articles of our Christian faith to believe that two complete persons, singly considered, *viz.,* the second person in the Trinity, and a human person, do constitute, by an hypostatical union, but one person.

4. But as to his own scheme, besides the absurdity of making the same *individual numerical consciousness* necessary to constitute the *same person,* I think there follows another absurdity from his making the same numerical being necessary to constitute *self,* or the *same person.* For how can he account for the resurrection in the following case? Suppose a man lives and believes as a good Christian ought to do for forty years, and then has a distemper in his body which obliterates all the ideas lodged in the numerical individual immaterial substance, so that on his recovery there remains no memory, no consciousness of any idea that he perceived for forty years past. And further, suppose this numerical individual immaterial substance to get ideas again as a young child does, and, until its separation from the body, leads a dissolute and debauched life. Here, on my principles, is the same being at different times—as much two persons as any two men in the world are two persons, or as the same man mad or sober is two persons. Now I ask him whether or no they are two distinct persons? If he answers they are two

distinct persons, I ask him how one of them can be punished eternally, and the other eternally rewarded, on supposition that the same numerical individual substance is necessary to continue the *same person?* And if they are two persons, whether personal identity must not consist in consciousness alone, without any regard to its existing in the same or different substances? If he answers that they are not two persons, but one person, I ask him whether he can suppose this being rewardable or punishable? And what kind of consciousness it will have when it is either rewarded or punishable? When he has answered these questions to himself, and will give himself the trouble to consider Mr. *Locke's* chapter of *Identity* and *Diversity,* he will see that, let him frame what imaginary schemes of *personal identity* he pleases, if there lie not unanswerable objections against them all, except that of *personal identity consisting in consciousness,* yet at least that experience perfectly contradicts his notion of *personal identity* which consists in *an individual numerical being with the same numerical consciousness.* And when he sees the impossibility of the *same numerical consciousness* continuing a moment in a finite being, but that every moment's consciousness is a new action, and nothing but bringing the idea of a past action into view, he may perhaps see the needlessness of contesting whether *self* or *personal identity* must inhere in the same or different beings at different times. Because he may then as easily conceive that the *same consciousness* may exist in different beings at different times, as in the same numerical being at different times, and may have as clear an idea of *personal identity* continuing under the greatest change of substance—as he may have an idea of animal or human *identity* which, consisting in a continued life under a like continued organization of parts, cannot be destroyed by the greatest change or flux of particles imaginable. Though after all, was a flux of particles absolutely inconsistent with personal identity, God almighty could as easily preserve the most loose particles from a separation, as he can an immaterial or unextended being from annihilation.

As to what Mr. *Clarke* says about the injustice of punishment, on supposition that *personal identity* consists in consciousness, and that consciousness is a mode of motion in a system of matter, it is to no purpose to enter into that question until we are agreed on the ends and reasons of both temporal and eternal punishments—which he has not as yet assigned. And when he assigns what I take to be the true ends of punishment, both in this world and the next, it will be then time enough to show that they may all take place on my principles as they can on any principles whatsoever.

CLARKE'S FINAL WORDS

In Clarke's "Fourth Defense of an Argument" he replies to what Collins says in his reply to Clarke's third defense (Clarke, Works, pp. 902–4).

Upon the question *whether individual personality can be preserved by a continual transferring of consciousness from one parcel of matter to another in so flux a substance as the brain or spirits,* you repeat what you had before advanced in your *Reflections.* In answer to which, I shall not repeat, but only desire the reader to compare what I offered in my *Third Defense,* pp. 288, 289, and 302, 303, *vol.* 8. And I shall here make only some brief incidental observations on what seems new in your reply.

In the first place, you disown none of the absurd consequences I charged on your hypothesis. You deny not but *one substance may be conscious of an action's having been done by itself which really was not done by it, but by another substance;* you make *individual personality to be a mere external imaginary denomination, and all self-consciousness a mere dream and delusion;* you own that *one man may possibly be two persons, and two or two hundred men one person—that is, not persons exactly like one another, but all really and truly one and the same individual person, at the same time that they continue* so *many distinct, intelligent, rational men.* These absurdities, I say, you have not denied to be unavoidable consequences of your hypothesis, nor have you done anything towards clearing them from being absurdities, but instead thereof have only offered some loose objections against what I propose under this head.

You say you *are sure* that my *calling* your *hypothesis* an *impossible* one, *and, instead of saying a word to prove it impossible, immediately arguing on the supposition of its possibility, is begging the question, and supposing what I was to prove.* The particular hypothesis here referred to *(viz., that memory may be preserved in a fleeting substance by continually repeating the ideas, and imprinting them afresh upon new particles of matter perpetually succeeding in the room of those that pass away)* was, I said, an impossible hypothesis, and an impossible hypothesis it will always appear to be until you can find out some new hypothesis by which to make it intelligible how it is possible that new ideas printed upon new particles should be a *memory* of old ideas printed upon old particles. But I did not enlarge upon this, because, supposing the *possibility* of it, yet it would avail nothing towards your main purpose, the question being, not whether the *memory* in general of such or such an action's having been done might possibly be preserved in the manner you suppose, but whether the *consciousness* of its being done by *me,* by *my own individual self* in particular, could in this manner be continued. Now how it was in me a *begging of the question* to argue that, even on supposition of the possibility of the hypothesis now mentioned, yet it would nevertheless be impossible for you from thence to make out the conclusion you were to prove, I confess I understand not. Neither do I understand how you can prevail upon yourself to dispute in such a manner.

A man, you say, who, during *a short frenzy, kills* another, *and then returns to himself, without the least consciousness of what he has done, cannot attribute that action to himself,* and therefore *the mad man and the sober man are really two as distinct persons as any two other men in the world, and will be so considered in a court of judicature.* Extraordinary reasoning indeed! Because in a *figurative* sense a man, when he is mad, is said *not to be himself,* and in a *forensic* sense is looked upon as not answerable to his *own actions,* therefore in the *natural and philosophical* sense also *his actions* are not *his own actions,* but *another person's,* and the *same man* is *really two distinct persons!*

You add: *should there be* so *strong a representation to my understanding of a murder done by me (which was never done at all) so that* I *could not distinguish it in my mind from something really done by me,* I *can no more help attributing this to myself, etc.* It is true, I could not *help* it indeed—but it would be (as Mr. *Locke* well expresses it) a *fatal error,* and not (as you would have it) a making me to be really the person I am not. So *that it* is *evident* (you go on) *that self or personal identity consists solely in consciousness* though a false one—that is, it consists in a *false representation,* in *a dream,* as Mr. *Locke* well expresses it again. And so all mankind, it seems, are nothing but a dream. Unless rather your opinion itself be a dream, as, I presume, it will be found to be by every man whose reason is awake.

The restoring, you say, *the power of thinking to the same or to a different body at the resurrection, with a memory* or *consciousness extending to past actions, will be a raising the same person, and not creation of a new one.* If so, then the restoring the like power of thinking to twenty different bodies with false memory (a dream), or a consciousness extending to imaginary past actions, will be a making them all (as I said, and as you expressly allow) to be, not persons like one another, but one and the same individual person, at the same time that they continue different, intelligent, rational men. That is to say, if twenty of your clocks happen to go exactly alike, they are no more twenty clocks, but one and the same individual clock.

Your distinction, between *raising the same person* and *creating a new one,* is a distinction without the least difference. For the *memory* or *consciousness extending to past actions,* which you suppose makes the *same person* in the one case, does exactly as well make the same person in the other case. It being evidently as easy for God to add an imaginary *consciousness extending to past actions that never were* to a new created body *now,* as add an imaginary *consciousness extending to past actions that were done by one body* to another body at the *Resurrection.* So that from your opinion it unavoidably follows that I may now, at this present time, as possibly be created anew, and have another *self, existing* at the same time with me, by God's adding to *the understanding* of a new-made body so *strong a representation* of my past actions, that that other my-self *could not distinguish them in his mind from things really done by him* (as you express yourself in a like case). This, I say, is exactly as possible, in your hypothesis, as it is for me to be raised again at the Resurrection.

Your argument, by which you endeavor to retort upon me that, according to my notion of individual personality, there can be no Resurrection, nor any such thing as personal identity at all, is founded upon a fallacious representation—as if, by the *same individual numerical consciousness,* I understood the *same individual numerical act of thinking.* Whereas the *individual numerical consciousness,* which identifies the person, is that perception by which the person is sensible that his *past acts of thinking* were his *own thoughts* and not *another's.* Which *perception,* in the same continued being, is a *true memory,* and can be *true* in that one numerical being only. But in your fleeting being, it would be a *false memory,* a *mere delusion,* and might be impressed on any number of beings at one and the same time. All which, distinct, intelligent, rational beings, because they happened to be in the same *dream,* you would affirm to be one and the same individual person. And, for the same reason, if twenty pieces of money happen to be stamped with so like an impression that they could not be distinguished one from another, you must affirm them all to be one and the same *individual shilling,* notwithstanding their being different *pieces of silver.* Having granted that if *ever so many thinking beings* have—not *one and the same numerical consciousness,* as by your comparison of a *vast bulk of senseless matter* being added to a man's body, you would very artfully insinuate, in contradiction to the whole course of your argument and most express concessions, but—having granted, I say, and contended, that if *ever* so *many distinct thinking beings* have within themselves a like *consciousness,* or a like *present representation of past actions,* they *can all constitute but one and the same person,* you ask me whether each of these distinct thinking beings must not unavoidably *think* himself the *same person* that did the action, and the *same person* that everyone of the rest will likewise distinctly think himself to be? I answer as before. They must indeed *unavoidably think* so, but in so doing, they must also *unavoidably be mistaken.* And so, according to your notion, we are all *unavoidably we know not who,* and do but *fancy and dream* ourselves to be the persons we think we are, and write and read about *we know not whom nor what.* To your taking refuge in the *justice* of God, I have already answered that the question is not whether God *will* do an absurd thing, but whether in the nature of things it be possible to be done. And whereas you allege that *if God should cause to exist twenty present representations of the same past sinful actions in* so *many distinct beings, the consequent punishment would be twenty times as much as the sinful actions deserved and his justice required,* and that therefore God *will not* do any such thing, I reply the difficulty does not lie there. Because the punishment due to the single person's sinful actions might be divided proportionably among the twenty distinct intelligent being's— which, in your way, are one and the same individual person, and so, *according to you,* there would be no injustice done, because the punishment would not be more that the offenses deserved. And yet it is manifest that, *in reality,* nineteen at least of these twenty distinct beings would be punished unjustly, how small a proportion soever they bear of the punishment, because they would be punished for what they had never been guilty of at all—however, by a false *consciousness,* they might *imagine* themselves to have *done* what they *never did.*

The case you put, of a person living well for some years, and afterwards forgetting that he had done so, and then living for the future in all manner of debauchery, is so far from being an *absurdity,* as you call it, upon my notion of personal identity, that, on the contrary, there is no manner of difficulty in it. The man is not *two persons, as much as any two men in the world are two persons* (which you declare he must be, in consequence of *your* principles—a consequence sufficient to have convinced almost any man of the falsity of the principles from which he sees and owns such an absurdity to follow). But he is, I confess (as you add in the next words), *as much two persons* as *the same man mad and sober is two persons—that* is, he is *not at all two persons,* but plainly *one and the same person—and* shall justly be punished as his iniquities deserve.

You urge that my argument is no more useful to the ends *of religion* than yours, because, *unless the soul, as an immaterial being, did perpetually think, a proof of the immateriality of the soul,* would not necessarily *prove a future state of rewards and punishments.* And upon this you are pleased to make yourself merry in a very needless manner. Now what connection there is between the soul's *immateriality* and its *per-*

petual thinking has been considered elsewhere. In this place it may be sufficient to add that whether the *immateriality and immortality* of the soul necessarily infers its perpetual actual thinking, or not, yet *my* argument is evidently *useful* to religion, by proving at least the *possibility,* and *great probability,* of a future state of rewards and punishments.

And *yours* is evidently *destructive* of religion, by making a future state of rewards and punishments not only *improbable,* but *impossible—seeing* it infers (as I have at large shown) an absolute *impossibility* of a *resurrection of the same person;* and if a resurrection were possible, yet, by introducing such an absolute and fatal *necessity* of all human actions, as Mr. *Hobbes* and *Spinoza* formerly attempted to establish by the same *numerical* argument (though from your *thinking in the same way,* I would not conclude you all to be the same *individual* person), it manifestly makes all future *reward unreasonable,* and all *punishment unjust.*

William Uzgalis

18

Locke and Collins, Clarke and Butler, on Successive Persons

In the "Appendix on Personal Identity" to his *Analogy of Religion* (1736), Bishop Joseph Butler writes regarding John Locke's account of personal identity in *An Essay Concerning Human Understanding:*

Mr. Locke's observations upon this subject appear hasty and he seems to profess himself dissatisfied with suppositions he has made relating to it. But some of these hasty observations have been carried to strange lengths by others; whose notions when traced and examined to the bottom, amounts, I think to this. [Chap. 5, p. 100]

There is then a footnote referring us to Anthony Collins' answer to Mr. Clarke's third defense of his letter to Mr. Dodwell in the Clarke-Collins correspondence of 1706–8. Butler then appears to quote Collins:

"That personality is not a permanent, but a transient thing: that it lives and dies, begins and ends, continually: that no one can any more remain one and the same person two moments together, than two successive moments can be one and the same moment: that our substance is indeed continually changing; but whether this be so or not, is, it seems, nothing to the purpose; since it is not substance, but consciousness alone which constitutes personality; which consciousness, being successive, cannot be the same in any two moments, nor consequently the personality constituted by it."

William Uzgalis wrote this essay expressly for this volume.

Butler's use of quotation marks leads us to think that he is quoting Anthony Collins, but he is not. He is only paraphrasing or summarizing what he takes to be Collins' position. The summary does not quite make sense. Personal identity is constantly changing. After all, our substance is continually changing, but that is not to the point, because it is consciousness that constitutes personality, and not substance. But consciousness is successive, so it also does not make personality the same over time either. So the language of the summary suggests there is a transition from substance to consciousness that will solve the problem of sameness of personal identity over time. But then consciousness is declared to be successive as well, and so cannot provide sameness of personal identity over time. A successive person is one where there is a new person at each successive moment, and so no sameness of person over time. Clearly whatever Butler is doing, he is attributing to Collins the view that persons are successive entities, and he is claiming that in doing so Collins is carrying to strange lengths some of Locke's hasty observations on personal identity.

Some philosophers think the idea of successive persons is a good idea. Butler did not. Butler claims this is the strange length to which Locke's account of personal identity leads. He holds that this (among other things) shows the absurdity of Locke's views on this subject. For, if persons really were successive, this would make any doctrine of responsibility in this life or personal immortality in the next ridiculous. He goes on to contrast the Locke/Collins account of personal identity with what he takes to be a better account. The account he gives is the same as that of Samuel Clarke, the other protagonist in the Clarke-Collins correspondence of 1706–8. Thus we have a battle about personal identity with Locke and Collins on the one side and Clarke and Butler on the other. Many of the positions about identity and personal identity taken by philosophers in the seventeenth and eighteenth centuries have been given new life by philosophers in the twentieth-century debates over personal identity. Rodrick Chisholm resurrected the Clarke/Butler distinction between identity in the strict and philosophical sense and identity in the loose and popular sense against the neo-Lockean views of Sydney Shoemaker. Paul Grice and John Perry among others have also defended neo-Lockean accounts of personal identity against the kinds of criticisms that Butler offered. So it is very likely still worthwhile, both for reasons of historical accuracy and for present philosophical interest, to determine whether the charges that Butler made against Collins' position are fair or not.

In this paper I propose to consider whether Collins really holds the successive person view that Butler attributes to him and whether the doctrine of successive persons really is a consequence of Locke's account of personal identity. My answer to both questions is an emphatic no. In order to get to that answer, however, we ought to contrast briefly the opposing positions and then consider what things Collins said that might have given Butler the impression that Collins believes in successive persons. Then I will explain why Butler turns out to be wrong.

LOCKE, CLARKE, AND BUTLER

One way to get at the most fundamental difference between Locke's account of identity and personal identity and that of Clarke and Butler is to focus on the role substance plays. Locke downplays the importance of substance in determining the identity of living things, and that of substance and soul in determining personal identity.

Locke's account of personal identity is based on an analogy between the identity of plants and animals over time and personal identity. We can begin with the distinction between masses of matter and living things. The mass of matter that composes an animal at a given time changes every time a new atom is added or an old one removed. But the horse that is composed of a mass of particles at any given instant stays the same horse over time because the functional organization of the particles remains the same, allowing the same life to be communicated to the new mass of particles that constitutes the horse at the next moment. Locke explicitly draws the analogy to personal identity:

Different substances, by the same consciousness (where they do partake in it) being united into one Person; as well as different Bodies, by the same Life are united into the same Animal, whose *Identity* is preserved in that change of Substances, by the unity of one continu'd Life. [II. XVII, 10.14–18, p. 336]

Consciousness is a reflex act that goes along with thinking and that makes us aware that we are thinking, perceiving, meditating, and so on. For Locke, consciousness is what ties a person together into a unity over time. Note that when Butler complains that on Collins' account "it is not substance, but consciousness alone which constitutes personality" this is true of Locke as well. This is presumably one of those "hasty observations" of Locke's about which Butler is complaining.

In section 13 Locke brings up an important feature of this analogy. He raises the question of "whether the consciousness of past Actions can be transferr'd from one thinking Substance to another" (II.XVII, 13.31–32, p. 337). In effect the same issue holds for the other side of the analogy. There, life is being transferred continually from one substance to another as atoms are added or subtracted from the mass that makes up a plant or animal at any given moment. In personal identity, the issue is about memory being transferred from one substance to another rather than life.

In II.XXVII, 13, Locke makes the point that we need to know more about the nature of the substances involved in order to know if transference of consciousness from one substance to another is possible. We also need to know more about consciousness. Either consciousness is the same individual action or it is a representation. If consciousness were the same individual action, then it could not be transferred from one substance to another. If, on the other hand, consciousness involves a representation, then while the transference of consciousness is possible, there are going to be difficulties with error and injustice. Given that the first alternative precludes the transfer of consciousness, Locke proceeds to explore the problems involved in the second alternative. The problems Locke considers are fascinating, but for present purposes it is simply worth noting that the result of the discussion is that for the remainder of the chapter Locke clearly assumes that memories and hence consciousness can be transferred from one substance to another. So, given his own dichotomy between acts and representations, he is taking consciousness of past actions or memory as representations and not as actions. Let us now turn to Clarke and Butler.

Substance is fundamental to Clarke and Butler's account of personal identity. Barresi and Martin note of Butler: "One of the things he did do is to reassert the immaterial substance view of personal identity, often merely repeating Clarke's criticism of relational views" (p. 39). Butler explicitly rejects Locke's analogy between the identity of plants and animals and people: "The inquiry, what makes vegetables the same in the common acceptation of the word, does not appear to have any relation to this of personal identity" (Chap. 5, p. 100). In setting forth their own account of identity and personal identity Clarke makes and Butler names the distinction between identity in the strict and philosophical sense and identity in the loose and popular sense. On this account, only sameness of substance gives identity in the strict and philosophical sense. Clarke and Butler regard the kind of identity that Locke attributes to plants and animals as fictitious, or identity in the loose and popular sense (Chap. 5, pp. 100–101).

One of the reasons why Clarke and Butler insist on the necessity of sameness of substance for identity is because they believe that it is impossible to transfer properties from one substance to another. But this is precisely what happens on Locke's account. The life of an oak gets transferred from one mass of matter to another as the oak grows. Further, in his account of personal identity Locke makes consciousness constitutive of personal identity, rather than substances of any kind whether material or immaterial. One is the same person as the one who stole the apples from Farmer Brown's orchard because one can remember having done so. Clarke and Butler reject consciousness as constituting personal identity. They make the soul (a simple substance) the bearer of personal identity. Consciousness makes us aware in memory not only that certain acts were done but that they were done by the same simple substance that now remembers having done them. Without sameness of substance, memory would be a fraud that would make us believe that we were the same person when in fact we were not. We have, then, a clear set of contrasts.

COLLINS' DIVERGENCES FROM LOCKE

When the topic of personal identity arises in the Clarke-Collins correspondence of 1706–8 Collins refers Clarke to Locke's chapter "Of Identity and Diversity" for an answer to his concerns

(Chap. 17, p. 307). Thus Collins is taking that account as his own. Collins explicitly endorses the analogy between the identity of plants and animals and personal identity (Chap. 17, p. 304). He also takes consciousness and memory to be constitutive of personal identity. Still, while Collins says he accepts Locke's account of personal identity, and there is certainly strong evidence that he does, there are ways in which Collins' account of personal identity must diverge from that of Locke. One also might get the impression from concessions that he makes to Clarke that Collins was giving in to Clarke on a number of crucial issues in respect to personal identity and in doing so was departing from Locke's account of personal identity in several crucial respects. I want to go over these points because they are the relevant ones in deciding whether Butler has accurately captured Collins' position about personal identity.

One reason why Collins' account of personal identity cannot be exactly the same as Locke's is that Locke's theory is neutral about what kind of substance or substances compose us. Thus Locke writes:

Self is that conscious thinking thing, (whatever Substances made up of whether Spiritual or Material, Simple or Compounded it matters not) which is sensible or conscious of Pleasure and Pain, capable of Happiness and Misery, and so is concern'd for it *self,* as far as that consciousness extends. [II.XXVII, 17, p. 341]

But Collins is starting from the proposition that it is possible for matter to think, and so he is committed to a materialist account of personal identity. This, in itself, is not a crucial divergence from Locke. Since Locke's theory is neutral in respect to the nature of thinking substances, it is possible for it to be adapted to a materialist account of personal identity without significant modification being required. But it is a difference worth remembering. Collins has modulated Locke's account of personal identity into the materialist mode. Still, if this is the most significant difference between Collins and Locke on personal identity, we might well agree that any consequences that genuinely follow from Collins' position will follow from Locke's as well.

More serious divergences seem to follow as Clarke presses

Collins. One of the issues that Collins seems to give in on has to do with the transfer of properties from one substance to another. At the end of his second defense Clarke puts his argument in the form of fifteen propositions. The eleventh proposition reads: "No individual *Quality* can be *transferred* from one *Subject* to another" (Chap. 17, p. 289). The twelfth reads: *"The Spirits and Particles of the Brain, being loose and in perpetual Flux, can not therefore be the Seat of that Consciousness, by which a Man not only remembers not only things done many Years since, but is also conscious that he himself, the same individual Being was the doer of them"* (Chap. 17, p. 289). The force of these two propositions is that no property can be transferred from one substance to another. Consciousness is a property, and it cannot be transferred from one collection of brain particles to another.

Collins comments on most of the fifteen propositions at the end of his "Reflections on Mr. Clarke's Second Defense." Concerning proposition 11 he writes:

This proposition I allow to be true: The Quality of a subject can only be the quality of that Subject wherein it exists, and not of another Subject. The motion of a system of Matter can only be the Motion of that System. The Consciousness of any being can only be the Consciousness of that Particular Being. [Chap. 17, p. 295]

This really seems like a disastrous admission. Collins seems well on his way to justifying Butler's claim that he believes in successive persons. And things really seem to get worse with his comments on Clarke's twelfth proposition:

Though the Spirits of the Particles of the Brain cannot by being in a perpetual flux be the Seat of that Consciousness by which I know myself today to be the same individual conscious Being that I was a Year ago (for I deny that we have any Consciousness at all that we continue the same individual Being at different times) yet if it be not absurd for Matter to think, Matter must at the same time know that it thinks, or be conscious of its thinking; and if it can know at this instant that it thinks, I can see no reason why it cannot remember To-morrow what it thinks To-day, though some Particles will then be wanting which it has at present. And if it can remember at all, then the memory of things may be continued even after we have lost all the Particles of Matter that we had at the time of the doing them, by continual intermediate repeating, or imprinting afresh our Ideas before they are quite lost or worn out. And it is thus as intelligible to me that memory of things should be preserved by a Being in Flux, as by a Being that is not so. [Chap. 17, p. 295–96]

Collins continues:

For the individual Consciousness To-day, can neither in an individual nor a divisible Being be the individual Consciousness tomorrow; that Consciousness is a perfectly distinct action in both Beings from the preceding Consciousness the day before. [Chap. 17, p. 296]

So Collins is denying that we know ourselves to be the same conscious Being that we were the year before, and in fact we have no consciousness that we continue the same individual Being at different times. This seems to show that Butler is indeed correct and Collins has a doctrine of successive persons.

In addition, when he says that the individual Consciousness today cannot be the individual consciousness tomorrow, Collins is treating consciousness as an act rather than a representation. In fact, he regularly treats thinking and consciousness as actions. So it would appear that on his view (unlike that of Locke) consciousness cannot be transferred from one subject to another. This, along with the parenthetical remark quoted above that "I deny that we have any Consciousness at all that we continue the same individual Being at different times," seems to strongly suggest that he believes in successive persons, as Butler charges.

WHY THE CHARGES TURN OUT NOT TO BE TRUE

First we should begin with Locke and note why the claim that the Lockean account of personal identity is not one of successive persons. The reason why this is so is that Locke has a quite different account of identity from that of Clarke and Butler. On Locke's account it is quite possible for an entity to stay the same through changes of substance. This is not possible on the Clarke/Butler account. So it is only if you apply Clarke and Butler's definition of identity to Locke's account of oaks, horses, and people that one gets a concept of successive plants, animals, or persons. But since there is considerable reason to think that Locke would have rejected such a definition of identity, there is no reason to think *his* theory has such a consequence. It is only if you apply the

Clarke/Butler account of identity to Locke's account of plants, animals, and people that you would get such a result. And why do that?

When we turn to Collins' account of personal identity he basically says he agrees with Locke about this topic. He accepts Locke's revolutionary view that consciousness, and not the substantial soul, is the bearer of personal identity. Again agreeing with Locke, he regards both memory as crucial to personal identity and feelings of pleasure and pain as important concomitants of consciousness. Collins also defends the concept of memory involved.

Still, Clarke holds that Collins' account of memory violates a basic principle of Clarke's substantialist account of identity— that properties cannot be transferred from one substance to another. Collins' response to this is to claim that annexing consciousness to the brain explains the phenomena of consciousness far better than positing an unchanging immaterial substance (Chap. 17, p. 290–91). It is also a perfectly reasonable sense for properties to be transferred from one substance to another. In his "Reflections on Mr. Clarke's Second Defense" Collins writes:

For if we utterly forget, or cease to be conscious of having done many things in former Parts of our Lives which we certainly did, as much as any of those which we are conscious that we have done; and if in fact we do by degrees forget everything which we do not revive by frequent Recollection, and by again and again imprinting our decaying Ideas; and if there be in a determinate Time a partial or total flux of Particles in our Brains: What can better account for our total Forgetfulness of some things, our partial Forgetfulness of others, than to suppose that the Substance of the Brain is in a constant Flux? [Chap. 17, p. 291]

As for the problem of transferring consciousness from one substance to another he writes:

I will suppose myself conscious at Forty of having been carried to a Market or Fair at Five Years old, without any Particle of Matter about me, the same which I had at that Age: now in order to retain the Consciousness of that Action, it is necessary to revive the Idea of it before any considerable Flux of Particles, (otherwise I must totally lose the Memory of it (as I do of several things done in my Childhood) and by reviving the Idea of that Action, I imprint afresh the Consciousness of having done that Action, by which the Brain has as lively an Impression of Consciousness (though it be not entirely composed of the same Particles) as it had the day after it did the Action. [Chap. 17, p. 291]

This account of how memory works nicely fits the model of the preservation of organization through change of matter that Locke uses to explain the identity of living things. Still, what are we to say of Collins' treatment of consciousness as acts that cannot be transferred from one substance to another, and his remark that he does not believe that we are conscious of being one individual being from one time to another? Hasn't he conceded way too much to Clarke?

There are, I think, really two issues about the transference of properties. The first is to explain why Collins would accept Clarke's eleventh and twelfth propositions as true. I think the answer to this is that in the text of Collins' "Reflections on Mr. Clarke's Third Defense" there is a crucial qualification that he does not make in discussing the propositions in his "Reflections on Mr. Clarke's Second Defense." When he discusses the issue of transferring properties, Collins says: "And if there is every now and then a Recollection of a Past Action, a Man may be conscious of things done by him, though he has not one Particle of Matter, the same that he had at the doing of those things, without *Consciousness's being transferred from one Subject to another,* in any absurd sense of those words" (Chap. 17, p. 291). So it appears that there is some absurd sense in which one might foolishly think consciousness can be transferred from one substance to another, and then some perfectly reasonable sense for consciousness to be transferred from one substance to another. The sense that is absurd is the sense of consciousness as an act. This leads us to our next question.

How can Collins treat consciousness as an act rather than a representation and still have any transference of consciousness? The answer is that he does not do this. Collins is treating consciousness as both an act and a representation. It is a clear case of the inclusive "or." As an act, consciousness cannot be transferred from one substance to another while as a representation it can. Thus the answer to the question about the difference between the two kinds of transference is this: to transfer acts from one substance to another is absurd; to transfer representations is not.

So, on the one hand, he says: "Any particular act of Consciousness is incapable of the Continuation of its Existence; wherefore its Identity can only consist in it being that very Numerical Act of Consciousness that it is" (Chap. 17, p. 304); and, on the other hand: "That present *Consciousness* or Memory *is nothing but a present Representation* of a past Action, and that *personal Identity* consists only in having such a *Consciousness* or Memory" ("An Answer to Mr. Clarke's Third Defense (Chap. 17, p. 306). Thus Collins is still staying with the Lockean account of personal identity. Still, what about Collins' response to Clarke's propositions 11 and 12? How could he agree with those propositions when they are completly unqualified? We get the answer, I think, in the comment that Collins makes in his discussion of proposition 14:

From all which it is plain that all Mr. Clarke's Propositions are founded on his considering Consciousness to be something else than what I contend it is; and so though he may demonstrate the impossibility of Matter's being conscious in his Sense of the term Consciousness, yet I deny that he has said one word to prove the impossibility of Matter's Thinking in the sense for which the term Consciousness stands with me, and I suppose with all those that contend for the possibility of Matter's Thinking or being conscious. [Chap. 17, p. 296]

I think it is perfectly plain that Collins is following Locke in making the distinction between consciousness as an action and consciousness as a representation and agreeing that in the first sense consciousness cannot be transferred from one substance to another while maintaining that in the second it can.

What about Collins' remark that we do not know ourselves to be the same individual being that we were yesterday or the year before? Does not this strongly suggest that Butler was correct and that Collins believes in successive persons? The answer is surely not. What Collins is rejecting here is not the notion that persons stay the same over time; rather he is rejecting the claim that we are conscious from one time to another that we are the same simple substance. Thus he is rejecting a basic doctrine of Clarke and Butler's account of personal identity. He has a different account of identity, where personal identity does not depend on sameness of substance.

What then are we to say about Collins' account of personal identity? Does it contain a doctrine of successive persons? The answer is not at all. Butler came to the conclusion that he did by applying his own metaphysical principles to the account of persons that Collins gives. Just as I suggested that there is no plausibility in doing this for Locke, since Locke would reject the crucial definition of identity that Clarke and Butler accept, the same applies to Collins. Neither Locke nor Collins has a doctrine of successive persons. Nor does anything they say imply such a doctrine. Butler is simply applying his own account of identity to Collins' doctrine to illegitimately produce what he regards as an unacceptable result. If one goes back to that pseudo-quotation one can see Butler attributing a position to Collins on the basis of his own metaphysical principles that Collins would never accept. This is surely a significant philosophical sin.

John Perry

19

Williams on the Self and the Future

Is personal identity simply bodily identity? Or is it based on a different principle, continuity of consciousness or links of memory? Locke thought the latter, and so, with various important qualifications, do Sydney Shoemaker and a number of other contemporary philosophers who have written on the problem of personal identity. (See Chap. 2 and Chap. 8 of the present volume). Both Locke and Shoemaker bolster the case for the memory theory by appealing to cases of putative body transfer. In a body transfer case, a person has one body at one time, and a different body at a later time. In other words, there is personal identity without bodily identity. The advocate of the view that personal identity consists in, or at least implies, bodily identity must resist taking these cases to be real cases of body transfer. This Bernard Williams has done in a number of essays, culminating in the imaginative and elegant "The Self and the Future" (Chap. 13 in this volume). In this essay, I try to understand the arguments Williams has given for resistance.

PUTATIVE EXAMPLES OF BODY TRANSFER

The most famous examples of putative body transfer are Locke's cobbler and prince and Shoemaker's case of Brownson. Locke

This is a reworked version of a review of Bernard Williams' *Problems of the Self.* The review originally appeared in *The Journal of Philosophy* 73, no. 13 (1976): 416–28. This version originally appeared in John Perry, *Identity, Personal Identity, and the Self* (Indianapolis, 2002).

doesn't explain why the cobbler he imagines comes to have memories of a prince, but says that the cobbler would be the same person as the prince, but not the same man. Shoemaker gives us more details. Brown's brain is transplanted into Robinson's cranium. The survivor of this operation Shoemaker calls "Brownson." We can represent this sort of case with a diagram in which the horizontal rows represents sameness of body:

1. Shoemaker's Case	
Earlier Time	Later Time
Brown	Brown's body, no brain
Robinson	Brownson [Person with Robinson's body and Brown's brain]

The diagram is neutral as to the question of personal identity. We can ask whether Brownson is Brown, Robinson, or neither. Shoemaker says that, assuming Brownson has the memories of Brown, we should cautiously conclude that Brownson is Brown. If we conclude this, then this is a case of body transfer, though Brown still has part of his original body, his brain.

Since Shoemaker put forward the Brownson case, writers, including Shoemaker, have considered more abstract examples, in which the brain itself isn't transferred (see Chap. 16). The properties of the brain that are relevant to memory (and any other mental traits deemed important) are somehow duplicated in another brain, whose owner is imagined to have a mental life exactly similar in relevant respects to that which actual brain transfer would have produced. Since this more abstract case is the sort variations on which Williams discusses, I'll call it "the basic case":

2. The Basic Case	
Earlier Time	Later Time
A	Left open
B	B-body-person [B's body, A's memories]

Is the *B*-body-person *A?* Or *B?* Or neither? In Shoemaker's case, it was the memories and not the brain that were important in arguing that Brownson was Brown. The brain's importance derived only from the fact that it was the physical basis of the memories. It seems then that the same arguments would apply in the basic case. Williams himself states these arguments very effectively in "The Self and the Future," (Chap. 13, pp. 181–85)— but only as a preparation to rejecting them.

Williams thinks that persons are material objects, that personal identity is bodily identity, and that the putative cases of body transfer should not be accepted as real. His strategy is to lead us to consider variations on the basic case. When we explore our intuitions about these variations, we find the force of the arguments for the memory theory based on simpler cases fading away. In an early paper, "Personal Identity and Individuation," Williams puts forward his reduplication argument.[1] Later, in "The Self and the Future," he puts forward what I shall call the non-duplication argument. I shall consider each of these.

THE REDUPLICATION ARGUMENT

In the reduplication argument, Williams asks us to consider a variation on the basic case. Instead of having one person at the later time with *A*'s memories and someone else's body, we imagine having two. Given that the basic case does not involve an actual transfer of the brain, we can suppose that the very same process that in the basic case led to the *B*-body-person having *A*'s memories is applied twice. Thus both the *B*-body-person and the *C*-body-person have *A*'s memories.

3. The Reduplication Case	
Earlier Time	Later Time
A	No person has *A*'s body
B	*B*-body-person [*B*'s body, *A*'s memories]
C	*C*-body-person [*C*'s body, *A*'s memories]

This sort of case presents the memory theorist with a dilemma. Both the *B*-body-person and the *C*-body-person have that relation to *A* that was deemed sufficient for personal identity in the basic case. But then both of them should be *A*. But they clearly are not identical with one another. They have different bodies, will have different perceptions when they awake from the operation, and so will soon have different memories. They can't find out what each other is thinking or doing by introspection. But since identity is a "one-to-one" relation, we can't consistently maintain all of the following:

(1) The *B*-body-person = *A*
(2) The *C*-body-person = *A*
(3) The *B*-body-person ≠ the *C*-body-person

Which of these will the memory theorist give up? It would be absurd to give up (3). Giving up either (1) or (2) undermines the idea that personal identity consists in links of memory. (There can be no sufficient reason for giving up (1) and (2) without the other, since the claims have exactly the same basis.) Thus the reduplication argument forces us to rethink the power of the basic case.

The logic of this argument seems to be this: A description of some basic case is given, neutral on questions of personal identity. From this description, we can see that some relation obtains between the memory donor and the survivor (*A* and the *B*-body-person). Is this relation sufficient for identity? If it is, changing the example in ways that do not affect it should not affect the question of identity. But certain changes give us a variation in which the relation is clearly not sufficient for identity, namely, adding another survivor (the *C*-body-person) who also has the relation in question to the memory donor. Of course, one can make these changes only if the relation in question is "duplicable"—is the sort of relation that can obtain between *A* and both the *B*-body-person and the *C*-body-person.

In Williams' "Personal Identity and Individuation," Charles claims to be Guy Fawkes and supports this claim with detailed memory-like reports of Fawkes' life. "Appears to remember events from Fawkes' life in great detail" is a duplicable relation, which two people might have to Fawkes. But this relation would surely not be supposed, even by those most sanguine about transfer of bodies, to be sufficient for personal identity. Any inclination to suppose that Charles is Fawkes must be based on the assumption that this relation is good evidence for some other relation, itself sufficient for identity. The real question is the duplicability of this other relation.

Consider the Shoemaker case. Suppose Charles is to Fawkes as Brownson is to Brown: Charles actually has Fawkes' brain, which has somehow survived with all of its memories intact. The possibility of a competitor with similarly accurate sensory impressions is not a problem for the advocate of body transfer. This competitor would simply seem to remember being Fawkes. But Charles, because his current memory impressions have the right sort of causal link to Fawkes' life, could be said to really remember. The advocate of body transfer could say that the important relation, the one that permits there to be one person where there are two bodies, has not been duplicated.

Williams notes that it is an advantage of the Shoemaker example that it does not seem to admit of the reduplication problem. But he points out in "Are Persons Bodies?" that a natural extension of the example does: "Consider, not the physical transfer of brains, but the transfer of information between brains."[2] The relevance of this to the Shoemaker case, and to the project of rebutting the argument that personal identity is not bodily identity, is not perfectly clear because it seems that only one successful example of bodily transfer needs to be provided to disprove the claim that bodily identity is sufficient for personal identity. The following line of argument is open to Williams. Whatever considerations there are in favor of counting brain transfer as body transfer are also reasons to regard information transfer as body transfer. But the reduplication argument shows we cannot regard information transfer as body transfer, so these reasons must not be good enough. Further, as Williams points out, the reduplication argument is certainly an embarrassment to any memory theorist who doesn't want possession of a particular brain to be a condition of personal identity, and the motivations behind memory theories are such that most would not.

But what sort of embarrassment is it? Williams says the principle of the argument is that "identity is a one-one relation, and that no principle can be a criterion of identity for things of type T if it relies on what is logically a one-many relation between things of type T."[3] What the reduplication case shows (with the details suitably filled in to be relevant to a particular account of personal identity in terms of memory) is that the memory relation proposed as the criterion of identity is not logically one-one.

Does it follow from the fact that identity is logically one-one that any criterion for identity must be logically one-one? It is not even clear that it follows that it must be, as a matter of fact, one-one. For example, "has the same fingerprints" is perhaps, as a matter of fact, but surely not as a matter of logical necessity, a one-one relation, yet this is certainly, in the ordinary sense, a criterion of personal identity. It would still be so even if in every couple of million cases two or three people did share the same fingerprints. A relation that is not one-one can be quite good evidence for one that is one-one, so long as there are not too many exceptions. Presumably then some special philosophical notion of "criterion" is at work here. Even if we require some "conceptual" or "logical" connection between the criterion and what it is a criterion for, the inference in question may not hold. Using, for example, Shoemaker's explanation of the term in *Self-Knowledge and Self-Identity*,[4] a criterion for personal identity would be a relation that could not possibly not be good evidence for personal identity. All that seems to be required of such a relation is that, in each possible world, it is good evidence for personal identity. All this seems to require is that in each possible world the relation in question be one-one with but a few exceptions.

Perhaps by "a criterion of identity" is meant some relation between persons that can serve as an analysis of the very meaning of "is the same person as." Williams's remark that his point could be made more rigorously in terms of "sense and reference of uniquely referring expressions," suggests this.[5] Such analyses are often developed in terms of equivalence relations and equivalence classes.

An equivalence relation is one with the following properties:

It is transitive, which means that if x has the relation to y, and y has it to z, then x has it to z. It is symmetrical, which means that if x has it to y, then y has it to x. And it is weakly reflexive, which means that if x has it to anything, x has it to x. Equivalence relations break populations up into equivalence classes. These classes contain only things that have the relation in question to everything inside the class, including themselves, and nothing outside of it. For example, "having the same mother" is an equivalence relation among children. If we pick any child and consider the class of things that have the same mother as her, they will all have the same mother as each other, and none will have the same mother as anything outside of the class. On the other hand, suppose we say that x is y's brother if x is a male and x and y have the same mother or the same father. Then "having the same brother" would not be an equivalence relation, because it is not transitive. It will not break a population of children up into equivalence classes. If we start with one child and consider the class of children that share a brother with that child, we may have people in the class that have this relation to people outside of it.

Memory theorists often explain the notion of personal identity by starting with a relation that obtains among stages or phases of persons or their minds. Persons are then taken as being or corresponding to equivalence classes of these entities, generated by the relation given as the "criterion of identity," or, as I prefer to call it, the "unity relation." For example, with an analysis Grice suggests, the relation is roughly "A and B are end points of a series of person-stages each member of which has an experience of which the next could have a memory."[6]

In this framework, Williams' requirement for a logically one-one relation amounts to the following: The unity relation must be an equivalence relation not merely as a matter of fact, but as a matter of logical or metaphysical necessity. But I don't think the memory theorist needs to accept this requirement.

In the actual world, if we take a person-stage and consider the class of other states that have Grice's relation to it, the population of person-stages breaks up into equivalence classes. Now suppose that in some other possible world w this is not so because there is frequent "fissioning" in the following sense: A person-stage *A* has an experience, which two successor person-stages, *B* and *C*, can remember. *B* and *C* have experiences, which successors of theirs, *B'* and *C'*, can remember. But no successor of *B* remembers any of *C*'s experiences, and vice versa. Now if we start with *C* and generate the set of stages that have Grice's relation to it, *A* will be included. And if we start with *B*, *A* will be included. But *C* will not be included in *B*'s set, and vice versa.

In world *w*, the notion of a person will not be as useful as it is in ours. We might say that the presuppositions of using it the way we do, to pick out individual nonbranching streams of thought and experience, are not met. But the fact that this notion would not be very useful in *w* does not mean it doesn't work fine in the world the way it actually is. It does not mean that this is not the notion of a person that we actually have in our world, where R is an equivalence relation.

The memory theorist can be even more flexible about the logical properties of the unity relation. Suppose that such "fissionings" of streams of experience happen in our world, but only very occasionally. The notion of a person could still be very useful, even though not applicable in a clear-cut way to those particular cases. Consider the notion of a "nation." This is a pretty useful notion, although occasionally, as in the case of Germany and Korea, a sort of fissioning takes place. When we are talking about the history of Germany or Korea, we have to be careful about the way we use the concept of the "same nation" to describe things. If streams of experience were occasionally to split, as is imagined in the reduplication case, we would have to be careful in applying the concept of "same person" to those cases. This does not show that an analysis, like Grice's, that allows the logical possibility of fission, is mistaken.

So I think it is open to the memory theorist to reply to Williams' reduplication argument by saying that it imposes a requirement on analyses of personal identity that they do not need to accept. The possibility of body transfer only requires that our notion of personal identity may be correctly analyzed in terms of a relation that (*i*) is as a matter of fact an equivalence relation, and (*ii*) is a relation that could obtain between person-stages that involve different bodies.

The memory theorist can go further, I think, and note that the analysis implied by those who reject the possibility of bodily transfer is also subject to the reduplication argument. Williams himself notes that one could claim that "even a criterion of identity in terms of spatio-temporal continuity is itself not immune to this possibility. It is possible to imagine a man splitting, ameba-like, into two simulacra of himself."[7] He states that there is "a vital difference between this sort of reduplication . . . and the other sorts of case." The difference is that the procedure of tracing the continuous path between two occurrences of what is taken to be a single person will inevitably reveal the duplication, if "ideally carried out." Thus "in this case, but not in the others, the logical possibility of reduplication fails to impugn the status of the criterion of identity."[8] This is unconvincing for several reasons. Even if we grant that the spatio-temporal continuity requirement has the advantage described, having that advantage does not make it "logically one-one." How can such a difference between the spatio-temporal continuity criterion and others exempt it from what are alleged to be logical requirements of a criterion of identity? Perhaps the force of the "logical requirement" simply reduces to this advantage. But why should we think, after all, that this advantage is not shared by the memory criterion? Among other things, we should have to know what it is to "ideally carry out" the application of that criterion. Williams asserts that memory is a causal notion (Chap. 13, p. 180). As Shoemaker has observed, this seems to suggest that application of the memory criterion ideally carried out would disclose the existence of competitors, since the causal chain involved would presumably involve a spatio-temporally continuous chain of events.

I conclude that the reduplication argument does not show that memory theorists are incorrect in allowing for the possibility of body transfer. Let us now turn to what I shall call the "non-duplication argument."

THE NON-DUPLICATION ARGUMENT

Williams begins his discussion in "The Self and the Future" by introducing an example whose structure is that of two basic cases superimposed:

4. The Master Case (Superimposed Basic Cases)	
Earlier Time	**Later Time**
A	*A*-body-person [*A*'s body, *B*'s memories]
B	*B*-body-person [*B*'s body, *A*'s memories]

Williams then poses a problem for *A* and *B*. Each is asked, at the earlier time, to choose one of the bodies to be tortured at the later time, the other to receive $100,000. This choice is to be made on selfish grounds. Williams assays the results of various possible combinations of choices and seems to find in them a strong argument for describing the case as one of body transfer. For example, if *A* chose that the *B*-body-person be rewarded, and this is done, then the *B*-body-person will be happy about a choice he will seem to remember making. It is natural to report this as "Someone got what he wanted," and this someone must be someone who had body *A* and then had body *B*. Williams' discussion (Chap. 13, pps. 181–85) puts the case for the possibility of body transfer about as effectively as it has been put.

But then he pulls the rug out from under us: "Let us now consider something apparently different. Someone . . . tells me that I am going to be tortured tomorrow . . . when the moment of torture comes, I shall not remember any of the things I am now in a position to remember . . . but will have a different set of impressions of my past" (Chap. 13, pps. 185–6). To be tortured is a frightful prospect, and the additional bits of information about loss of memory and acquisition of false belief just make things worse. But this is just a variation on the master case. Instead of adding a character, as in the reduplication argument, character(s) are subtracted—or at least knowledge of them is. We represent this variation by simply striking out half of the last diagram:

(With the information in the bottom half left out, the force of "*B*'s memories" in the previous case is simply "memories that are not *A*'s"; for all *A* is to be told, the memories of the *A*-body-person might not belong to anyone.) As Williams says, "for what we have just been through is of course merely one side, differently represented, of the transaction which was considered before;

5. The Non-duplication Case (Top Half of Master Case)	
Earlier Time Later Time	
A	*A*-body-person [*A*'s body, but not *A*'s memories]
B	~~*B*-body-person [*B*'s body, *A*'s memories]~~

and it represents it as a perfectly hateful prospect, while the previous considerations represented it as something one should rationally, perhaps even cheerfully, choose out of the options there presented" (Chap. 13, p. 187).

Going back to the choice about torture and money in the master case, Williams tells us that these and other considerations leave him "not in the least clear which option it would be wise to take if one were presented with them before the experiment." But his cautious advice is that "if we were the person *A* then, if we were to decide selfishly, we should pass the pain to the *B*-body person" (Chap. 13, p. 198).

Williams suggests that his opponent might claim that, in terrifying *A* with his one-sided description of what is to happen, it is the omission of mention of the *B*-body-person that clouds the issue. The objector would maintain that this "is to leave out exactly the feature which, as the first presentation of the case showed, makes all the difference: for it is to leave out the person who, as the first presentation showed, will be you " (Chap. 13, p. 190). Williams challenges this objector to draw a line somewhere in the following series. At which point should *A*'s fear of torture give way to anticipation of $100,000?

(*i*)   *A* is subjected to an operation that produces total amnesia;

(*ii*)   amnesia is produced in *A,* and other interference leads to certain changes in his character;

(*iii*)   changes in his character are produced, and at the same time certain illusory "memory" beliefs are induced in him; these are of a quite fictitious kind . . . ;

(*iv*)   the same as (*iii*) except that both the character traits and the "memory" impressions are designed to be appropriate to another actual person *B;*

(v)   the same as (iv) except that the result is produced by putting the information into A from the brain of B, by a method that leaves B the same as he was before;

(vi) the same happens to A as in (v), but B is not left the same, since a similar operation is conducted in the reverse direction. (Chap. 13, p. 190)

It is case (vi) that the memory theorist seems to suppose should leave A looking forward to receiving $100,000. This is, it must be admitted, an odd reaction to (vi), if we take everything up to (v) as describing an increasingly troubling description of surviving as an amnesiac. But should we react to cases (i) to (v) in this way? This depends, I suggest, on what we mean by "total amnesia."

Let's return for a moment to the diagram of the master case and the non-duplication case to note a crucial point about the logic of Williams' argument. For the non-duplication argument to work, there must be a certain relation that obtains between A and the A-body-person both in the master case and in the non-duplication case, which is supposed to be part of it differently presented. The relation will have to be clearly sufficient, in the non-duplication case, for the identity of A and the A-body-person. Then the argument will be that the addition of body B and the B-body-person to make the master case should make no difference—just as eliminating the strike-throughs in the bottom of the diagram would not alter the top. The A-body-person would still be A, and not have suddenly become B instead.

I believe the plausibility of the non-duplication argument turns on leaving the details of the master case hazy. I shall argue that filling them in one way leaves the argument with no force, while filling them in the other way reduces the argument to a fancy version of the reduplication argument, which I found unconvincing in the last section.

The haziness derives from the ambiguity of the term "amnesia" and the phrase "extracting information." "Amnesia" is a slippery word. It means one thing to a physician, another to a television writer, and perhaps something still different to Williams. In ordinary fiction amnesia is consistent with, and indeed implies, survival of memory traces. The picture is of a person whose memories are inaccessible, but, in some sense, still there. The disposition to remember is present, but not triggered by the ordinary conditions. Photographs, diaries, and the sight of loved ones will not do the trick; perhaps a fortuitous blow on the head or electric shock therapy will. In introducing the procedure whose consequences he wishes to discuss, Williams says: "[S]uppose it were possible to extract information . . ." (Chap. 13, p. 180). This is ambiguous. Compare photocopying a book to ripping its pages out. In either case, one has extracted information from the book. A possible interpretation is this: The information is extracted in a way that leaves the brain with all its memory dispositions in some way intact, although no longer capable of being triggered in the usual ways. On this interpretation, the case he envisages seems to involve a sort of programming of new memory dispositions over the old, in such a way as to leave the old dispositions no longer capable of being triggered. I'll call this the "information overlay."

A second interpretation I'll call a "brain zap." The information in the brain is extracted in the "ripping out the pages" sense. The information, the dispositions to speak, imagine, infer, and the like are destroyed. The brain is "wiped clean," to be a suitable receptacle for a completely different set of memory dispositions. Efforts to trigger the disposition would be to no avail because the disposition is not there to be triggered.

If we think of Williams' case as an information overlay, it simply leads to a complex version of the reduplication argument. A plausible analysis of personal identity in terms of memory will have to be flexible enough to allow for amnesia, even amnesia together with delusions of an alternative past. The identity theorist who allows for these possibilities will be confronted with two reduplication cases. Stage A will have the unity relation to the A-body person-stage and to the B-body person-stage. Stage B will also have the unity relation to both of these stages. We have two intertwined cases where the presuppositions of the concept of person have broken down. The memory theorist should certainly not say, in this case interpreted this way, that A should have unalloyed feelings of joy about getting \$100,000. He will have a ready explanation, in terms of the breakdown in the presuppositions of the concept of a person, of our feeling of not knowing where to draw the line in the series (*i*) to (*vi*). This feeling of bafflement is just what the memory theorist could predict. If personal identity is analyzable in terms of a certain relation, and if Williams' case involves a double intertwined breakdown of an empirical presupposition of that concept, namely, that the relation is an equivalence relation, then we have a case in which we should not expect to be able to apply our ordinary concepts.

I think there is good reason to suppose that Williams was giving "amnesia" a reading closer to what I am calling a brain zap, however. If Williams intended an information overlay, the whole point of his discussion becomes rather obscure. Let us review the logic of the situation. The interest in putative cases of body transfer is as counterexamples to the necessity of bodily identity as a condition of personal identity. If a case is presented as a counterexample, it's no good to pick another case something like it, but different in essential respects, and point out that this new case is not such a clear-cut counterexample. I think we have a right to assume that Williams' example is intended to be more or less the same sort of example that advocates of body transfer have offered. Moreover, the fact that he develops his example as a sort of moderate alternative to Shoemaker's original case, where a brain was transferred and there was no question of superimposition of one set of memory dispositions over another, and the fact that he speaks of replacing the information extracted from each brain with information extracted from the other suggest that a brain zap is what is involved.

This suggests it might be a relevant and helpful exercise to think through the non-duplication argument as applied to Shoemaker's original case. The removal of a brain and its replacement with a different one, with no transfer of information between them, seems like just an extreme way of achieving the same effects, so far as information goes, as a brain zap. Let's suppose, for a moment, that in the master case the *A*-body-person has the actual brain *B* had at the earlier time. Then the relation between *A* at the earlier time and the *A*-body-person at the later time is "having the same body but not the same brain." This will also be the relation in the non-duplication case, the variation where *B* is left out. Consider what we should tell *A* were we to fully represent to him one side of the transaction: "Tomorrow your brain will be removed from your body. Another man's brain will be put in its place. Then your body will be tortured." This certainly represents a frightening prospect. But it is far from clear that it is torture that is to be feared, rather than death and defilement. We could, of course, give a superficial description that would both be true and inspire fear of pain: "Your body is going to be whipped, and it won't be a corpse when it happens." But the fear of torture inspired by this description might be a consequence of the omission of such details as the removal of the brain. The principle, to which Williams appeals in considering his case, is that "one's fears can extend to future pain whatever psychological changes precede it" (Chap. 13, p. 198). It's a little hard to get a grip on how this principle is supposed to work, since it seems that fear can extend to any future pain whatsoever, no matter whose it is, so long as the fearful person believes it will be his pain. The principle is surely only dubiously applicable to the Shoemaker case, for loss of one's brain is not, in the ordinary sense, a "psychological change." Williams' argument, that addition of another body to the scenario in the non-duplication case cannot affect the identity of A and the A-body-person, has no force unless the identity is clear to start with. If we were dealing with a brain transplant case, it would not be clear at all.

Perhaps this is all irrelevant, since Williams explicitly chooses not to deal with a case involving a physical transplant. He says: "Hence if utterances coming from a given body are to be taken as expressive of memories . . . there should be some suitable causal link between the appropriate state of that body and the original happening" (Chap. 13, p. 180). But one need not imagine, in order to secure this link, that a brain has actually been transplanted. "[S]uppose it were possible to extract information from a man's brain and store it in a device while his brain was repaired or even renewed, the information then being replaced: it would seem exaggerated to insist that the resultant man could not possibly have the memories he had before the operation. . . . Hence we can imagine the case we are concerned with in terms of information extracted into such devices from A's and B's brains and replaced in the other brain" (Chap. 13, p. 180).

Thus the relation between *A* and the *A*-body-person is not as it would be in a transplant case: having the same body but different brains. The relation is that they have the same body and the same brain, but information about *A*'s life has been extracted from this brain, and other information has replaced it.

But should this make any difference, either to *A* or to the memory theorist? I cannot see that the situation is importantly changed when we deal with a brain zap rather than a brain transplant. When it's not clear that *A*'s brain will be zapped, he fears torture. When that is clear, but he is left to assume the worst about the survival of the information in his brain, he fears death, or perhaps doesn't know what to fear. When he is told that this information will be appropriately put into another brain, itself previously zapped, that might change the focus of his fear considerably.

Consider now the non-duplication case, in which *B* has been left out. What is the relation between *A* and the *A*-body-person? Is it psychological change, through which *A*'s fears could, by Williams' principle, appropriately extend? Or is it simply the death of *A*? Or something else? For the non-duplication argument to work, it must be psychological change. *A* would react to the description of what is to happen with fear because he regards what is to happen to his body as something like his forgetting, and assimilates how he will be to a "completely amnesiac state" (Chap. 13, p. 186).

If the relation between *A* and the *A*-body-person is that the latter has the very brain the former had, but it has been zapped, then the case seems unimportantly different from a case in which they share no brain at all. A superficial description of the case might evoke fear of pain, but when the details are known, fear of death seems more appropriate. If one were tempted to draw a line between the case in which *A* and the *A*-body-person do not share a brain and one in which they share a brain, but it gets zapped between the earlier and later time, we could appeal to a point Williams makes. He argues that, if the sort of information-parking operation he envisages were possible, "a person could be counted the same if this were done to him, and in the process he were given a new brain (the repairs, let us say, actually required a new part)."[9] Apparently, so long as no transfer of bodies is at issue, it is the retention of information, and not of the brain, that is crucial for survival. Why shouldn't the same be true for non-survival?

In considering the series (*i*) to (*vi*), the memory theorist can simply point out that, if a brain zap is involved, "amnesia" in (*i*) to (*v*) is simply a euphemism for "death." After all, it is the cessation of the sort of activity of the brain whose role is to preserve that which has here been destroyed that is known as "brain death." The use of the pronoun "him" simply begs the question at issue. In case (*vi*) the trauma of gaining a new body should probably be feared, offset perhaps to some extent by gaining $100,000 if one made the right choice.

If we understand that a brain zap is involved, Williams' non-duplication argument fails. The non-duplication case was supposed to remind us that *A* really was the *A*-body-person. Then the argument is that *A* doesn't cease to be the *A*-body-person simply because the *B*-body-person is hanging around. Since, given that it involves a brain zap, the non-duplication case doesn't show that *A* is the *A*-body-person, it's possible that, when the facts about *B* and the *B*-body-person are added, *A* will be seen at the later time to be the *B*-body-person, an unusual but unambiguous case of personal identity with transfer of bodies.

NOTES

1. I am ignoring certain historical niceties here. In "Personal Identity and Individuation" (*Proceedings of the Aristotelian Society,* 1956–57, reprinted in Williams, 1973, 1–18) Williams doesn't discuss why the competing survivors both (seem to) remember being Guy Fawkes, so it wasn't quite presented as a variation on what I call the basic case.

As Wiggins points out in *Identity and Spatio-Temporal Continuity* (1967), we can imagine this sort of duplication even in the original case if we suppose that the halves of the brain are roughly equivalent in function, and imagine them being transplanted to different recipients.

The first version of the reduplication argument appears to be due to Samuel Clarke, in his controversy with Anthony Collins about the merits of Locke's approach to personal identity within the context of the issue of whether matter can think (see Chapters 17 and 18 of the present volume).

For treatments of reduplication cases, see David Wiggins, *Identity and Spatio-Temporal Continuity* (Oxford, 1967); Sydney Shoemaker, "Persons and Their Pasts," (Chap. 16); my "Can the Self Divide," *Journal of Philosophy, 69,* September, 1972, reprinted in Perry, 2002; Derek Parfit, "Personal Identity," (Chap. 14); David Lewis, "Survival and Identity" in Rorty, 1976; Terrence Leichti, *Fission and Identity* (Doctoral Dissertation, University of California, Los Angeles, 1975).

2. Bernard Williams, "Are Persons Bodies?" in Stuart F. Spicker, ed., *The Philosophy of the Body.* Quadrant Books, 1970. Reprinted in Williams, 1973, pp. 64–81. The quote is from page 79 of the reprint.

3. Bernard Williams, "Bodily Continuity and Personal Identity," *Analysis,* 1960. Reprinted in Williams, 1973, pp. 19–25. The quote is from page 21 of the reprinted version.

4. Sydney Shoemaker, *Self-Knowledge and Self-Identity,* Ithaca, 1963.

5. "Bodily Continuity and Personal Identity," p. 21.

6. See Grice, "Personal Identity," Chap. 4, section C, and the discussion in the Introduction, pp. 16ff.

7. "Bodily Continuity and Personal Identity," p. 23.

8. "Bodily Continuity and Personal Identity," p. 24.

9. "Are Persons Bodies?, p. 80.

Suggestions for Further Reading

Barresi, John, and Raymond Martin, eds. *Personal Identity.* Oxford, 2002.

Broad, C. D. *The Mind and Its Place in Nature.* London, 1937. See especially the chapter "The Unity of the Mind."

Campbell, C. A. *On Selfhood and Godhood.* London, 1957. See Chapter VI, "Self-Consciousness, Self-Identity, and Personal Identity."

Cassam, Quassim, ed. *Self-Knowledge.* Oxford, 1994.

Flew, Antony. "Locke and the Problem of Personal Identity," *Philosophy* (1951).

James, William. *Principles of Psychology.* New York, 1950 (originally published 1890). See Chapter X, "The Consciousness of Self."

Nagel, Thomas. *The View from Nowhere.* New York, 1989.

Noonan, Harold W. *Personal Identity.* London, 2003.

Parfit, Derek. *Reasons and Persons.* Oxford, 1986.

Paton, H. J. *In Defense of Reason.* London, 1951. See the essay "Self Identity."

Penelhum, Terrence. *Survival and Disembodied Existence.* London, 1970.

Perry, John. *A Dialogue on Personal Identity and Immortality.* Indianapolis, 1978.

———. *Identity, Personal Identity, and the Self.* Indianapolis, 2002.

Prior, A. N. "Opposite Number," *Review of Metaphysics* (1957–58).

Rorty, Amelie, ed. *The Identities of Persons.* London, 1975.

Shoemaker, Sydney. *The First-Person Perspective and Other Essays.* Cambridge, 1996.

——. *Identity, Cause, and Mind: Philosophical Essays.* New York, 2003.

Shoemaker, Sydney, and Richard Swinburne. *Personal Identity.* Oxford, 1984.

Unger, Peter. *Identity, Consciousness, and Value.* New York, 1992.

Uzgalis, William. *Locke's Essay Concerning Human Understanding: A Reader's Guide.* London, 2007.

Wiggins, David. *Sameness and Substance Renewed.* Cambridge, 2001.

Williams, Bernard. *Problems of the Self.* Cambridge, 1973.